INDIAN CULTURES AS HERITAGE

THE INDIA LIST

Also by Romila Thapar from Seagull Books

Voices of Dissent: An Essay

Gazing Eastwards: Of Buddhist Monks and Revolutionaries in China, 1957

The Past as Present: Forging Contemporary Identities through History

INDIAN CULTURES AS HERITAGE

CONTEMPORARY PASTS

ROMILA THAPAR

Seagull Books

LONDON NEW YORK CALCUTTA

Seagull Books, 2021

Printed in Arrangement with Aleph Book Company, New Delhi, India

First published in India by Aleph Book Company, 2018

This edition is not for sale in the Indian subcontinent (India, Pakistan, Sri Lanka, Bangladesh, Bhutan, Myanmar and the Maldives).

ISBN 978 0 8574 2 887 5

British Library Cataloguing-in-Publication Data
A catalogue record for this book is available from the British Library

Printed and bound in the USA by Integrated Books International

CONTENTS

Preface vii
Introduction: Defining Cultures ix

1. Cultures as Heritage 1
2. Heritage: The Contemporary Past 20
3. Time Before Time 38
4. Science as Culture 59
5. Women Decoding Cultures 81
6. The Culture of Discrimination 102
7. Knowledge as Heritage 134

Epilogue 179
Acknowledgements 207
References and Further Reading 209
Index 217

PREFACE

The questions that I asked when I was putting together this book were many and they revolved around the broader issues of heritage and culture. Some were questions that are generally not asked when heritage and culture are under discussion. Three centuries ago the definition of both was clear and uncomplicated. But now there are a range of definitions that recognize the many cultures that make up a society and the multiplicity of its heritage. My attempt here is to consider just a few among the many, merely to suggest that there is much that we miss out when we speak of culture as it was defined in earlier times.

Both culture and heritage require a context that refers them to their past or the present, so that they can be recognized as representing what we perceive as patterns of living, patterns that we are now beginning to concede give a direction to cultures. Their links may not be visible to historians. Or, possibly, my concern was with searching for the context of cultures—even if I was considering just a few—and in no particular order. This too underlines the connectedness. My focus, therefore, is on contexts rather than on objects. As it had been said, objects have an aura. I would argue that seeing each in its context heightens that aura. But this may again be just the obsession of an historian.

My other argument in this book is that we have in the past often thought of culture as single, as representing everyone in that singularity. For this singularity we have generally selected, or at least given it pride of place, the pattern of living and thinking of the elite. 'High' culture was what made for civilization, and the 'rest' did not matter too much. But now we know that in searching for the contexts of cultures, much comes from a hierarchy of sources, from high all the way down, and has to be acknowledged. My concern in this book is with a few of the many varied contexts that give an identity to cultures. My argument is not that every item of what we call culture has to be taken through a span of contexts, but that it might be worth investigating whether there are contexts other than the obvious ones.

In writing this book, I have drawn partly on some lectures that I have given in recent years to diverse audiences, and partly on published essays. These I have revised and rewritten in the last few months. My intention was to select a few themes and consider how they may be viewed as having contributed to the articulation of Indian cultures.

I would like to thank David Davidar and Aienla Ozukum at Aleph for their helpful comments and reactions to the text.

Romila Thapar
New Delhi
December 2017

INTRODUCTION: DEFINING CULTURES

We use the word culture quite casually when referring to a variety of thoughts and actions. I would like to begin my attempt to define cultures by a focus on three of its dictionary meanings that I think are significant to our understanding of the general term—culture. We often forget that its more essential usage is as a verb rather than as a noun, since the noun follows from the activities involved in the verb. Thus the verb, to culture, means to cultivate. This can include at least three activities: to artificially grow microscopic organisms; to improve and refine the customs, manners and activities of one's life; to give attention to the mind as part of what goes into the making of what we call civilization, or what was thought to be the highest culture. In short, one might argue that culture is the intervention of human effort in refining and redefining that which is natural, but that it gradually takes on other dimensions in the life of the individual, and even more in the interface between the individual and society.

When speaking of society, this word also requires defining. Society, it has been said, is what emerges from a network of interactions between people that follow certain agreed upon and perceptible patterns. These are determined by ideas of status, hierarchy and a sense of community governing the network. They are often, but not invariably, given a direction by those who control the essentials in how a society functions, as for instance, its economic resources, its technology and its value systems. The explanation and justification for who controls these aspects of a society introduces the question of its ideology and often its form.

The resulting patterns that can be differentiated from segment to segment of the society are frequently called its cultures.

Most early societies register inequalities. The access of their members to wealth and status varies. The idea of equality therefore has many dimensions. All men and women may be said to be equal in the eyes of God but may at the same time be extremely differentiated in terms of income and social standing, and therefore differentiated in the eyes of men and women. There may be small social segments such as jatis (castes) that may each have a hint of equality—although even among them there is a hierarchy. This would not apply to the entire society. There may be times when societies conform to a greater degree of equality, but such times may be temporary. It has been argued that on a pilgrimage, the status of every pilgrim is relatively similar but at the end returns to inequalities. Societies are not static and change their forms and their rules of functioning. Cultures are reflections of these social patterns, so they also change.

My attempt in this introduction is to explain how the meaning of a concept such as culture has changed in recent times and has come to include many more facets than it did earlier. This perhaps is pertinent to my choice of subjects included in this book. What we understand as the markers of culture have gone way beyond what we took them to be a century or two ago. The items of heritage that I have included in the first few chapters are an example of this change.

Apart from items of culture, which is the way in which culture as heritage was popularly viewed, there is also the question of the institutions and social codes that determine the pattern of living, and upon which pattern a culture is constructed. The later chapters are concerned with this aspect, where I comment on the perceptions of women in Indian society and the role of caste in providing contexts to determining attitudes to Indian culture. Finally, there is the process of socialization into society and culture through education. There is a historical dimension to each of these as culture and history are deeply intertwined. There is also an implicit dialogue between the present and the past reflected in the way in which the readings of the past changed over historical periods.

Every society has its cultures, namely, the patterns of how the people of that society live. In varying degrees this would refer to broad categories that shape life, such as the environment that determines the relationship with the natural world, technology that enables a control over the natural world, political-economy that organizes the larger vision of a society as a community or even as a state, structures of social relations that ensure its networks of functioning, religion that appeals to aspirations and belief, mythology that may get transmuted into literature and philosophy that teases the mind and the imagination with questions. The process of growth is never static therefore there are mutations and changes within the society. There is communication and interaction with other societies through which cultures evolve and mutate. There is also the emergence of subcultures that sometimes take the form of independent and dominant cultures or amoeba-like breakaway to form new cultures.

Although cultures coincide with history and historical change, the consciousness of a category such as culture, in the emphatic sense in which the term is popularly used these days, emerges in the eighteenth century in Europe. The ideal was the culture of elite groups, therefore sometimes a distinction is made between what came to be called 'high culture' that of the elite, and 'low culture' that of those regarded as not being of the elite, and sometimes described as 'popular'. Historical records of elite cultures in forms such as texts and monuments for instance, received larger patronage and symbolized the patterns of life of dominant groups. They were and are more readily available as heritage than the objects of the socially lower groups in society whose less durable cultural manifestations often do not survive. This also predisposed people to associate culture as essentially that of the elite. Such distinctions were implicit in terms such as marga (the cultivated) and deshi (the local) in India.

The nineteenth century in Europe witnessed the great breakthrough in natural sciences with the introduction of the idea of evolution, the focus being on the evolution of Homo sapiens, treated as the culmination in the evolution of living creatures. Evolution was the growth of simple forms into more complex forms, from the microscopic to the complex human. The growth was not linear but nevertheless had a teleology leading to the human species, thought of as the most evolved and maximally superior. Some forms fell by the wayside, others developed horizontally and yet others met the assumed trajectory. Some who were working on the history of human societies found the idea of evolution to be a plausible and scientific explanation for the hierarchy in human societies moving from the primitive to the highly evolved. Evolution became a central idea in assessing past cultures such as in archaeology and came to be applied to living cultures as well.

Colonialism brought the European world into contact with others at a close range and in large numbers. The success of the colonizers was further explained as the survival of the fittest. The rest were those that had missed the unidirectional flow of evolution. Race science had powerful supporters in the nineteenth century and biological origins were claimed to assert superiority. The notion of race was then extended to include all aspects of culture. It also became a staple in the idea of civilization. Race science attempted an identification of races and their placement in a hierarchy, and again the superior race was that of the colonizers from Europe.

The earlier definition of civilization had referred to those societies that could provide evidence of having had a high culture. Defined in terms of the humanistic studies of the time, these focused on activities of the mind that included philosophy, religious texts and literary forms such as poetry, drama, epics and professional texts; and with aesthetic values expressed in visual artistic forms such as sculpture, painting, architecture and forms that were heard—such as tonal structures in music. Added to this was the understanding of the universe through forms of knowledge using not only philosophy but also an extensive study of astronomy, mathematics and medicine. Occasionally, astrology crept in somewhat surreptitiously in the guise of knowledge, claiming derivation from the supernatural.

Civilizations were demarcated territories where these characteristic activities were central. The identity of each was marked not just by territory but also by professing a single major religion and using a single language, both emanating from the elite. Cultural frontiers however are difficult to demarcate. Historical events often alter frontier zones lying between states. Cultures have no boundaries. Buddhist shrines or ibexes etched or painted on rocks spread across a huge geographical range of Central Asia. Temple and stupa architecture in parts of Southeast Asia is tantalizingly both similar to its Indian counterparts and also dissimilar. Do we continue to ask questions about assimilation or do we explore the idea of juxtaposition and osmosis? There was a substantial degree of coincidence between what was viewed as 'high culture' and what was required of a civilization. Needless to say, the majority of the people in a society were regarded as being of low culture and non-elite and whose cultures found little place in the delineation of civilizations. This was in part owing to their having a lesser degree of literacy—the major form of communication among such groups was oral. This survived but was limited usually to a small group who embedded it as foundational knowledge in their pattern of living. So, too, with the crafts that encapsulated the aesthetics of the occupational group involved. The distinction between objects made by professional artists as 'art' and objects made by craftsmen as 'craft' persists. Sometimes, it is conceded that an object produced by a craftsman, although one of many identical objects and not therefore unique, may require a sophisticated aesthetic appreciation. In premodern societies this distinction between art and craft was perhaps more limited, since so much of what we today call art came from the hands of the craftsman.

Given the interface between history and culture, the latter had a historical context that had to be known for its fuller understanding. The context was determined by two initial questions: what was the chronological context of an item of culture, and whose culture does the item refer to? The first question is not merely a matter of dating an object or an idea, but also knowing its juxtaposition to other objects and ideas, at a point in time that gave shape to a culture. The second question relates to the place given to the creators of the object and to the intended audience in the social hierarchy. This can be more complex than it seems. The craftsman sculpting an image would come from a low-income community of artisans, whereas the patron for whom the object was made could be a wealthy person. The balance or even tension between the creator and the patron cannot be set aside, as we have tended to do in many studies, for instance of art historical objects.

In the last century, the concept of culture came to the forefront in another area of thought and activity—in discussions of excavated sites and in anthropological studies. This led to its incorporating a somewhat different definition especially in the light of the many current theories seeking to explain how society functions. In archaeological and anthropological studies culture came to mean a pattern of life associated with a community or a group in society that sometimes determined the more important facets of that society. There were of course multiple patterns and therefore many cultures had to be included in constituting a society. Those familiar with archaeological data also began to organize typologies of objects that indicated patterns of social forms. The explanations of these forms provided historians with indications of changes in history other than just dynastic changes.

Initially culture was seen as evolving from the simple to

the complex, a mutation that took a period of time. The earlier cultures of hunter-gatherers were simple compared to those of pastoralists and these in turn were less complex than those of the agriculturalists. The most complex were of course the patterns of living that took shape in urban centres. Premodern societies were charted along a path of evolution. Cultures came to be defined by dominant characteristics—thus the Harappan was urban and used a system of written communication; the Megalithic had a typology of burial forms; the Vedic was agro-pastoral dependent on cattle herding and some agriculture; the later cities of the Gangetic plain were recognized by the presence of certain kinds of ceramic ware and by structures within their houses. These were one level of identification in all these different societies, but there was also the need to observe other levels in order to understand the context.

In the social sciences culture gradually came to refer to the pattern of functioning in a society with its multiple facets, extending from the foundations to the many manifestations of actions and ideas. This widened the variety of objects included in the articulation of a culture, as for example, some textiles and items of clothing moved from being treated as a craft to being considered as objects of art. The articulation of groups that were not the elite came to be located in the cultural pattern, recognizing at the same time the interface between what had earlier been differentiated as being either art or craft. The two were not treated as definitively dichotomous and culture was not the creation of just the one.

How did this affect the perception of what came to be regarded as Indian culture in the nineteenth century? This was when it came to be recognized as a distinct category and a subject of study. Today, when we speak of culture, the objects and ideas may well be taken back to the ancient past, but our definition of culture is rooted in how culture was perceived in the nineteenth century. The hierarchies in culture were determined largely by the studies of Indian and non-Indian scholars writing on the culture of the upper castes and the elite of varied backgrounds.

The larger Indian society functioned through demarcations of community and sect. Identity was determined by the jati one was born into which in turn conditioned rules of marriage and inheritance and often occupation; the sect determined the rites of worship and belief. The self-definition of these castes and sects was at the root of the diversity. Their ranking was less easily recognizable since there were multiple rankings. This is evident even from the multitude of languages spoken. The analysis of each language provides a narrative of the history of its speakers who lived either in isolation from or more frequently intermingled with speakers of other languages. The form in which a language underwent change through its own evolution or from an intermingling with another language, points to the nature and history of the interaction between those speaking the languages.

In theory social groups were rigidly separated and ordered their daily life on the basis of strictly enforced social codes. In practice there was a considerable degree of accommodation between some groups in some activities, but not in others. Both were culturally determined. The categories of varna distinctions could transcend prescribed rules about occupations, as I hope to show in Chapters 5 and 6. But the segregation of those included in the various varna categories and those outside the pale of caste, the Avarna, was more emphatically observed from a certain period onwards.

Religious categories could also allow for accommodation. There is a considerable difference between how religion is formulated at a simple level and the form it takes when it becomes a social enterprise. In the latter case it controls crucial institutions involved in preparing the individual to be a member of society through prescriptions of behaviour and the practice of the religion, largely through institutions of education and through religious codes. Discussions on the social role of religion have to keep in mind that this role is man-made and in practice has a worldly aim quite apart from the benefits it may promise in the afterlife. It is distinct from the role of belief and faith. It refers itself to those who create religion and wish to control society through the ideology of religion. This is not dictated by any supernatural power, however much such myths may be propagated. The social role of religion, therefore, takes many forms. They range from the simple and direct ways of shamans who claim to be in communication with divine powers, to the complexities of the current political and economic control exercised by religious institutions through a variety of what are described as social organizations.

This is particularly significant when considering the interaction between religion and politics. At the level of royalty this has been studied, but perhaps not sufficiently. The religion of the rulers, be they Buddhist, Jaina, Vaishnava, Shaiva, Sunni or Shia or anything else, is stated and described and generally left at that. But historians are now delving into the political and social functions of these religious identities and assessing whether or not they dominated social institutions, and if they did, then why and how. Did Buddhist and Jaina rulers have different state policies as compared to the others?

The history of the Turks, Afghans and Mughals in India is generally still viewed solely and simplistically in terms of their being Muslim and ruling over a Hindu population. Yet historians know that there was a complicated web of politics and social relations that involved both the Hindu and Muslim elite, and even more variously was present in local populations, in ways that go beyond a simplistic view. In this matter, unfortunately, colonial views that are entirely out of date are still being propagated by some political and quasi-political organizations, whose concerns hover around building vote banks, and with using a falsified history to construct a new political identity.

When culture is defined in a broader way than it was in the nineteenth century then the reasons for either continuities or changes also cover a wider spectrum. Among them is redefining the concept of civilization, once so dominant in colonial times and continuing into the last century. The components of neatly demarcated civilizations were: a relatively unchanging territory as the location; a single predominant language in which its texts were written; and a single predominant religion that delineated belief and values. These components were treated virtually as static features but the fact of historical change forced a concession to civilizational change as well.

Important reasons for conceding change often follow from either rethinking one's own culture or from the impact of coming face-to-face with other cultures. What were once regarded as closely enclosed civilizations are now being found to be, not surprisingly, rather porous. Some historians are now writing histories of the larger movements that changed the world, what is sometimes called 'big' history, and the origins of change frequently lie in this porosity that is present in all cultures. This is evident in the recent histories of large areas of the world as in those of William H. McNeill, Andre Gunder Frank and Immanuel Wallerstein. The advance and expansion of technology that once was barely studied outside its history in Europe is now being examined both in terms of its having evolved through the interaction of knowledge and patterns of life of other cultures, as well as its role in contributing to cultural change the world over. However, in the case of some civilizations, there still remains some hesitation in integrating it into the study of 'high' culture. Where this is so, it is despite the fact that technology and the scientific thinking that goes with it is often intrinsic to humanistic values and vice versa.

How a technology is used by a culture has a historical context. Primitive societies lived by hunting and gathering. The hunting and clearing was done with hardly any weapons other than flaked stones, or sticks fitted with small stone blades or microliths and such like. Metal spearheads became more efficient. Stalking animals on horseback was even better. Royal hunts became the subject matter of epic poetry and romance and developed their own symbolism. It is the opening action of the Kalidasa play *Abhijnana Shakuntalam*. The hunt was no longer a search for food but was instead a mark of status, and the stage for heroic acts only a little short of minor battles, as in the hunts described in the *Mahabharata*. The successful hunter was the hero, and in a sense the same impetus carried him into battle. Idioms drawn from the major sacrificial rituals, the royal hunts and battles, featured in literary texts. Hunts became more elaborate as time went on with beaters and many more hunters, and the animal was the prized predator, the tiger, rather than the animal that could be eaten, the deer. We are all familiar with the many photographs of Indian royalty and British officers posing with the tigers that they inanely decimated by the hundred, all for sport and status. These are changing vignettes of the cultures of societies through the ages.

Are these forms of representing a cultural identity intended to claim status? To answer this question we have to ask who were the hunters because they changed from period to period? What were they claiming through this activity? Who picked up the carcasses, and who skinned them, and who prepared them for display in the homes of the hunters? Interestingly what is regarded as a polluting animal carcass at the time of its death to be collected and skinned by what was said to be the equally polluting untouchable person is then converted into a trophy of victory over natural life, and of demonstrating excellence in shooting. It then adorns the homes of the wealthy who can afford to pay for organizing a hunt. Cultural values clearly are multifaceted.

Cultures as patterns of living are created by, and are acceptable to, most persons that constitute a society. Norms and practices come to be established. Mutations come about through a variety of reasons. However, not everyone observes the norms, even if the majority does. Some are permitted to act and think differently, as for example the shamans of early societies claiming to be in communication with the supernatural. Such deviance becomes part of social functioning. Similarly, in later societies, some men and women prefer to opt out, as it were, of normal society and create a different society of their own. This was done by renouncers of various kinds who set up their own monasteries with different rules for patterns of living. Where castes and religious sects work out their own norms of social life we need to see these as multiple cultures coexisting.

Culture emerges sometimes from how we relate to the world we live in. Or it can be a subconscious attempt to distil a pattern of life, sometimes as the comprehension of an individual experience. Individuals do not reflect an entire culture but only the segments with which they empathize and choose as their identity or have an identity thrust on them through social mores. Societies therefore have multiple cultures and one pattern alone cannot represent the entire society. This becomes problematic when one culture is chosen to illustrate the many cultures of a society, as for example, when reference is made to a particular cultural form as Indian culture, or similarly in European culture or Chinese culture. Distinctions, demarcations, differentiations have to be conceded within that label, but seldom are. The question then is whether there can be a single label for referring to a number of cultures within a society—a problem that has become acute in many parts of the world today, now that it is recognized that non-elite cultures and the cultures of minorities have also to be given a place when the culture of a society or a country or a nation is under discussion. This is not merely an admission of their presence but an attempt to recognize the logic of where various cultures are to be placed. This may require turning the objects of the culture inside-out—instead of speaking of which group created a particular cultural item it might be more appropriate to speak of the object and its role in a pattern of culture.

It could be asked as to what goes into the making of a pattern of living today that can be called its culture. This was earlier dependent on the family, the community and education, three crucial agencies of socializing an individual to his or her society. These factors are slowly giving way to the creating of cultures through social media, television, advertisements and cinema. Social media is easily accessible on a mobile phone. TV presents a virtual reality that can distort the actual reality with fantasy becoming more central to culture than reality. This trend will only be exacerbated with the development and adoption of technology like Virtual Reality. Exposing fake news through the Right to Information can be at the risk of one's life, but lives, whether of individuals or of publications, do not matter now, as long as the story is sensational. Journalism that once used to value serious enquiry and explanation, and reported on the basis of transparent evidence, now includes statements whose authenticity need not be vouched for.

There have been studies on the influence of advertisements on the beliefs and practices of those that took them seriously. If one looks only at the advertisements the image of Indian culture is strange. One wonders which reality is being projected, if any at all. Beautiful young women and their babies in these advertisements look more like their European counterparts than their Indian equivalents. Are advertisements addressed to real people or to an imagined society?

What I am trying to argue is that often the definition of Indian culture is an attempt to perceive what is thought to be an Indian reality as well as the visualization of an Indian imagination, and to create forms that accord with these ideas, and to select forms from existing historical experience that would support these ideas. It has been the construction of a group within society that has the wealth, the power and the status to select, dictate, and define the culture that they assume should reflect the entire society. In times past it was royalty or the upper castes that most frequently defined culture, with its finer points and nuances endlessly observed from various perspectives. Today, we accept this definition or there is insufficient questioning of it. This definition was legitimate for a small group and its appreciation remains within a small group. But there were other norms and forms observed by the larger part of society, and often by those who were creating these objects, whose aesthetic and skills are ignored in the belief that they were merely following what the patron told them. They were anonymous but that did not annul their creativity. Culture, we have to remember, is the end result of human purpose, and is dependent on those who have created it, or given it shape. Should we not learn to understand that purpose? Moreover, the diverse cultures of the majority remained confined to their own boundaries. These cultures are only now beginning to get reflected, and that too rather partially, in the broadening horizon of Indian culture.

◆

Let me stop for a moment at this point and ask a few questions. What then is the intention in recognizing that that which we perceive as culture is based on a pattern of living? To what degree is the pattern a conscious or a casual one, or else a play on fantasy? This may determine the extent to which conformity to the pattern is required. Is it a process or is it the end product of such an ordering? We like to believe that elements of culture such as heritage are givens. But we have to pause and ask how cultural ideas, forms and patterns of living are shaped, how they give rise to institutions, what is the range through which they are expressed, and how in turn do the answers to these questions condition our thought and action.

We speak of the pattern of living and of culture in the singular, yet in every society there are multiple patterns and more correctly we should speak of multiple cultures. That we do not, is in part the influence of thinking about individual civilizations in the singular and extending it to culture; and partly because a culture is generally defined only by the characteristics of the dominant culture with its particular perceptions of the rest of society, together with the biases and sensitivities of both those who perceive and those who are so perceived. That cultures have also to be associated with inequalities of various kinds is a thought of relatively recent vintage.

How have inequalities arisen in history? It has been argued that if one social group gathered to itself a major part of the wealth and thereby gained status, this gave it dominance in society and it could dictate the norms. To this can be added the argument that some groups exploited human belief in the supernatural and claimed to be in communication with divinity—this gave them power over society and enabled them to dictate the norms.

Perhaps a more simple way of explaining this was what early thinkers said. The *Digha Nikaya* (III.84.4-93.210) mentions that the Buddha, for instance, held that the utopian beginnings of egalitarian society slowly gave way to social inequalities with accompanying conflict, when groups split up into families and when ownership was asserted over cultivated fields. Texts from the Brahmanical tradition also projected a pristine utopia and the equality of all, which then declined. This gave rise to the varna hierarchy of society and the gods having to appoint a king who agreed to protect the *Vedas* and who was said to be of divine origin as mentioned in the *Mahabharata* (12.59.1ff). Presumably hierarchy would have begun within the family with the competition for the eldest female or the eldest male to assert greater authority, a process that led eventually to the establishing of patriarchy. This in turn resulted in gender inequality that became an accepted feature in many cultural patterns. Added to this was the broader social segmentation, which in India took the form of jati, and was systematized by the upper castes as varna.

Necessary features of this culture were identity being determined by the caste one was born into, maintaining a social hierarchy among the castes and the preservation of a distinct caste through rules of endogamy and exogamy; patriarchy reinforcing caste. The insistence on following occupations designated by caste was rigid in some cases but more flexible in others. The type of occupation contributed to the location of the caste in the hierarchy and obviously those that laboured for others had a low status. This segmentation of society meant that each segment acquired an identity and these identities had differing statuses. The identities were reinforced by norms specific to each.

Early historical societies were concerned with establishing norms of individual ethical behaviour, and in some instances social ethics, but there was less concern regarding social justice. Utopian times of the past and golden ages as encapsulated in the construction of civilizations hardly focus on social ethics although there were groups in these societies that spoke or wrote on this subject. The two major groups of teaching in early Indian society, Brahmanism and Shramanism (Buddhists, Jainas, Ajivikas and such others) had divergent views on social ethics. The assumption was that the correct observance of the prescribed norms ensured a society committed to duties and obligations. Rights were largely thought of as marginal. These have become central to philosophical discourse in relation to the institutions of society only in recent times, presumably because social ethics and justice have priority in our definition of modernity. This new condition requires us to discard some older identities in favour of those more apposite to contemporary norms. For example, in the nation state, the identity of community, based on religion, language, or ethnicity, has less centrality than the identity of the citizen of the nation that is now the more appropriate primary identity. Religious nationalisms in present times in the various nations of South Asia are battling the secular identity of the citizen that they wish to replace by giving priority to a particular religious identity—be it Muslim in Pakistan and Bangladesh, or Hindu in the concept of Hindu Rashtra, or Sikh in that of Khalistan, or Buddhist in Sri Lanka.

Identity is a demarcation of a segment of society and, by its own logic, may require not only separation but even in some instances, the exclusion of the Other. But nationalism introduces the reverse of insisting on an inclusive identity, where all are to be included as citizens of a nation. Exclusion can be self-imposed although more often it can come of being excluded by others. The greater the emphasis on a particular identity, the greater will be the emphasis on the exclusion of the Other. Texts such as the *Dharmashastras* keep reiterating identities, yet in practice there were divergences. How then was the lack of fit between theory and practice negotiated in the past and how is it to be negotiated in the present? Conceding that there is a difference, the theory can be adjusted to suit the practice. It can also be done, as it has been more often, by conceding a change in practices but maintaining at the same time, that the façade of the theory remained unchanged. Texts confirming the continuation of the theory have to be carefully investigated. Colonial reconstructions of the past, therefore, saw gender and caste as static and historically unchanging. This reading is continuing in the ideologies of religious nationalisms but is being questioned by social scientists who ask searching questions of the data. When social practices are studied then the many forms of social negotiations are revealed as ways of change. With reference both to the history of women and of lower castes and outcastes, one has to ask whether the rules of exclusion were altered and if so why and in what circumstances, and if not then why not?

A new identity and a new type of exclusion became prevalent in the nineteenth century, and that was race. Among other ideas, this concept drew on the theory of evolution as propounded by Charles Darwin and others, and also on his ideas of the survival of the fittest. Race itself was a useful idea in legitimizing the superiority of the colonial powers by describing them as more advanced on the evolutionary scale. Some civilizations were conceded a position a little below the top-ranking ones, but many were societies placed low on the scale and referred to as primitive peoples. The concept was new to history and was unfamiliar even to those societies that had been granted the status of civilizations.

The question had to be asked as to the point in history when the identities that we use today came to be used. Can we trace these concepts or their application to the earliest histories? This is problematic for India as despite social segmentation the concept of race is absent. But there was no shortage of terms used for excluded segments, some more sharply excluded than others, terms such as Dasa, Mleccha, Chandala, Avarna, Yavana, Turushka. None carried the meaning of race. Modern translations of texts referring to race often used the word jati, and this of course was not only incorrect but resulted in much confusion. The choice of this word was probably because birth in both cases was seen as a source of identity.

In the world of today, the term 'race' has no scientific basis and has been discarded. But this has not unhinged its popular usage, especially where the term carries a basketful of characteristics, generally in utter confusion. In India the label of race has been and continues to be used for anything under the sun—people, language, religions, custom—you name it. But as with many myths, it distorts reality and hides our understanding of the world. In the construction of the concept it draws on fantasies relating to culture and history.

At the time when race was being invented, the notion of nation, nationality and nationalism also became central. Nations were built on a new consciousness of communities coming together and tracing common cultures and histories as binding forces. The self-perception of societies underwent change. Earlier medieval kingdoms declined and were replaced by new alignments among erstwhile subjects and communities. In the colonies, nationalism took the form of opposition to the colonial power by the colonized. The latter saw this as what bound them together and permitted them the identity of a nation. There was a demand for independence by the new polity that had been shaped as a result of colonial conquest. Boundaries were redefined using colonial boundaries and history had a teleology tied to the creation of the nation state. The need to claim a single culture inevitably led to appropriating the culture of those that had been dominant and had wielded power. This was the culture that was taken as having survived the destruction of time. Its monuments had been better built with greater care, it had a rich textual tradition and there were people in authority who endorsed it. It became the national culture inherited from the past. Cultures at lower levels of societies were probably less open to change and may have survived better.

It is convenient for the national culture to be singular but it seldom can be since there is a competition between the various identities that have to coalesce to become a nation. In India the confrontation involved three obvious claims to nationalism, two on the basis of religious identities—Hindu and Muslim—and one contesting these as a secular anti-colonial identity. Hindus and Muslims each had other identities in pre-colonial times some of which coincided and some conflicted. But the new political identities based on religion, whether Hindu or Muslim, but claiming to be national were created and nurtured by the colonizer. In this process the secular anti-colonial process was, to some degree, undermined.

If history is essential to nationalism as has been frequently said, so too is the claim to a national culture frequently curated from this history. The problem arises when selections have to be made as to what goes into the construction of a national culture. At the official level there is a continued use of the colonial terms: majority and minority, derived from figures of those following different religions. Instead of looking for more valid descriptive terms, the configuring of culture as majority and minority cultures, however inept, is reinforced by saying that whereas the majority culture will be prominent, the cultures of the minorities will also figure. What this means is that Indian culture more often is defined centrally by what is projected as Hindu culture, with an addition if required of items associated with those that come from minority communities.

In India today Islamic and Hindu monuments dominate the landscape. Should they be juxtaposed or should there be an attempt to place each of them in the larger context where their relationship to each other and to the many more cultural items can be observed? Many today, either out of ignorance or for reasons of political ideology, propound theories that can only be called ridiculous—such as, that the Hindus have been victimized by Muslim rule and have been slaves during the last thousand years. The degree of ignorance contained in such a statement is astonishing, because it is actually a denial of the most effective, evocative and cherished religious articulations in various facets of Hinduism that took place during the last thousand years.

At the level of philosophy there was a continuation of the earlier debates across the spectrum of various schools of thought as is evident from the fourteenth-century compendium *Sarvadarshana-sangraha*. The worship of Krishna and Rama as avataras of Vishnu gained immense popularity with the Vallabhacharya sect establishing pilgrimage points associated with Krishna at Brindavan, and with the Ramanandins defining locations linked to the worship of Rama at Ayodhya. Versions of the story of Rama were composed in various regional languages and widely recited such as Krittibas's *Ramayana* in Bengali and Tulsidas's *Ramacharitamanas* in Hindi. At the same time there was a range of Bhakti sants in every part of the country who propagated various ways of worshipping either Hindu deities, or a deity that was an amalgam of many deities across religions, or else did not conform to any existing religious icon. Pilgrimage centres flourished and bhajans were sung in every emerging regional language. Many aspects of belief and worship that are central to Hinduism today found expression and patronage during the second millennium AD such as the worship of Krishna and Rama and many Shakta sects. In some cases, popular aspects of Hindu and Islamic religions were interwoven, as indeed was the courtly culture.

Composers of the more popular hymns included Muslim poets and Sufis, such as Ras Khan, whose verses in praise of Krishna are still sung as part of classical Hindustani music. Classical Indian music, both Hindustani and Carnatic, emerged substantially from the many musical forms that were being explored five hundred years ago, by musicians from a variety of religious sects. This was not a one-off but a reflection of multiple dialogues.

Major commentaries on texts of the earlier period such as the *Mahabharata*, *Ramayana*, *Manu Dharmashastra* and other *Dharmashastras* were written and discussed in this millennium. Sayana wrote his famous commentary on the *Rigveda* in the fourteenth century and it was used in the many centres of Sanskrit learning that were active at the time. Brahmana and Jaina scholars worked with Persian scholars at the Mughal court on the translations of Sanskrit texts into Persian.

Rajput royal families intermarried with Mughal nobility. Apart from personal relationships this also meant that palace rituals reflected more than one tradition. Rajputs or other high caste Hindus, such as learned Brahmanas and Kayasthas, frequently manned the more responsible levels of Mughal administration. The Mughal army that defeated Rana Pratap at the Battle of Haldighati was commanded by Rajputs, a command that was given to them on more than one occasion. Conversion to Islam was on a lesser scale than is claimed in the exaggerated accounts of court chronicles since the percentage of the Muslim population remained a minority even in pre-Partition India. This may well have been because Hindus were not invariably forced to convert.

This is not to say that there was no confrontation at the political level but this should not be confused with claiming that there was massive victimization of the Hindus bringing about Hindu resistance in the late Mughal period. Political relations should be examined in terms of the politics of the time. Conflicts of a routine kind were clearly local and more casual than has been assumed. Relations between communities in general tend to be governed by some degree of accommodation and some degree of confrontation. It makes greater sense to try and analyse the reasons for either.

The British conquered India but did not settle in the land. They drained its resources to enhance industrial capitalism in the home country and find markets in the colonies. Unlike the British, the Turks, Afghans, Arabs and Mughals—commonly bunched together as 'the Muslim rulers'—invaded India, but also settled in the country. New communities and new patterns of thought and expression came into being. To treat all Hindu and Muslim cultures as separate cultures, entirely segregated and demarcated from each other, is historically untenable, nor is it viable in cultural terms. The form taken by facets of these cultures, and from earliest times, from the architecture and ornamentation of monumental buildings to the compositions of music whether as ragas or qawwalis, derives from the interplay of more than even two cultures. The recognition of this multiplicity gives authenticity to a cultural form.

It is as well to remember that confrontations in India relating to religion go back to a period when Islam did not even exist as a religion. We may insist today that Buddhism and Jainism have always been a part of what we now call Hinduism, and therefore there was no conflict between them and Hinduism. But their teachings were distinctively different as were the social institutions that they instituted, as for example the monastic orders of the Buddhists and Jainas in particular. There are references to hostility between what were in the past called the dharma of the Brahmanas and that of the Shramanas. The much-respected grammarian Patanjali, writing in the second century BC, compares the relationship of the two dharmas to that of the snake and the mongoose.

The inheritors of Brahmanism appropriated some of the Shramanic tradition and the second millennium AD saw the decline of Buddhism. The two parallel religious and cultural traditions are no longer visible today. Jainism tried to preserve the Shramanic tradition in at least the few areas where it prevailed—Karnataka and Gujarat and Rajasthan. In terms of inheriting the culture of each and their interaction, it would be more meaningful to investigate the kind of negotiations that occurred between Brahmanism and Shramanism and what were the outcomes. We have yet to investigate how a caste society negotiates or confronts the friendliness or the hostility of its neighbours.

If victimization is to be associated with the second millennium AD then it is of two kinds: the slow driving out of Buddhism from India, which curiously seems to have coincided with Buddhism becoming the influential religion of other parts of Asia, such as central, eastern and southeastern Asia; and the unmistakable victimization of the Avarna, untouchable sections of Indian society, by the caste Hindus.

But to return to our times. Nationalism can determine the selection of what we project as national culture. This helps in the preservation of what otherwise might have declined, or it highlights ideas and objects that might have been neglected. This might be called a positive role even if the selection of what is to be preserved may not have unanimous support from the nation, or that citizens may feel that some cultural items were deliberately or inadvertently left out.

But there is also the problem of the destruction of culture in the name of nationalism or a similar sentiment. This is generally a systematic, deliberate, destruction of a prominent aspect of culture, in order to make a statement and attract attention. It is essentially a political act and may actually have little to do with sentiment. There have been some rather dramatic cases of this in recent times. The Greco-Roman monuments in Palmyra and Aleppo in Syria were destroyed by Islamic extremists of the Islamic State; the massive Buddhist statues at Bamiyan in Afghanistan were destroyed again by Islamic extremists, the Taliban; and the Babri

Masjid in Ayodhya was destroyed, by Hindu extremists claiming, among other things, to be avenging the raid of Mahmud of Ghazni on the temple of Somanatha that took place a thousand years ago, as well as assuaging a supposed subsequent Hindu trauma. Historically there is no mention of such a trauma in the ancient texts. It is mentioned for the first time in 1842 in the course of a debate in the House of Commons in Britain when a member of the British parliament suggested that the raid might have created a trauma among the Hindus. The Babri Masjid was a sixteenth-century mosque that in the name of history and culture, had been deemed a protected monument of the Indian state, but in the name of Hindu nationalism it was destroyed by those antagonistic to its presence at a site that they claimed was sacred to them marking a temple to Rama.

Culture and nationalism in the colonies have another aspect that is now surfacing in many parts of the world: migrations. In India migrations from various directions have played a significant role in the creation of culture. Archaeology, ancient textual sources, and now DNA analyses are all informing us that ours has been and is, a very mixed population, as indeed have been the populations of many large areas. We have had varieties of people from diverse cultures who have settled in the subcontinent. At the same time traders, craftsmen, and ritual specialists from the subcontinent, have settled in smaller numbers in different parts of Eurasia.

These processes have been part of the essential history of premodern culture in India and Asia. Over the centuries, the nuclei of elite centres in areas that had earlier been peripheral required a structural change in the local society to make them conform to the mainstream, creating a new elite and other social segments. When new states were formed in erstwhile remote areas—and this was a continuous process through the centuries—the seven limbs of the state as enumerated by Kautilya in the *Arthashastra* had to be established: the king, the territory, the administration, the capital, the treasury, force of various kinds and the ally. This involved a process of acculturation with the locals who had earlier identified with their own culture. The process continued under the sultanates and the Mughals. It may even have continued to a minimal extent under the British who showed some initial interest in living in India and adopted elements of the local culture. But it was terminated after 1857 when India became a colony. After this, the demands of capitalism and imperialism required an altogether different cultural idiom, when formulating the culture of the colony.

The concept of Indian culture as constructed by British colonial policy was based partly on the definitions that were being discussed in Europe, but more on how the colonial power understood its colony, and how it wished to project this understanding. Indian culture was an alien culture yet it had to be studied, classified and described in ways comprehensible to colonial administration and thought. What was familiar and therefore more comprehensible was rated high. In this the culture of royalty, of the upper castes and generally of the elite, was given priority as was the case in all concepts of civilization. The selection included some remarkable and varied cultural achievements that had survived many centuries. The imperial concern was also to direct its choice to the culture of the elite that it now controlled. Colonial interventions encouraging the aesthetic that went with it was another aspect. There were some controversies but these were subsumed in the debate on what was foreign and what was indigenous and therefore assumed to be national. What this undermined were the earlier dialogues and differences between various diverse social segments, who despite observing variant cultures, were ready to integrate cultural idioms.

The debate should have been on how we define 'national culture'. But our understanding of the cultures that constitute the national remains incomplete, without adequate explanation for the choice and suitability of being regarded as such. Should there still be, for example, a differentiation between objects of culture and ethnic objects? Ethnic as a label has many meanings as it can be exotic, having an aesthetic that is outside the cultural mainstream, authored by an anonymous group rather than by known people, and sometimes even viewed as a trifle inferior. The debate on 'high' culture and ethnic culture has yet to take place. It will of course also hinge on who are the patrons and who the creators, and their relationships.

A more complete picture would be helpful in studying culture if we keep in mind its broader aspects. Culture after all is not limited to the past but has also to do with what might be called the contemporary past. This is not a contradiction in terms but gives rise to what we call our cultural heritage. What do we select of heritage and what do we reject and why? Are we selecting heritage in order to define our culture? Are we trying to mask the culture that comes from the past or are we being deliberately selective to a point where we may be excluding the culture of those we think are not representative? This is a question that is sensitive to identity politics. Above all do we weave in the context, essential to what we call culture? Does our selection reflect the dialogues that shaped cultures in the past, or do we give it the shape that we, in the present, think is appropriate?

There are many situations that call for defining a national culture. One of the more challenging among them is migrations. In the colonial period the state controlled the migration of labour from India to British colonies elsewhere, as distant as the Caribbean and Polynesia, to work on plantations, as well as encouraging a few settlements of commercial professionals, as for instance, in South and East Africa. Independent migration in the postcolonial period was largely of middle-class professionals settling in economically advanced societies. So we now have an Indian diaspora and this provides another dimension to the interlinking of culture with nationalism.

Migrants carry their cultural identities and are anxious to

protect them and keep them intact. But ethnicity undergoes change and so do cultures, especially those grafted, however tenuously, onto a new host society. Over a period of a century or more, the home society also changes. The diaspora, in part, tends to cling to its memory, somewhat redundant, of the home society and is constantly inventing traditions; or else where the migration has brought success to the migrants, it becomes the role model for the home society even if its own culture is changing differently, given the difference in context.

This might explain the cultural crisis among some of Indian origin in Europe and the United States. There can be conflicting situations of the two cultures—the homeland culture and that of the host country. There is often a romancing of the first peppered with fantasies, and only a small acculturation with the host culture focusing on language, dress and mundane routine. This can lead to some rootlessness despite the search for acculturation, syncretism or even hybridity.

Irrespective of where one lives the images that one carries of one's homeland and especially its past—regarded as the source of its culture—are shaped by one's conception of its history, and its interpretations. Culture is not only interwoven with history, as I have said earlier, but is even often dependent on the history that we carry in our minds. Interpretations of history are not static. They change when new sources come to light, or when new questions are asked of existing sources that provide answers different from the earlier ones.

In some ways, it is becoming somewhat anachronistic to speak of national culture. In the minds and activities of those for whom religious cultures carry a political message of identity, the constituents of national culture can be changed by political diktat. National cultures are not static. They too mutate, dependent on those who create them. What was regarded as national culture by Indians a century ago is not identical with what some Indians today would describe as national culture, for the latter are busy trying to expunge what they maintain are alien elements and not part of the Indian tradition as they see it.

And then there is globalization. The rush to be globalized brings two contradictory trends: one is to be open and participate in a global economy and society, and the other is to create citadels in the name of religion that are in effect self-contained citadels. It could be said that there is an element of continuity in this. In the past, there were viharas (monasteries), mathas and khanqahs (hospices) that had contacts with similar institutions in other parts of the known world. Donations from patrons allowed them to be independent of state interference and if they were powerful enough—as some were—they intervened in politics. But with this difference—that whether they saw themselves as another kind of social institution or not, their transparency was also a source of their strength. They were not citadels. Patronage is a significant facet in the making of culture and in protecting what is defined as culture. Who is providing the patronage and for whom and what is being protected and why, are all relevant questions, and in turn raise a host of further questions in their answers. Where patronage takes the form of gift-giving it acts as a method of exchange between donor and recipient, and creates a relationship that has cultural implications. A tangible gift may be given in exchange for an intangible aura and status that is claimed by the donor. Patronage and gift-giving provide many glimpses of cultural readings of a society.

When we speak of national culture today we concede that the state as patron is also involved in determining the content of this culture, as it has always been in the past to varying degrees. What we do not concede but should, is that alternative definitions of culture have also to be protected. This can only become a practice when the defining of culture ceases to go to only one source and is able to induct other sources.

◆

In conclusion, I would like to suggest that perhaps we should reconsider existing definitions of terms such as culture and heritage. Culture is the pattern of living of all segments of a society, and since there are many patterns there are many cultures, with many activities that sustain a society. Cultures of the past are the ingredients of heritage. We know only that which has survived, dependent on the patronage of those that cultivated that heritage. We seldom enquire into who and what ensured its survival and what has been its individual history. Nor do we consider what might have been the forms that have not survived but are perhaps hinted at or incipient in what survives. Or, has a particular heritage been deliberately revived or even invented, or else suppressed, and if so then why? I am not arguing for counterfactual history but only for an extension of what we know, and that too in the form of enquiry.

Civilization is an amalgam of cultures, of patterns of living, with much interaction. The interaction is a process that is vertical between higher and lower social strata, as well as horizontal, through the crossing of civilizational borders that we historians have artificially created. Our current definition of civilization is too rigid and in some ways ahistorical. It misses out on the significant areas of overlapping cultures, and therefore the layers implicit in heritage.

The creative link to the past has been seen largely in the form of elite cultures. We accept the assessments of heritage by its current consumers, perhaps forgetting that heritage was given form and meaning originally by its creators and patrons. We have a right to our assessments but we must also know who the constituents of heritage in earlier times were, and how they were perceived.

The concept of an Indian heritage will possibly have greater validity when the range of heritage from the varied pasts of our diverse communities is juxtaposed, and understood, each in relation to the other or, as part of the other. No item of heritage is an island unto itself. Equally significant is how we explain heritage since we cannot return to the time to which it belongs and observe it as it was. Are we reading it as it was meant to be read or are reading it as we want to read it? Both readings are subject to debate drawing on historical evidence. This has to remain a continuing question since the answer cannot be definitive. When we comprehend heritage as the interface of the cultural memories, identities, aspirations and utopias of a range of people, and try and explore what their meanings were for those creating the heritage, only then will we understand heritage as a viable cultural entity.

◆

In the chapters that follow, my attempt is to touch on a few themes that have been present in varying degrees, essentially as part of a context to the shaping of Indian cultures, but which themes are seldom brought directly into the discussions of Indian cultures as they should be. The initial chapters on multiple cultures consider items of heritage in terms of what we select and what we ignore, and implicitly who does the selecting. These are aspects of the interface between the objects and ideas reflecting a selection of cultures from the subcontinent and what may be called their context. It is imperative to ask who determines the importance of what is selected. The relevance of such questions has increased with the wider definition of culture.

The other chapters have a rather different focus, more on the background ideas and conditions that determine cultural attitudes. The way in which they are expressed as social attitudes or norms affect patterns of living, as indeed the pattern of living is also influenced to some degree by what is defined as culture. Of the more abstract ideas, concepts of time are discussed. These we are either unaware of or else take for granted. We seldom pause to consider how they may have defined the way life was lived in the past or consider the cultural implications of what they signify. Concepts of time were part of what might be seen as two ends of a spectrum, from mythology to scientific thought. They were linked to belief systems as well as to mathematics and astronomy. We rarely give attention to the neglected field of scientific, or as some prefer it, proto-scientific thought, giving shape to culture. Yet the nature of this kind of thinking and the understanding of why it took the form that it did, is foundational to other strains of thought in early India.

Science has roots in society and articulates some of the thoughts, questions and actions of its segments. That is its context as an aspect of the cultures of the society. If it is made sacred as some of it was, and in a sense was thereby frozen, then its meaning changed and it ceased to be part of active knowledge. This would perhaps have isolated it as heritage.

At a less abstract level, the more immediate context for society is the way in which we perceive and present what is permitted to women as legitimate activity, and how this alters in accordance with different social patterns. What are the implications of these social attitudes for patterns of living? These would also be linked to the application of inclusion and exclusion of segments of Indian society as it works in caste, which in turn is both socially and culturally determined. This social segmentation creates diverse cultural groups of a kind that are sometimes problematic in relating the values that in theory shape cultures and the actual functioning of society. Upper caste culture, across society, tells us little about how this culture was perceived by the large numbers that constituted the segregated Avarnas ghettoized beyond the settlement.

In the process of cultural socialization and the acquisition of knowledge, education is a major factor, yet we are increasingly disregarding education as a significant factor in this process. If we concede the centrality of education to creating cultures then we have to consider, more seriously than we have done, the importance of the content of education and how it is to be communicated. The final chapter is a narrative of my one extensive experience of the interface of pedagogy and cultural issues, in which I was personally involved when establishing the teaching of History in Jawaharlal Nehru University in New Delhi. Questions arose at many levels as also did the answers to these questions. I feel a certain poignancy in attempting this narrative, as would others as well, since we did succeed in giving JNU an academic quality that was conceded and respected by the best universities anywhere. The poignancy lies in the fact that the current authorities seem to be bent on de-intellectualizing JNU, annulling its quality and reducing it to being nothing but a teaching shop.

What this book is then, is not a book on the history of Indian culture in the conventional sense. It is not a history of monuments, art, literature and philosophy and the usual components of what is called 'culture'. It is drawing on patterns of living that provide a social crucible for what are viewed as cultures. It is an attempt to suggest that when one assesses an object or an idea from the past or even from the present, one should be familiar with the context that gave rise to it, in addition to merely appreciating the result. Observing the context would add a dimension to the assessment.

1

CULTURES AS HERITAGE

'Heritage' is that which is inherited, and can refer to objects, ideas, or practices. It is recognized in various ways—from genes to geometrical structures, from the ways in which societies were organized to how people belonging to various strata of society were treated, from property to economic activities. It goes into the making of our cultures and our civilization linking the past to the present. It was once assumed that heritage was what was handed down to us by our ancestors, neatly packaged, which we then passed on to our descendants, unchanged. Heritage is thought of as static whereas tradition is said to mould our way of life. But the more we seek to understand heritage the more we realize that each generation changes the contents, sometimes marginally and sometimes substantially.

More recently it has been argued that tradition is actually the interplay of what we believe existed in the past, combined with our aspirations for the present. In exploring this interplay and the new ideas it generates, our concept of heritage takes shape. Rituals and ceremonies thought of as ancient are often, on investigation, found to be recently invented. The traditions of the past therefore, can even be invented in order to legitimize our actions. Historians now investigate what is sometimes called the invention of tradition.

The ongoing discussion of what constitutes heritage or tradition leads to analysing concepts such as culture and civilization. There is no easy definition of these and there have been intense arguments about their meaning especially at times when existing norms are questioned. The European Enlightenment in the seventeenth century resulted from striking historical changes and became a time when new questions were asked. Basic concepts needed fresh exploration. In India, too, we are experiencing similar change and the constituents of our heritage need to be examined afresh.

Heritage can be of two kinds. One is natural heritage that came from the physical creation of the earth. This is the heritage that we are currently busy depleting because we cannot control our greed for the wealth that comes from destroying natural resources. By linking the environment to history, this heritage is now being seen as essential to the other one.

The other heritage is the one that was cultivated and created by human effort. This became what we call 'cultural heritage'. It includes objects and ideas that determine our pattern of life. They define our concepts of culture and civilization. What needs explanation, and this I shall try to do in this chapter, is how the historical assumptions that go into the making of these concepts have changed. Consequently, historians now see heritage not so much as something inherent and inexplicable, but as constructed and therefore subject to differing assessments for various reasons.

Let me begin by defining the terms that I am using. Culture was once linked to the achievements of a society in literature, the visual and performing arts, architecture, philosophy, and in extending the frontiers of knowledge—of what we would call the life of the mind. In premodern times these activities were associated with the elite who had the wealth and leisure to focus on these pursuits and for whom these were, at some levels, symbols of status, apart from their practical value. So it was viewed as 'high' culture to differentiate it from popular forms. But this was too narrow an assessment of its source. The essentials of these activities come from a wider social range. The definition of culture needed to reflect this range. So culture came to mean both the pattern of life of the segments that constituted a society, and the forms in which they expressed their ideas.

Culture then can refer to something as simple as the pattern of life of hunter-gatherers, pastoral people, farmers or urban dwellers. Out of this simplicity rise the complexities of what people make and do to render life more meaningful and to understand the world and the cosmos within which they live. But then it was found that cultures change and are both vulnerable and porous. Patterns have changed often enough in history. So we speak of successive cultures registering these changes.

The past therefore does not conform to a single culture as some would like to believe but is made up of multiple cultures. The cultures of the elite were dominant, as elite cultures have been everywhere. These were linked to the pattern of life of royalty, the upper castes, and those that controlled power and economic resources. But the cultures of the rest of society sustained the elite culture and therefore were essential.

A number of questions arise. Were all the multiple cultures in society integrated as we assume they were when we speak of golden ages of the past, or were they segregated by caste, language and religion? Are we doing something different now in our attempt to integrate them? The attempt seems restricted to the slogan of 'unity in diversity'. I call it a slogan because we have never defined, as far as cultures go, what constitutes unity or how far we extend the diversity. Are we instead trying to indirectly justify the segregation through using colonial categories such as majority and minority communities identified by religion? And when we look back at the cultures of the past do we confine ourselves to the easily recognizable dominant cultures or do we attempt to search for the ways of life of the rest of society?

There was, additionally, as there still is, a tension between change and permanence. A seeming continuity, when analysed, can point to change. For example, it is said that the four-fold system of caste society, with its established hierarchy, has been prevalent in the subcontinent for many centuries. Yet the hierarchy differs quite noticeably in various regions. The dominant caste is not always the same. In the Punjab it was Khatri traders, whereas in some other regions it was the Brahmanas, or it was rulers claiming Kshatriya status. And in some areas the varna stratification is absent. Such differences invariably affect the form of the local culture as I shall be suggesting at greater length in a later chapter.

The presence of dominant and subordinate groups is characteristic of all societies. Who belongs to them can change over time, as do the cultures that they patronize. A single dominant pattern is neither uniform nor eternal. Until recent times, the upper levels of society were in a better position to leave records and markers of their culture. Reading between the lines has been one way of trying to ferret out the culture of those of lesser status who have not left records. Archaeology provides some information. Even the culture of the elite can be better understood if we can follow its interactions with the rest of society.

Cultures, as we know, can also change because of external factors. The effect of ecological change is now being noticed. Deforestation, a changing river course, climate change, also happened in the past. These are now among possible explanations for the decline of the Indus cities in around 1750 BC. Technological innovations as well as adjusting to social and economic changes are often required in such situations.

Contact with new people through trade or incoming migration, or the political dynamics of conquest introduces new patterns of living. Conquest is easily recognized as a new political pattern. Trade and migration are defining features because they are long-lasting, yet we always give greater prominence to invasions. This is illustrated by what happened at the turn of the Christian era in the northwest of India and Afghanistan with what are called Indo-Greek or Greco-Bactrian forms. One aesthetic style that evolved from this was called Gandhara art.

The art highlighted the aesthetic differences between Buddhist art in this region and in Mathura and central India, as well as further south, as in Amaravati. These differences were sharply debated among art historians during the last couple of centuries, in defining the Indian aesthetic. Were the Indian artistic forms, resulting from contact with Hellenistic forms, superior to those not influenced by the Hellenistic? Among art historians writing on Indian art, some regarded this as the apogee of Indian art because of its obvious Hellenistic features, and some others called it hybrid art and therefore of little aesthetic consequence apart from its limited influence in the subcontinent. Nineteenth-century art historians did not think to ask the craftsmen still sculpting icons and friezes to give their reactions to these earlier forms. The art under discussion had all come from guilds of artisans. By way of contrast and unlike the art, the languages of the region remained distinct. Greek, Aramaic and Prakrit were used.

The same region, a thousand years later, saw the arrival of Turkish, Afghan and Persian migrants from Central and Western Asia. We dismiss this experience as one of invasions and conquest, and leave it at that. But the flip side of invasions is that they enhance trade connections and attract migrants. As I have mentioned, the impact of these can sometimes redefine the culture of a region to a greater degree than invasion. This time around it was not the style of sculpture that changed, but language intertwined with religious belief.

I am not referring to the introduction of formal Islam but to the possibly more creative side of the infusion—the Sufis and for instance, their influence on local languages. New ideas entered the indigenous languages requiring the induction of new words, or else existing words were given a new meaning. With a large popular usage of these ideas, the languages themselves took new forms. A new word for God—rab—entered the Punjabi language. Derived from Arabic it had common currency among all religions using Punjabi. Poets and teachers of the likes of Bulleh Shah, Waris Shah and others composed their poetry not in Persian or Sanskrit but largely in this commonly spoken language, creating a new cultural idiom. This would extend to other cultural aspects as language always does.

All languages change, traces of which are carried in vocabulary, grammar and the style of writing with each generation that uses the language, introducing new forms of expression. The grammarian Panini (c. fourth century BC) makes a distinction between the Sanskrit of the Vedas, and the more commonly used Sanskrit. Checking linguistic form is one way in which we can date texts that have been composed over long periods of time. For example, the text of Kautilya's *Arthashastra* as we have it now took a few centuries to take its present form from the fourth century BC to the third century AD. It registers recognizable linguistic differences between the earlier sections and those added later. Where a language is in contact with other languages there is bound to be mutual borrowing. The nature of what is borrowed is the clue to recovering the relationship between the speakers of the languages. For example, the word for the plough, langala, in Vedic Sanskrit is thought by scholars to be of Dravidian origin. This raises a host of questions about one aspect of the relationship between the speakers of the two languages, Indo-Aryan and Dravidian, not to mention the technology of agriculture.

◆

Migrants arrive in various ways. There are pastoral groups searching for pasture lands who establish themselves and their annual circuit in a region. These are often carriers of oral traditions as is evident in their songs and stories. The establishing of trade routes brings in settlements of traders that foster new communities and create new cultural patterns.

Migrant communities settle in new places for a variety of reasons. This has happened repeatedly in India, with the coming of peoples from Central and West Asia. They settled, intermarried locally and became a part of the Indian population. These communities identified themselves with the local culture by adopting facets of that culture and internalizing it. Caste (jati) names, such as Huna, and Durrani, among many others, confirm this. Some of these names are used jointly to this day by diverse religious communities.

The coming of the British was different. They did not settle in India. Their interest was in reorganizing the economy of India to enable the new rulers to take its wealth back to Britain. Nevertheless, they were curious about the Indian past and applied new ways of advancing the knowledge of this past. The techniques they used to investigate the past were often insightful and incisive. However, some of their readings of Indian culture led to generalizations that have become problematic today, such as their formulations of the structure of Indian society and of religion.

Dominant cultures backed by wealth leave the maximum traces on a society. They have texts describing their ideas, icons in stone and metal, and their architectural forms indicate their religious and social preferences. As I have said, subordinate groups leave few such traces. They do not have the wealth to build monumental temples and mosques or to house manuscripts in institutions and libraries. Those at the lower end of the social ranking provide the wherewithal for the wealth, but are not participants in elite culture—for example, they are excluded from some sacred places such as temples. Their culture has been different and much of it has been inferred so far from how they are viewed by the elite. This information inevitably carries the perspective of the author, not always free of bias. But we should recognize that the living patterns of the wealthy are ultimately also dependent on the aesthetics and the expertise of those who make the artefacts and work the resources.

Culture, even where it constitutes heritage is not static, whether as object or idea, or the social structures on which society rests, although it is often treated as such by us in the present. In claiming an ancestry for it, we are inducting the past into the present and thereby giving it continuity. We should perhaps investigate what has been retained, replaced or discarded in this believed-to-be-unchanging continuity.

Claiming ancestry is also a way of acquiring legitimacy from the past. Such a claim can be a stamp of desired status and thus a demonstration of social success or it can be an attempt to deny questioning an identity that may be accepted by some but questioned by others. By insisting on a particular ancestry for a cultural item we may be denying its other possible ancestries. There could be many reasons for this if it is deliberate. Possibly, its other ancestries come from sources that earlier were quite acceptable but have now become less so. But recognizing the other may be crucial to understanding the cultural form. By not recognizing it we are either distorting or inventing a tradition.

To take a much discussed example. It is generally agreed that some among the forms of performing arts that we treat as classical are traced back to the Devadasi performances, of premodern times, together with ideas derived from textual sources. Is it enough to know the technicalities of the form or should we not also relate it to the context? In this case it was women choosing or being chosen for a profession that was contrary to the normative caste code. They created their own social nucleus distinct from the mainstream. Did this give them the flexibility of experimenting with their professional performance? How did they relate to the bigger civilizational context through both their performance and their social culture?

The concept of civilization has now become so complex that one almost prefers to set it aside. As I have noted, the earlier simplistic definition of its conforming to an elite culture is now giving way to the idea that it encompasses many cultures. This approach comes from the new ways in which historical connections of the past are being viewed, arising from the awareness that societies function at many levels, and that the cultures of these levels are not identical.

By about the early eighteenth century, the core of a civilization was a classical period from the past. 'Classical' referred to a style, seen as the high point in a culture, chosen from the many manifestations of a historical period. It was the exemplary norm, typifying excellence and against which successors were measured. There was a suggestion of the static in this description and it was not expected to change. All societies with a long history had to have a classical age that was viewed as the cultural and intellectual pivot.

◆

Today, it is generally understood that the concept of civilization was based on at least four components, each of which is now being configured differently from before. The four components are territory, language, religion and the classical. Each civilization had a demarcated territory. This was feasible when cartography became common and boundaries of territories could be mapped. Prior to that, frontier zones between states were marked by natural features, such as rivers, mountains, forests, deserts etc. These frontier zones were often the meeting point where people came from and went to various directions, so the cultures of these regions were more mixed or overlapping than in others.

The borderland of northwestern India functioned as a frontier zone for centuries. It hosted peoples from Afghanistan, Central Asia, Iran, and Gangetic India. Nodal points of trade and of the spread of religions were located there and it also provided springboards for invasions in various directions. Buddhist monks travelled with traders and established important monasteries in Afghanistan, Uzbekistan and eastward through the deserts to China. A few centuries later, similar routes were taken by Sufi orders coming from Western and Central Asia to India.

For the east coast of India, the sea was the frontier but this was transgressed in close links with Southeast Asia and southern China, as is evident from the impressive monuments still standing in those regions. The long coast of western India had its own history of large settlements of Arab traders that intermarried and founded new communities of Indo-Arab cultures, different from the Indo-Islamic culture of the royal courts. Passes in the Himalaya were entry points to Tibet and what lay beyond. The northern frontier zones were land based, and in communication with cultures across Eurasia. The peninsula experienced another factor, the geographically extensive networks of the Indian Ocean, projecting as it did as a landmass into the centre point of the ocean. These provided a different perspective that we now have to induct into our narrative of Indian civilization.

Where then should we mark the territorial boundary of Indian civilization? We have defined our civilization from the perspective of the Gangetic heartland, the perspective from which histories were written. But civilization, when seen from the rim, reflects other more distant but significant contacts. Cartographic boundaries enclose and isolate lands, but the notion of frontier zones instead of linear boundaries, extend and open them. The concept of civilization has become territorially open-ended.

We apply labels of indigenous or foreign to people of past times. But the boundaries of British India, that defined the concept of Indian civilization according to colonial writers, had far less meaning in precolonial times. Foreignness in the past was assigned by cultural features—language, custom, ritual—and not by boundary lines. The term Mleccha, can mean alien or out-of-caste but was also applied to some who were indigenous to the subcontinent. There were areas of alien cultures within the subcontinent as, for example, the communities of forest dwellers, marginalized in Sanskrit texts and described sometimes as rakshasa (demons). Looking east, the rulers of Cambodia built Angkor Wat with its magnificent sculptured panels depicting the *Ramayana* and the *Mahabharata* in their versions and in Khmer style; or the rulers of Java built Borobudur as a gigantic stupa to honour Buddhism. Did they think of themselves as patronizing a foreign culture? Or had they internalized aspects of what we today claim as Indian culture through which they were articulating what they perceived as their own distinctive culture?

A second component of civilization was a single language of culture and communication. It was said to be Greek and later Latin in Europe, Arabic in West Asia, Chinese in China, and Sanskrit in India. This meant that the texts written in this language had priority and were treated as the norm encapsulating the entire body of local cultures. However, to research the past using the texts largely of one language in a multilingual area is historically untenable.

The earliest deciphered records pertaining to Indian cultures are inscriptions in Prakrit and date to the first millennium BC. The earliest surviving dated written text in Sanskrit is again among inscriptions, and dates to the early first millennium AD. Manuscripts from a slightly later period have survived. Vedic and epic texts composed in Sanskrit were earlier than the inscriptions but were initially part of an oral tradition. Sanskrit continued to be the language of Vedic Brahmanism and inevitably a slightly different version also became the language of some elite groups. The major ideologies that opposed Vedic Brahmanism, such as Jainism and Buddhism, initially taught and wrote in the Prakrits, with Pali being the one preferred by the Buddhists. Those who patronize the Shramana dharma used these languages. In the south the language was the early form of Tamil.

From the turn of the Christian era, Sanskrit began to replace Prakrit as the language of the elite. But Prakrit continued to be used, although with a lowered status, spoken by women and lower castes. Colonial scholars investigating the Indian past, began with the Sanskrit texts given the highest status by their Brahmana informants. It was a while before attention was directed to texts in other languages such those of the Buddhists and Jainas.

This differentiation was also made in defining the religion of Indian civilization as Hinduism. This was before it was discovered that Buddhism had once been a major Indian religion, and had been exported to other parts of Asia, where in many places it was the dominant religion, although in others it had subsequently declined. Making religion the third component of civilization and maintaining a priority for Hinduism in India and Confucianism in China, tended to eliminate Buddhism in Asia, whereas it can arguably be described as the main religion of the early history of Asia. That other religions, Jainism (frequently classified as a part of Hinduism), for instance, had been important in specific times and regions in India, was not thought so relevant. Islam was excluded as being West Asian in origin.

Since the structure of Hinduism was different from Christianity and Islam, the attempt was to formulate it in a manner comprehensible to European scholars and colonial administrators. This created problems of another kind. Hinduism did not grow around the teaching of a single, historical personality with a relatively precise chronology. It was instead a mosaic of independent sects each associated with a particular deity and its rituals. Its extraordinary survival lay in the legitimacy of the segment, namely, the sect. It was not a monotheistic religion with a uniform belief system that cut across all believers and it did not preclude reverence for other deities. As has been often said, more attention was given to the performance of rituals—orthopraxy, rather than the dogma of theology—orthodoxy. It did not have an overall ecclesiastical authority. The sectarian identity could be and often was linked to particular categories of castes. Inevitably the ranking of sects was not impervious to the hierarchy among castes.

The fourth component of civilization is, as we have seen, the existence of what was called a classical age. For Greco-Roman civilization it was Athens under the rule of Pericles, and Rome in the time of Augustus, for Islam it was the Caliphate based in Baghdad, and for India it was the Gupta period. But neither cultures nor civilizations can be confined to a single period. That makes them static, and stasis is not what governs a golden age.

Different aspects of a culture develop in different periods and they are all inheritors and contributors to an ongoing evolution.

Dynasties are more often chronological labels, rather than the handlers of cultural idioms. Exceptional rulers chose to patronize particular cultural forms. For example, when a new form of devotional worship, Bhakti, with its multiple new sects that virtually reconstructed much of Hinduism emerged from the seventh century onwards, some rulers in the area patronized some of the diverse Bhakti sects. Patronage came in a small but continuous way from those who chose to be part of the sect or to follow a particular sant. Substantial patronage came from royalty and the wealthy, depending on personal inclination, and in the case of royalty also on the popularity of the sect. The advantages, political and social, could be worthwhile for the ruler if the following was large.

Patronage could take the form of a small gift or a considerable grant of land providing a regular income. This enabled the building of stupas, commemoratory pillars, monasteries, temples, mosques, khanqahs and gurdwaras. Monuments, however, require maintenance and when the income from the grant dried up, the structure fell into disrepair. Sometimes a few of the structures of one religion would be vandalized by the supporters of another religion, or would be converted for use in the other religion. Buddhist stupas were sometimes built over, or built adjacent to, the sacred space of Megalithic cultures as at Amaravati; Buddhist chaityas were sometimes converted into Hindu temples as at the Trivikrama Temple at Ter; and much later some Hindu temples were converted into mosques, the most obvious being the Quwwat-ul-Islam in Delhi.

There are very few examples from the early period of the conservation of dilapidated structures of the past by either royalty or wealthy merchants. Some references occur in Jaina texts where conservation or repair of a sacred site is an act of merit. Merutunga, the fourteenth-century Jaina chronicler, describes the rebuilding of the first temple at Somanatha by the Chalukya king Kumarapala. According to Merutunga, the temple was in a dilapidated condition because of its neglect by the ministers who had charge of maintaining it, and through weathering by sea spray since it stood on the edge of the sea. Interestingly its condition is not ascribed to Mahmud's raid.

Pre-eminent among those who might be called conservationists was Sultan Firuz Shah Tughlaq, who ruled Delhi in the fourteenth century. He was the first important Indian conservator who gave conscious attention to a particular set of objects from the past—the pillars of Ashoka Maurya. He moved the Ashokan pillars from out-of-the-way places to secure and prominent locations where they would be protected. He recognized them as heritage even though no one could tell him what was written on them or what they signified. He seemed to have intuitively recognized their historical importance hence his relocating them. But he was the only Tughlaq to do so. The Mughals, however, were remarkably creative in interweaving cultures. Emperor Akbar was curious about the ancient Sanskrit texts recommended by Brahmana and Jaina scholars, and had some of these translated into Persian. This doubtless facilitated his famous discussions with religious scholars. He would probably have received a rather different picture of the tradition of belief and practice if his discussions had included more from the range of 'holy men', such as the yogi, sant, pir and fakir. His interest in the Nathapanth would suggest this. The Mughals were not hesitant about incorporating ideas and objects from the earlier past and recognizing them as part of their heritage.

As a contrast to this, Indian cultural items were not a source of heritage for the British. They were a source of information on the colony and fed their curiosity about its culture. Nineteenth-century Europe held the view that the world consisted of the civilized, the barbaric and the savage peoples. The civilized was the society, predictably, of the European colonizers and a few carefully selected cultures that could boast of a golden age. The Others constituted the primitive. This incorporated both the barbaric and the savage depending on the area colonized.

So deeply rooted was the distinction between the civilized and the primitive that it was even included in British Indian law courts as a valid legal differentiation. The transgression of laws by the natives was explained as due to their being primitive and not civilized.

The concept of the classical age underwent a radical change in the late twentieth century. Instead of a single classical age it was argued that any age with the required characteristics could be a classical age. This emerged largely from the efforts of archaeologists and historians to periodize the past. In India, the dual division of history into Hindu and Muslim periods was discontinued as it was an inaccurate explanation of historical change. The changes in material culture noticed by archaeologists also called for a systematic explanation.

Civilization now meant a society that lived in cities and communicated through a writing system. Control by a state system and a stratification of society was assumed. The city manufactured articles that could be traded. It was dependent for food on surrounding agricultural settlements. There was no single period of urbanization and city cultures arose in different regions at various times for diverse reasons. The culture of cities, both material and intellectual, was believed to give rise to the sophisticated manifestation of aesthetics and the life of the mind, accompanied by a distinct improvement in material conditions.

The new definition opened up many hidden aspects of cultural expression and brought them together in diverse ways. There was a move away from seeing just a narrow vertical space of a dynasty, or a text or a monument. The horizontal lateral view provided an entry into far more than had been earlier seen as contributing to either culture or civilization. What was evident was already known but now the search began for the less evident or for the hidden within what was thought to be the evident. The making of a cultural item began to be viewed as the consortium of many ideas and artefacts. Civilization was no longer a static entity. It had developed a kinetic form.

What this allowed for was the idea that everything did not have to be traced back to its earliest historical beginning or to a single point. Some facets of culture may have evolved later and this process reflects on what went into their making. This, in turn, introduced the idea that items of heritage were selected by a society. Who did the selecting and what went into the making of heritage was another question. This is reflected, although sometimes rather sadly, in some of the current formulators of culture such as state patronage, Bollywood and the visual and social media. But citizens can and do demand alternatives even if the alternatives remain the cultures of the few. The pluralities of South Asian culture require that we give such questions more thought than we have done so far.

Cultural innovation can give new meaning to heritage. Earlier forms presented in contemporary ways have often been the trajectory of cultural items. This not only links the present with the past but can convey additional meaning. The contemporary presentation opens up new ways of understanding the item. This is most commonly seen when the aesthetics of elite groups have to be extended to include those of other segments of society. What is incorporated, no matter how different it may be in origin, can create new forms. The juxtaposition of these with existing ones tells its own story. Dialogues between the presumed authors of existing forms and the new authors making the transposition, become meaningful.

An example from literature comes to mind. In the early eighteenth century, when a royal court wanted to host a performance of the story of Shakuntala, the drama of Kalidasa was adapted to the occasion. The language was changed from Sanskrit to Braj Bhasha, then used in some royal courts of north India and commonly spoken outside the court. Shakuntala was portrayed as a feisty, forthright woman not quite like the more shy, demure woman of the Kalidasa version. The episodes of the ring and the curse were deleted. Unlike the Kalidasa version that has largely remained within upper caste-upper class cultural norms until recently, the Braj version had a wider audience. Such extensions are appropriated by a changing aesthetic. Maybe one day we too shall see Shakuntala performed in a contemporary adaptation.

Much is made of the centrality of memory as a component of heritage. But memory is amazingly short and few cultures take pains to remember the past. When they do, the earlier memory is restructured to serve present purposes. Slivers of remembrance can hardly go beyond a couple of generations after which they are grist to oral narratives. For example, even something so visible as Buddhist rock cut monasteries went into oblivion with the decline of Buddhism and a lack of use and patronage. Even when texts are memorized their previous contexts are forgotten. When scripts change, as they inevitably do, texts can no longer be read. The edicts of the Emperor Ashoka (c. 268-232 BC) that we quote today as valuable heritage were unread and ignored for a over millennium until their script was deciphered in the early nineteenth century. That is a long cultural hiatus for the message that they carried of non-violence and tolerance from a king. And when the edicts were initially read none knew who the author was. The *Vishnu Purana*, for instance, merely lists him as one among the Maurya rulers. Only the Buddhist texts tell us about him in some detail. But these Pali texts ceased to be read in India when Buddhism declined, as will be discussed in more detail in the next chapter.

The colonial definitions that we have internalized have often been divisive in slicing apart common cultures, separated by religion and caste. Within these divisions, as I have mentioned, the cultures of the elites were given priority. This often disallows dialogue between cultures. So now that we are searching for a national heritage it is again these that surface whilst much remains hidden. Heritage can give prominence to, or submerge aspects of, its own history. Earlier forms may continue or new ones be described as the old. My argument is that we need to explore in greater depth what we refer to as our traditions and to recover from these explorations the diverse strands of our cultural inheritance that might currently be submerged. If heritage is not a fixed item and can be added to or subtracted from, then we have the opportunity to argue over its representation.

Defining national heritage is invariably contested since there are many competing for inclusion, especially in societies that host multiple cultures. Sometimes the contestation leads to the deliberate destruction of heritage, often for political reasons, as for instance the destruction of the Mughal period Babri Masjid. Contestation is often but not invariably linked to competition among dominant groups. Sometimes the opposite happens and an item of heritage over time absorbs much more than it started with and takes on incarnate forms. This quieter and gentler history of heritage is more often linked to those of lesser status with smaller ambitions and aspirations. Knowing the link between cultural forms and the societies from which they come helps in assessing these connections.

An interesting case of both absorption and contestation is the current confrontation over the narrative of the Rama Katha. There are a few hundred versions familiar to the Indian subcontinent and Southeast Asia and some go back many centuries. Each version is special to its authorship and its audience. This plurality has always been viewed as the strength of this particular cultural idiom. Versions have fissioned off, each segment growing and absorbing diverse ideas and incarnated in a new form, including dramatic presentations and exquisite poetry. The range is quite remarkable. Then comes the contestation when the story becomes a pawn in modern politics. The Valmiki version is declared to be the sole acceptable version, encapsulating a religious and social identity, to the exclusion of other versions. Where such political moves are successful, the definition of this cultural idiom will inevitably change and shrink. National heritage will then include only the items that survive. The *Valmiki Ramayana* is undoubtedly of the highest quality, but can we exclude the other versions? Some of these give us extended insights into the meaning of the story as well as the communities that associate with it.

We are ambivalent about constructing our heritage. When it suits us we accept without question the colonial interpretation of our culture, but at other times we question it. I would argue that this is a somewhat casual and insufficient exercise. To give priority to elite cultures is easier but it overlooks the subordinated or alternate cultures, and leaves the exercise incomplete. So too is the emphasis on the culture of one religion to the more token inclusion of the others. I would like to suggest that we have to think once again and debate what we mean by heritage. That is why I have tried to explain the redefinition that is now being given of culture and civilization by some historians. We have to accommodate many more aspects of our diverse cultures. Such an accommodation requires sensitivity to the constant adjustments that cultural forms make to a changing history. A reliable, rational study of history, not just as a narrative but as an explanation of the past, becomes essential to constructing heritage.

2

HERITAGE: THE CONTEMPORARY PAST

Heritage is a possession—an object, or an idea that is expressed in an act—and is inherited from the past. But when claimed as heritage, it can also be used to define an identity in the present. It carries a meaning from the past yet its meaning in the present could be similar or dissimilar. Does it encapsulate for us the same value as it might have done for those associated with it in the past?

A Gupta period sculpture or a Chola temple or a Mughal miniature painting, are all legitimate items of heritage. But if heritage links the past to the present we need to understand what its meaning was in the past, and whether it remains the same in the present. We should also be aware of what aspects of whose heritage we are selecting, and why.

As we have seen in the previous chapter, heritage comprises both the natural heritage of landscape and environment and the one created by men and women. This latter can be either tangible or intangible. Tangible heritage consists of objects ranging from small coins and beads to enormous monuments and to cities such as Mohenjo-daro, Hampi, Fatehpur Sikri and now even the Delhi built by Edwin Lutyens. Tangible heritage is more easily recognized. The intangible is the heritage of ideas and values that may be associated with objects, or may be articulated differently, for instance as performance; or, they may even be the institutions of society that give form to the heritage. These have all to be interpreted. As we know, interpretations inevitably result in debates and controversies that either liberate thinking or else silence the mind.

In this chapter, I shall discuss some visible forms of objects but also enquire into the intangible heritage sometimes associated with them. The German philosopher and cultural critic Walter Benjamin wrote that every object in a museum has an aura. This aura should be made accessible to visitors else the significance of the object eludes them. I would like to highlight this by arguing that the context enveloping objects and ideas from the past also needs to be presented in order to create the aura. This generally comes to us from that which is written in inscriptions and books, or it can be suggested by an oral tradition. When we imbue an object with only our contemporary aesthetic values, we could be annulling its real time and space. The object or idea from the past is converted to a contemporary use, irrespective of its original intended use. Through comprehending its aura, as it were, we are locating the object or idea in its own time and space. As a historian I do tend to see time and space in terms of the historical context.

Then there is the question of survival into the present. Heritage of any kind requires patronage to survive. Enquiring about its patronage is therefore important because there can be contradictions. An interesting example is the Somanatha Temple in Kathiawar that I have referred to in the previous chapter. In 1026, Mahmud of Ghazni raided the temple. The chroniclers of the sultans attribute its subsequent dilapidation to repeated attacks by their patrons, the various sultans. However, as I have noted earlier, Merutunga has an altogether different explanation for the temple being in poor condition—due to its being neglected by incompetent ministers and from weathering by sea spray. Therefore, the Chalukya king Kumarapala, ruling in the early second millennium AD, built a new temple on the same site. A couple of centuries later, a lengthy Sanskrit inscription issued by a Persian ship captain describes Somanatha as a hub of Indian and West Asian trade. We have here a choice of explanations regarding patronage or the lack of it.

The link between heritage and history needs careful attention given that absurd fantasies are often woven about the past by people ranging from tourist guides to major politicians, not to mention the deliberate distortions resorted to for ideological purposes in various ways, as for example, sometimes in school textbooks. Such distortions affect the choice of heritage objects and the reasons for the choice. The explanation of heritage is central to constructing a cultural memory therefore its absence or its distortion can erase memory. We are still at the stage where mythology is frequently taken as history, other than among historians. Mythology illumines the dimensions of a society's imagination and its assumptions. But it should be taken as doing just that. It cannot replace an analytically researched reconstruction of the past, as implied in history.

Given this background of my understanding of heritage, I would like to turn now to three specific questions. The first is historical since every item of heritage has its own history. Can we assume that what we view as heritage today was always understood in the way we now understand it? Do icons of heritage—whether objects or past personalities—undergo an uneven experience of either prominence or amnesia at various times? My example will be the Mauryan king, Ashoka, whom I have touched upon briefly in the previous chapter.

The second question relates to how we select our heritage, highlighting some aspects and ignoring others. I have chosen in this connection, the astrolabe, the instrument used by early astronomers and navigators. My third question arises from the fact that various social groups, such as the socially underprivileged, have objects and ideas specific to their concerns. Do we keep their heritage segregated or do we try and incorporate their sensibilities when we speak of Indian culture?

To start with the first question: how have Indians in the past two thousand years or so looked upon Emperor Ashoka? Not everyone was aware of him or saw him in the same way. In the Brahmanical tradition of the *Puranas*, he is a mere name, Ashoka, listed among the Mauryan rulers. Apart from this, the twelfth-century history of Kashmir, the *Rajatarangini* of Kalhana, makes a brief reference to him. And that's about it. The Buddhist texts however are fulsome in praising him with somewhat exaggerated stories of his conversion to, and patronage of, Buddhism. This difference in perception is not surprising. Many sources mention the Brahmanas and the Shramanas as having distinctively different dharmas where the premise of the one negates the other.

The Brahmana dharma was based on Vedic Brahmanism. This held that the *Vedas* are divinely revealed, the texts being sacred cannot be questioned, and that each human body has an immortal soul that is reborn after death into a new body until it achieves moksha or freedom from rebirth. This was foundational to Brahmanical theology. The Shramana dharma did not accept the existence of deities nor the *Vedas* as divine revelation, nor a belief in an immortal soul. The arguments and explanations of the Shramana dharma were based initially on reasoning, logic and causality. This tradition was common to a number of sects that emerged in the mid-first millennium BC such as the Buddhists, Jainas, Ajivikas and also underlined some of the philosophical schools such as that of the Charvakas. The dhamma of Ashoka drew from the Shramana tradition hence his emphasis on social ethics. As mentioned earlier, Patanjali compared the relationship of the two dharmas to that of the snake and the mongoose.

Colonial scholarship when investigating the Indian past initially depended largely on Brahmanical texts. They took their cue from learned Brahmanas and their recommendations of what constituted the authentic past. Buddhism by this time had been virtually non-existent in the mainstream of Indian religions, nor were there any Buddhist monks in India to suggest a reading of Buddhist texts since Pali was virtually never taught, even in departments of Sanskrit. Therefore, little was remembered about Ashoka. His edicts in which he comments on ethical values and good governance were inscribed on rock surfaces in many parts of the subcontinent, and on pillars that were mainly located in the Gangetic plain. The pillars were inscribed in the commonly used Brahmi script and in the language of the time, Prakrit.

A pillar with his edicts is now located in the Allahabad Fort. This pillar is an unusually significant item of historical heritage. Let me explain why. Six centuries after Ashoka, a Gupta king ordered an inscription to be engraved on the same pillar. It was written in the later Brahmi script of the Gupta period and composed in Sanskrit, not Prakrit. It eulogized the military conquests of Samudragupta and his uprooting of various peoples. These were statements endorsing sentiments contrary to those propagated by Ashoka. Although the basic Brahmi script continued to be used in the Gupta period, languages and scripts change their forms every few centuries. So some can continue to be read if the change is not excessive but others can no longer be read. If the Ashokan inscription could still be read, then was the statement on Samudragupta intended to denigrate Ashoka's message?

This enigma is also present in another object. At the site of Sannathi, near Gulbarga, there is a post-Gupta Kali temple. In a recent renovation of the temple it was discovered that the flat stone slab into which the tenon of the image of the goddess had been slotted, was in origin a slab that carried some Ashokan edicts engraved on one side. The slab may have fallen and much later a square-shaped hole had been cut into it destroying a part of the inscription. It was now used as the pitha on which the image could be fitted. This action raises questions. Buddhist sites in the vicinity such as Kanaganahalli may have hosted the Ashokan edicts. The stupa at Kanaganahalli, dated prior to the Gupta period, had reliefs of scenes where the label inscriptions referred to 'rayo asoko'—a reference to King Ashoka. The link is with Buddhism. Were those who supervised the building of the temple or its patrons unable to read the edicts? If they could read them, were they not curious to know what was written? Or did vandalizing an object from a Buddhist place of worship not matter by the Gupta period?

Another question presents itself. Was the Ashokan pillar itself, rather than the message on it, the actual object of attraction? It was a magnificent polished sandstone pillar that earlier had been surmounted with a sculpted capital, and was adjacent to a stupa and therefore revered by many people. Did the choice of the pillar arise, as I like to think, from a vague historical consciousness, since it seemed to be an important record from the past? Was it thought that the Gupta period inscription might gain further legitimacy by association with what seemed to be a significant object of heritage, even if inexplicable?

In the fourteenth century, the Ashokan pillars came into prominence again, but only partially. As we have seen, Sultan Firuz Shah Tughlaq was intrigued by them. Enquiries revealed that none knew what they were nor could anyone read what was written on them. Some referred to them as Latha Bhairon—the staff of Bhairon; in other places they were worshipped as massive lingams. Nevertheless, two were shifted and installed in Firuz Shah's capital in Delhi despite the immense problems of transportation as described in the *Tarikh-i-Firuz Shahi*. The one still located on the top of the citadel in Delhi has a dramatic placement suggesting a gigantic needle pointing into space.

Firuz Shah was a major conservator of Ashokan objects. He activated what is today called a cultural translation with some earlier objects. What meaning does an object from an older culture have for the newer culture? How can it be explained? But it would seem that he was also selecting those items of heritage that he thought were relevant to what he saw as his claims to legitimate rule. His choice is worth thinking about as it reflects his perception of what had meaning from the past. This is a continuous process in history, even if it is not always obvious and apparent.

The Mughals were equally mystified by the Ashokan pillars, and attracted by the mystique. The pillar that is now in Allahabad had, by Mughal times, acquired multiple graffiti by local rajas, mostly wanting their names to be recorded as is common in such graffiti. At some point it was shifted and erected prominently within the Allahabad Fort. Emperor Jahangir ordered his genealogy to be engraved on it, composed in Persian and in the Nastaliq script, arrogantly cutting into a part of the Ashokan inscription, as had been done with the earlier inscription referring to Samudragupta. As an object of historical heritage this pillar is probably the most impressive in India. It ranges across three millennia in time, and the inscriptions are in three different languages and scripts. Each inscription refers to a different theme but connected with the authority of the ruler. There was certainly something extraordinary about the pillar.

Nineteenth-century colonial scholars recognized its importance but the questions they faced again were: What did the inscriptions say and who was their author? It is interesting that none of the previous rulers tried to have the script deciphered. This was left to the British officer and scholar James Prinsep who, together with interested others, deciphered it in 1837. Having read the inscriptions, the next problem was to identify the author who referred to himself simply as Devanampiya Piyadassi—the beloved of the gods, the gracious king. No list of kings from Brahmanical sources such as the dynastic lists in the *Puranas* had this name. But in the late nineteenth century, ancient Buddhist chronicles from Sri Lanka were read, and in these Ashoka, the Mauryan ruler, was associated with this title. This was confirmed in 1915 when an inscription was discovered authored by Devanampiyassa Asokassa. This ended any lingering doubts.

In the twentieth century, when the contents of the edicts were widely discussed, Ashoka was applauded as an exemplary ruler. For the British author H. G. Wells, in his widely-read history of the world, *The Outline of History*, Ashoka was unique in world history for being a ruler who propagated ethical values. He became an icon for the Indian national movement, associated with a message of tolerance and non-violence. The wheel of law, taken from his pillar capital, was placed as a symbol on the national flag. For Nehru, he was something of an exemplar.

But now once again Ashoka faces a threat. A century ago, the historian H. C. Raychaudhuri in his book *Political History of Ancient India*, had argued that Ashoka's policy of non-violence had weakened the Mauryan Empire and opened it up to invasions by the Indo-Greeks, Shakas and Kushanas. Other historians demonstrated that this theory was untenable. But in today's world of glorifying violence, some politicians have revived the old argument. They maintain that Ashoka's propagation of non-violence was the cause of India's inability to withstand subsequent invasions. Historians see this as a specious argument as there is enough evidence to counter it. It carries echoes of the old antagonism between the Brahmana and the Shramana. In the current atmosphere charged with paeans to violence and intolerance, Ashoka's concern with social ethics seems to have little space.

I have tried to suggest that items of heritage, be they Ashokan pillars or his ideas as encapsulated in his edicts, have no guarantee of permanency as heritage unless they are conserved, and even when conserved their context has to be fully understood. They can be appropriated or banished, depending on what may be viewed as their usefulness to contemporary times. This function tends to be determined by those who set the political and cultural agendas of society. We are back at the question of who selects what we accept as heritage, and why.

I would now like to turn to my second question. Why do we choose some objects as heritage and not others? Architecture, sculpture and painting are readily recognized as heritage. In recent times some handicrafts are hesitantly being given this status. We continue to reiterate tolerance and non-violence as cherished values of Indian culture irrespective of the evidence to the contrary.

This is illustrated in the inscription I have referred to earlier, in praise of Samudragupta, projected as an iconic ruler of the 'golden age' of the Indian past—the rule of the Guptas. His conquests and the ensuing violence are described in glowing terms. Kalhana's *Rajatarangini*, a twelfth-century history of Kashmir, has an impressive presence of violent activities and intolerant behaviour. Other aspects have been either ignored or given low priority, such as essential objects related to scientific thought and action. I would like to consider the example of the astrolabe—literally, the instrument that catches the stars. It was a two-dimensional model of the celestial sphere: an instrument charting space by giving the position of the stars and planets, by giving local latitudes, and by giving readings of time. It was used in surveying. Varieties of the instrument could be used on land and on the high seas. It helped open up the navigation of the Indian Ocean eagerly sought by Arab and Indian maritime interests. It has been described as an ancient astronomical computer. An object of much aesthetic elegance, it was also a remarkable symbol of the integration of knowledge in the Eurasian world. Astronomers and mariners from different continents were dependent on it and contributed their knowledge to improving the instrument.

Navigation in parts of the Indian Ocean in the early centuries AD used information gathered by the geographer Ptolemy. This was mapped in later centuries. Focusing on the arc of the Arabian Sea, the western coastline of India in this map did not lie approximately north-south but tended to go west-east, with a small area of land to the south of it that was Sri Lanka. Clearly something was wrong yet the map was consulted.

Then came the astrolabe, a generic name for a number of such instruments. They had been used by the Greeks and became familiar to the Indian Ocean navigators by the mid-first millennium AD. Arab and Indian astronomers advanced on the earlier Greek and Byzantine calculations. Navigation became more reliable with the use of the astrolabe by Arab and Indian ships' captains in particular, who were navigating in the Indian Ocean. Maritime traders, who had much to gain from this accuracy, encouraged its use. Astrologers piggybacked on this new device because it was linked to astronomy. Since every court all over Europe and Asia had a court astrologer, kings were more impressed if the predictions were supposedly based on a mechanism for calculations.

The more advanced form of the instrument was common in the maritime activities of the Arabs. It could also indicate the direction of Mecca, useful to the Islamic world. Most astrolabes were flat—planispheric—but there were a few spherical ones. The earlier wooden ones were replaced by metal ones, and some of the finest metal-craft was employed in their making. Unlike us, scholars in those times always had one eye on the beauty of the books and instruments they were handling. Manuals on their use in various languages became available. The numbers and letters on the instrument itself came to be written in all the languages of the areas where it was used—Arabic, Latin, Sanskrit and Chinese.

By the fourteenth century it was all the rage and was used both by astronomers and navigators. Mahendra Suri, who was the court astronomer to Firuz Shah Tughlaq, wrote about it in his work *Yantra Raj*. In the fifteenth century, Nilakantha Somayaji, who was part of a remarkable group of astronomers and mathematicians working in Kerala, refers to it in his studios.

In the second millennium AD, an incredible range of what we would today call amateurs, discussed the astrolabe in various parts of the world, unknown to each other. When mention is made of Amir Khusrau we automatically think of the qawwali and of his poetry. But he was also greatly interested in the working of the astrolabe, in part perhaps because he tended to agree that the earth went around the sun, contrary to the view of Islamic and other orthodoxies. And at the other end of the then known world was Geoffrey Chaucer, the author of the *The Canterbury Tales*, a source of formative poetry in early English. A keen reader of texts on astronomy, he wrote a book for his young son describing the uses of the astrolabe in detail.

The Renaissance in Europe that began in the fourteenth century, assisted in part by the Arab recovery of earlier Greek texts, brought about an increasing interest in science. New instruments were invented to improve on the work earlier done by the astrolabe. Maps took a dramatic turn from the late fifteenth century and became relatively more accurate. Improved navigation brought the world closer. The astrolabe gradually became an instrument of the past. Nevertheless, it is symbolic of how civilizations were not sharply defined self-sufficient blocks, as we have assumed, but rather were nebulous, porous forms, that constantly interacted with each other.

I would now like to take up the third question, which was addressed briefly in the previous chapter. Multiple communities make up the body that we now call Indian citizens. Some identities come from having been imprinted by elite society, others go back a long way and are distinctively different from those of the elite. The latter see their heritage as demarcated from that of others, having its own history of origins. Do we include all these in what is labelled as Indian heritage today, or do we prefer to set them aside? This is a question that will surface with repeated frequency in the future, as various communities become aware of being citizens with equal rights and will register their presence, but with distinct past identities. I shall refer to a couple of these, such as the worship of Ayyanar in Tamil Nadu and the Niyamgiri Hill of the Dongria Kondhs.

Many villages in Tamil Nadu have a shrine to Ayyanar near the entrance to the village. He is the deity who protects the village, depicted as a larger-than-life-sized figure riding a white horse. He can be placed inside the shrine, although frequently his large clay icons with his attendants are kept in the open. The image these days can also be of brick and cement and metal. His images are occasionally placed in the sacred grove that sometimes hosts or adjoins the shrine in the vicinity of the village. Very occasionally an existing image gets appropriated and painted over to conform to the iconography of Ayyanar.

He is not an upper-caste deity. This is clear from the form he takes that has a different aesthetic from the stone and metal images of the regular Hindu pantheon. The priest of the shrine often belongs to the Velar community of potters and is therefore of low caste. He is characteristically non-vegetarian. The potters make the many images of clay horses that are ritually donated to the sacred area. Clay horses as essential ritual objects are found in other parts of rural India as well. The horse was a special and expensive animal associated with royalty and status.

It was difficult to breed good quality horses in India. Pastures that could be used for horses were poor in quality of feed, and the tropical ecology and climate were generally unsuitable. Horses bred in India were, therefore, not of the finest quality. Horses of quality were imported from Central Asia or by sea from the Arabian Peninsula. Nevertheless, the horse was symbolically associated with power, owing no doubt to its continued use in campaigns as cavalry and in royal processions. Yet Ayyanar has been a rural deity and linked to those that were not so well off in society. Did the cult, apart from assuaging the fear of raids, also symbolize the aspiration to status?

The representation of a local hero as protector of the village, and occasionally shown with a horse, goes back two millennia, although this icon was stylistically different. The link between this hero and Ayyanar is unacceptable to many scholars but may, all the same, have had some tenuous connection, not necessarily of form but of a continuing idea. From the early centuries AD, images were sculpted on stone slabs of the hero who had died protecting the village or the village cattle. They are now called vira-kal, hero-stones, in south India and more frequently kirti-stambha in the north. They are frequently found in the border areas in what were once frontiers of kingdoms, or in environmentally marginal areas that witnessed attacks by predators, or frequent cattle raids on villages, or local skirmishes. They commemorate the local hero who defended the village.

The early ones are simple, showing just the hero or the hero with his weapons and occasionally a horse. Gradually they become more elaborate and provide more information generally in graphic form, although the horse is not prominent in all icons. The sun and the moon are symbols of eternity; there is an indication of the sect to which the hero belonged by the symbols linked to him; he is shown being carried away by apsaras to heaven so the cause of his death precludes him from rebirth; and there is a depiction of the incident, either a skirmish or a cattle raid. Even more elaborate are the later ones that carry inscriptions describing the hero and the incident. The hero, since he was sometimes worshipped, is known just occasionally to have morphed into a deity. This has been suggested as the origin of the cult of Vitthala in Maharashtra.

Is there continuity in these forms? In searching for the ancestry of a horse-riding deity should we not look beyond the texts? The iconography may be different in village cults and more so over a period of centuries, nevertheless there are similarities. Hero-stones and the cult of Ayyanar are both linked to villages and low status groups. Veneration is directed towards the person depicted who is seen as the protector. The cult seems initially to be outside the confines of elite worship; it epitomizes a local regional culture different from that of a recognizably royal cult. It also points to the frequency of raids at the village level that were fought off without the help of the king's army. Do the hero-stones and cults such as that of Ayyanar carry yet another message, that what mattered most to a village community was its ability to defend itself, and that this had often to be locally organized without dependence on the higher authority? There obviously was a difference between those defending the village and officers of the king's army defending the kingdom.

I would now like to turn to an Adivasi community that has been in the news. Their problem raises the issue of environmental heritage as well. I am referring to the Dongria Kondhs of Odisha and their defence of the Niyamgiri Hill that they worship as Niyam Raja whom they hold sacred. The area hosts sacred groves of sal trees and has some of the finest pristine forests in India. The many streams flowing down the hill nourish the forests, vegetation and villages—a fine example of biodiversity. It was proposed to set up a huge opencast mine across the top of the hill, in order to obtain bauxite. This would have destroyed the very area that sustains this biodiversity as well as being an assault on a site held sacred by the Dongria Kondhs.

The reaction in the media, in support of the Dongria Kondhs who resisted the mining of their sacred hill, was slight. Would there have been the same silence had a corporate company wished to mine bauxite from beneath a temple or a masjid or a gurdwara? Are we insensitive towards those whose culture we treat less seriously, and therefore towards their sentiments and fears? Such matters need to be discussed far more widely. They create precedents for the future and are likely to occur more frequently with further inroads into areas occupied by the Adivasis. The more pristine hilly areas are often rich in mineral wealth and no doubt such confrontations will not be occasional.

Claims to hurting sentiments are resorted to regularly in upper caste situations as a mechanism of silencing contrary opinion, irrespective of whether the claims are legitimate or not. But we barely discuss such questions when they concern Adivasi communities.Is this because they have lived throughout history in relative isolation, outside caste identities, having traditionally been regarded as inferior? Are we only becoming conscious of them now when their presence is seen as a barrier to our intentions?

Kautilya's *Arthashastra* refers to the forest people as a menace,

Ashoka Maurya threatens the atavikas, the forest dwellers, Banabhatta's *Harshacharita* treats them as primitive and alien, as indeed they are classified as Mlecchas, outside the social pale, in the caste ordering of society. These cultures had little recognition. They were either ignored or, at best, converted to low-caste Hindus.

The rejection by the Dongria Kondhs of intrusive activity by the outside world draws on their belief that their current lifestyle is idyllic, if not utopian. But this belief introduces another aspect of heritage, to which we give little attention, namely, its link to the notion of utopia. Utopias are often the golden ages of the past especially when they act as props to national identities. Alternatively, they can be projections of the future, as with Plato in Greece and Sir Thomas More in England. Utopias of the future assume that a better world will come, wiping away the inequities of the present.

Heritage is, of course, central to the construction of the golden ages of the past. In the *Puranas*, such an age was the imagined Krita Yuga, the utopia at the start of the four-age cycle of time. The first of the four was when dharma was upheld and the varnas or castes were well established. But in each succeeding age there was decline in the observance of dharma until the present age, the Kali Yuga, when the world has been turned upside down. Not only do the lower castes usurp the functions of the upper castes, but worse, even women are liberated. Dharma is compared to a bull that initially stood on four legs, but one leg dropped off in each yuga. Now the situation is truly precarious as it is standing on only one leg. There is no looking forward to a utopia, except that at the end of the Kali Yuga—many hundreds of years from now—the last avatara of Vishnu might come riding on a white horse and restore the utopian Krita Yuga. There are many representations of this event in sculpture and painting. (The yugas and the concept of time will be discussed in greater detail in the next chapter.)

The coming of a utopia may not in itself be an item of

heritage, although it could be argued that what goes into its formulation carries elements of heritage. There are two reasons for this. One is that it links the past to the present and the present to the future. The latter link may be rare in objects of heritage but does occur in the realm of ideas. The other is that if the presentation of the utopia is through a recitation or a performance that claims to come from the past, then that and what it conveys becomes an item of heritage. Ritual, is in essence, a performance. There is in our history a tradition of envisioning and reciting as ritual the utopias of a future world. But this has remained less recognized. These forms were more familiar in non-Brahmanical literature. They inevitably become part of the vision of society in the compositions of some Bhakti sants—such as Kabir, Ravidas, Tukaram, as has been discussed by various scholars. Their regular recitation on ritual occasions emphasizes the religious message and tends to hide their value as commentaries on existing society within a vision for the future. Frequently the utopia as envisaged is a critique of present conditions. From this perspective the concept of a utopia not only links the past to the present, and indirectly to the future, but also allows us to treat it as an aspect of heritage.

The fantasy of the utopia arises among communities of a common caste or class, where the community seeks an identity through drawing on the historical past or even claiming to so strengthen the fantasy. History and heritage are thus entwined. I shall take as my example a Dalit community from the Punjab, but the pattern is replicated elsewhere.

Religion in India was not monolithic. Its popular practice and propagation was via a multitude of sects, with founding ancestors of men and women, whose following became a community, as for example with the Bhakti sects. As I have noted earlier in the book, these sects either broke away, amoeba-like, from the mainstream or else arose independently and found their social location where they thought it was most suitable. However, religious sects, irrespective of their religious colouring or even where they denied links to any religion, as many did, had caste identities as well, and that is often forgotten. So when conversions took place, the caste identity often carried over into the new religion. Thus every religion of India, indigenous or imported, segregated the Dalits in their midst. Among those who became Sikhs in the Punjab, the upper castes continued to maintain a distance from the Dalit converts to Sikhism.

The Dalit Sikhs remained close to Guru Nanak's teaching but some among them had an additional trajectory as well. Many groups of Dalit Sikhs became followers of the Ad Dharmi, a newly formulated set of ideas and practices close to the needs of the Dalits. In the twentieth century, some of them revived the teachings of an earlier Bhakti sant of the sixteenth century, Ravidas. This was a reaching back into history for an appropriate link and deriving an element of legitimacy from the past. Ravidas was a Chamar, a leather worker in Benares, and social concerns were important to his teaching.

Among his compositions was one that has achieved iconic status. It is called *Beghampura*. Its religious message is not too different from that of some other Bhakti sants, which was that deity, where it exists, is approachable by all irrespective of caste. But his social message was embedded in his concept of a utopia of the future. Beghampura is a Dalit utopian vision as has been pointed out by scholars. It is the city—pura—that is without sorrow—be-gham. In this city there is no fear, no caste segregation, no taxes to be paid, no one is tortured, none have to labour to excess, and everyone is equal because there is no hierarchy. The urban setting facilitates a utopia. There is freedom from all that oppresses the Dalit, unlike the Benares of the sixteenth century. People are not known by their caste or religion but by their actions. The practice of untouchability is, of course, entirely absent.

Although the followers of Ravidas still venerated the Guru Granth Sahib, they also had their own granth, or holy book, a compilation of the poems of their guru, Ravidas. The recitation of the verses of Ravidas was a reassertion of what they regard as their particular heritage. In historical terms they claimed that their heritage went back to pre-Aryan, pre-Brahmana times, when Dalits were indigenous, free people. This utopia of the remote past would return when Beghampura became a reality. Some Ravidas Dalits have migrated to Canada, perhaps in search of a Beghampura.

We see here the coalescing of a community, establishing its identity by reviving the heritage of an earlier medieval period teacher, and asserting its link to it by the recitation of his compositions as part of the ritual. It is, in some ways, a radical revival. Structures marginalized by the mainstream are being brought to the centre. History can revive the recognition of heritage. Heritage, in turn, can create an identity that reinforces claims of legitimacy from the past. The history that is resorted to frequently connects to present-day aspirations. These are used as pointers to a cultural memory. The search for such a history necessarily requires understanding the need for heritage. And heritage can be used to assert pride or to galvanize protest.

As a counterfactual question, had the Brahmi script not been deciphered what would have been the history of early India in which Ashoka Maurya was absent? Our assessment of heritage is therefore dependent on what we know at a certain point in time, and this is subject to being viewed afresh and possibly differently, when more evidence becomes available. In packaging heritage and labelling it as being Indian, we have to be sure to include, or at least be aware of, the heritage of a wide range of cultures from the past, giving some attention to that which has been ignored so far, or treated as legitimately excluded. In selecting the items of heritage, constant reassessment of the role of neglected items may help contribute to a more enlightened vision of what we have inherited.

3

TIME BEFORE TIME

Concepts of time are closely tied to the self-perception of various segments of society. Even something as simple as the form in which time is measured is not universal as it varies in accordance with the function of time in a culture. Seasons as a measure of time are crucial to pastoral and agrarian societies, and these often carry over into rituals and festivals in societies that measure time differently as with people living in cities. The form in which time is measured or thought about, alters from associating objects with the measurement to virtually abstract measurements. The role of time in mythology has its own meaning and of course there is a close tie between time concepts and a sense of history.

The received wisdom of the past two hundred years describes the traditional Indian concept of time as cyclic, excluding all other forms and incorporating an endless repetition of cycles. This was in contrast to the essentially linear time of European civilization. Implicit in this statement is also an insistence that cyclic time precludes a sense of history. This contributed to the theory that Indian civilization was ahistorical. Historical consciousness, it was said, required time to be linear, and to move like an arrow linking the beginning to a final eschatological end. Concepts of time and a sense of history were thus interwoven. Early India was said to lack a sense of history.

Early European scholars working on India searched for histories of India from Sanskrit sources but were unable to discover what they recognized as histories. The exception was said to be Kalhana's *Rajatarangini*, a history of Kashmir written in the twelfth century. It is indeed a most impressive premodern history of a region, but it is not an isolated example since this genre finds expression in other regional chronicles, even if the others were not nearly so impressive. There was a short chronicle from the state of Chamba and from Nepal in the Himalaya and others from Rajasthan, Maharashtra and Odisha in the second millennium AD. These were ignored, perhaps because they were less known to European scholarship; and perhaps because if Indian civilization were to be characterized by an absence of history it would become all the more necessary that Indian history be 'discovered' through the research of scholars who came to be labelled as Orientalists. Some among these scholars did suggest that there was a strand of linear time in certain texts, but the dominant view remained that of insisting on the dichotomy of cyclic and linear, and reiterating that the Indian time concept was restricted to the cyclic. Whereas linear time had a teleology towards which history moved, this was lacking in cyclic time. Another aspect of this was the derision over the length of the cycle, which ran into well over a million years. For those observing the eighteenth-century Irish cleric Bishop James Ussher's calculation of about 6,000 years for the life of the universe, the figures given in Indian sources seemed absurd. But this derision changed to puzzlement when geology indicated that the universe had existed for a few million years.

Cyclic time in India, endlessly repeating itself and with no strongly demarcated points of beginning or end, was said to prevent a differentiation between myth and history, and to deny the possibility of unique events that are a precondition to a historical view. Repeating cycles would repeat events. This minimized the significance of human activities. The construction of the cycle was said to be a fantasy of figures intended to underline the illusory nature of the universe. Nor was there any attempt to suggest a teleology that history was moving towards the goal of 'progress', an idea of central concern to nineteenth-century Europe. In the supposed discovery of the Indian past the premise of investigation remained the current intellectual preconceptions of Europe. The colonial understanding of India drew in part on its comprehension of the European past and in part on what it believed to be an inherent absence of such a past in the civilization of India.

These preconceptions projected Asia, and particularly India, not only as different from Europe but essentially as a contrast to Europe. Asia was the Other of Europe. If Karl Marx and Max Weber were looking for contrasting paradigms in understanding the structure of the Asian political economy or the function of religion in Asia, lesser thinkers—but influential in some circles—such as Mircea Eliade, spoke of the Indian time concept as the myth of the eternal return of cycles of time, precluding history.

All this apart, a sense of time was essential to the creation of cosmology and eschatology as much as a calendar was essential to historical chronology. The existence of a historical chronology and a sense of history, which some of us are now arguing are evident in Indian texts, implies that there were in fact, at least two concepts of time, two forms in which time was projected. One was the view that time moved in cycles, found more often in the construction of cosmology. The other was time visualized as moving in a linear form, a form more commonly used in genealogies when counting generations and in inscriptions that claimed that they were narrating the historical past.

I would like to argue that not only were there distinct concepts of time such as the cyclical and the linear but that these were not always parallel and unrelated, but were sometimes interrelated. I would further like to argue that there was sensitivity to the function of each and a mutual enrichment of thought whenever there was an intersection of the two. My attempt will be to illustrate this by describing the use of both cyclical and linear time in early India, often simultaneous but arising from diverse perceptions and intended for variant purposes. Sometimes these forms intersected in ways that enhance the meaning of both.

Concepts of time can be influenced by the measurement of time through calendars. A terrestrial form of reckoning was culled from the changing seasons and the diversity they brought to the landscape. The heroes of the Kuru clan mentioned in texts of the first millennium BC set out on their cattle raids in the dewy season, returning with captured herds just prior to the start of the rains.

Parallel to these forms of time reckoning, a more precise measurement involved turning heavenward and was constructed on observations of the sun and the moon as the two most visible planets, and also the constellations. By the mid-first millennium BC such observations provided the scale of the lunar day—the tithi, with its multiple subdivisions—the muhurtas; the fortnights of the waxing and waning moon—the paksha; and the lunar month—the masa. But the longer periods of the two solstices—the uttarayana and the dakshinayana—were based on the course of the sun. The interweaving of lunar and solar calendars is reflected in the calculations that to this day determine the date of most festivals.

Some changes grew out of an interaction with Hellenistic astronomy. This was encouraged by the contiguity of Indian and Hellenistic kingdoms—the Mauryas and the Seleucids, in the northwest of the Indian subcontinent. Close maritime trading connections between the western coast of India and ports along the Red Sea and eastern Mediterranean also provided knowledge derived from navigational information. Alexandria was the location of considerable activity in these matters where Indian theories were also known. Hellenistic studies of astronomy and mathematics were translated and advances in knowledge were based on more than a single source in Greek and Sanskrit.

The Indian astronomer Varahamihira, of the mid-first millennium AD, remarked that although Greeks as Mlecchas were outside the social pale of caste society, and therefore socially inferior, they were nevertheless to be respected as seers, rishis, because of their knowledge of both astronomy and astrology. Interestingly, Indian scholars resident at the court of Harun al-Rashid in Baghdad exchanged theories on Indian mathematics and astronomy with the Arabs, the most widely quoted examples being Indian numerals and the concept of the zero. In later times, algebra was also regarded as a contribution coming from India.

A measurement of time large enough to reflect these changes was the adaptation of the idea of the yuga. This was initially a five-year cycle but gradually extended to immensely bigger spans. The word comes from the verb 'to yoke' and refers to planetary bodies in conjunction. The yuga was to become the unit of cosmological and cyclic time, described in the *Puranas* and similar sources. Those creating the projection of cyclic time measured the cycle in enormous figures, perhaps anxious to overawe their audience.

By far the largest of these cycles was the kalpa, infinite and immeasurable, the period that covers creation and continues until the ultimate cataclysmic destruction of the world. And how was this calculated? Some represented the kalpa spatially and these descriptions are such that they cannot be measured in temporal terms. Interestingly, they often come from sources associated with those who were regarded as heretics by the Brahmana orthodoxy. In one Buddhist text the description is as follows: if there is a mountain in the shape of a cube, measuring approximately three miles on each side, and if every hundred years the mountain is brushed with a silk scarf held, according to some, in the beak of an eagle which flew over the mountain, then the time taken for the mountain to be eroded is a kalpa. Another description in a text of the Ajivika sect is equally exaggerated: if there is a river which is a hundred and seventeen thousand six hundred and forty-nine times the size of the Ganga, and if every hundred years one grain of sand is removed from its bed, then the time required for the removal of all the sand would be one measure of time; it takes three thousand of these measures to make one kalpa.

The recurring refrain of 'every hundred years' introduces a temporal dimension of humanly manageable real time, but the image is essentially spatial. It indicates the impossibility of measuring such a length of time almost to the point of negating time. The length of the kalpa is a deliberate transgression of time and was thought up by those who were aware of historical time. At a literal level, the silk scarf would have quickly disintegrated. And who could remove the grains of sand from the bed of a flowing river?

Infinite time was, however, not the view of some contemporary astronomers who did suggest a temporal length for the kalpa. The suggestions differed. The most popular it would seem calculated the length as four thousand, three hundred and twenty million—4,320,000—earthly years, a figure that was to occur in more than one context. More closely related to astronomy, mathematics and cosmology was the theory that time should be measured in the great cycles—mahayugas. This could be expanded when cyclic theories came to incorporate other theories. For example, one theory maintained that a kalpa had fourteen manvantaras—period of Manus—each of which had a Manu as its creator. We are currently in the seventh manvantara, that of Manu Vaivasvata. There is, therefore, an interface between cosmology and astronomy in terms of the figures used for the length of the ages and the cycles. It remains unclear whether the astronomers borrowed the figures from the creators of cyclic time or vice versa. Perhaps cosmology was seeking legitimacy by borrowing the numbers used by the astronomers. Differences between the two become apparent in the figures used by later astronomers that differed from these.

Each mahayuga or great cycle incorporated four lesser cycles, the yugas, but not of equal length. The pattern in which the great cycle is set out and which holds together the cyclic theory does hint at some controlling agency. One evocative image presents time as being that which regulates the working of the universe, when it is said, asya loka yantrasya sutradharah (time directs the working of this world).

The four ages or yugas were perceived in the following order: the first was the Krita or the Satya consisting of four thousand divine years sandwiched between two twilight periods of four hundred years each; then came the Treta of three thousand years with two similar preceding and subsequent twilight periods, each of three hundred years; this was followed by the Dvapara of two thousand years with a twilight at each end of two hundred years; and finally the Kali of one thousand years with similar twilight periods of a hundred years each. These add up to twelve thousand divine years and have to be multiplied by 360 to arrive at the figure for human years. A great cycle therefore extends to 4,320,000 human years.

The play is on the number 432 and it increases by adding zeros. Did this fantasy on numbers arise from the excitement of having discovered the uses of the zero at around this time? The notion of cycles may have been reinforced by the notion of the recurring rebirth of the soul—karma and samsara—that was a belief among many religious sects. The names of the cycles were taken from the throws at dice, thus interjecting an element of chance into the flow of time. The present Kali Age has been called the age of the losing throw. The start of the Kali Yuga was calculated to a date equivalent to 3102 BC. Since it has a length of 4,320,000 human years, there are many thousand still to come, so we have an immense future of declining norms before us, until the cataclysmic end. By way of scale, we are also told that the length of a human life is that of a dewdrop on the tip of a blade of grass at sunrise.

The descending arithmetic progression in the length of the four cycles suggests that there was an attempt at an orderly system of numbers. Some numbers were regarded as magical such as seven, twelve, and even four hundred and thirty-two, which have parallels in other contemporary cultures. The cycles are not identical and therefore permit of new events. Because of the difference in length there could not have been a complete repetition of events. It is thus possible for an event to be unique. The circle does not return to the beginning but moves into the next and smaller one. Such a continuity of circles could be stretched to a spiral, a wave or even perhaps a not very straight line. Should these be seen as cycles or as ages?

The decrease in the length of each age was not limited to a mathematical pattern. It is also said that there is a corresponding decline of dharma—the social, ethical and sacred ordering of society as formulated by the highest caste, that of the Brahmanas. The first and largest yuga encapsulated the golden age at its start but subsequently there is a gradual decline in each age, culminating in the degeneration of the Kali Age. The symbols of decline are easily recognizable: marriage becomes necessary for human procreation and men and women are no longer born as adult couples; the height and form of the human body begins to get smaller; the length of life decreases dramatically; and labour becomes increasingly arduous and necessary. There is an abundance of heretics and unrighteous people. These are familiar characteristics of an age of decline in the time-concepts of many cultures. As we have seen, the decrease of dharma is compared to a bull that stands on four legs in the first age, but drops one leg in each subsequent age. There is a substantial change from one age to the next as is implicit in this image.

The decline inherent in the Kali Age is also underlined by the description of the caste order governing social norms being gradually inverted. The lower castes will take over the status and functions of the upper castes, even to the extent of performing rituals to which they were not previously entitled. This is in part prophecy but is also a fear of current changing conditions challenging the norms. Thus kings who are not of the Kshatriya or aristocratic caste but of obscure origin, and frequently low caste Shudras, or from outside the pale of caste society, can easily adopt higher status. They are referred to as degenerate Kshatriyas but this does not erode their authority. An even bigger disaster will be the liberation of women. This would also tie into the undermining of caste society since the subordination of women was essential to its continuing in accordance with the patriarchal social codes. It shall indeed be, as the text states, a world turned upside down. The coming future was a dystopia rather than a utopia. Part of the logic of cyclic time is that there are down-swings and up-swings in the cycle. The return to the golden age requires the termination of the entire set of cycles and that too in conditions that are the opposite of utopian.

When the condition of decline is acute then the faithful will flee to the hills and await the coming of the Brahmana Kalkin, who is said to be the tenth incarnation of the deity Vishnu, and who will restore the norms of caste society. Kalkin is a parallel concept to that of the coming of the last Buddha, the Buddha Maitreya, who will save the true doctrine from extinction and re-establish Buddhism. It is interesting that many of these saviour figures either emerge or receive added attention around the early Christian era, when the belief systems to which they belong—Vaishnavism, Buddhism, Zoroastrianism and Christianity—are in close contact in the area stretching from India to the eastern Mediterranean. The coming of Kalkin can be read as an alternative to the cataclysmic end of the mahayuga, since he initiates another golden age. History does not end and time does not cease, but eschatology is perhaps implicit, given the immense length of the great cycle.

The Kali Yuga was a concept frequently referred to in a variety of sources but the details of the cyclic theory come in particular texts. Among these were: the long epic poem the *Mahabharata*, initially composed in the first millennium BC; the code of social duty and ritual requirements, the *Manu Dharmashastra*, written at the turn of the Christian era; and the more accessible and popular religious texts of the early centuries AD, the *Puranas*.

The inclusion of theories of cyclic time in the epic are in the sections generally believed to be later interpolations and thought to have been inserted by Brahmana redactors when the epic was converted to sacred literature. The authorship of the *Dharmashastras* was also Brahmana. Although some of the *Puranas* are said to have been composed by bards, in effect, they were again largely edited by Brahmana authors. There is, therefore, a common authorship supporting these ideas.

The historiographical link with modern theories is that these were the texts studied and translated by Orientalists such as William Jones, Henry Thomas Colebrooke and H. H. Wilson. These studies were encouraged with the intention of enhancing British understanding of precolonial laws, religious beliefs and practices and in searching for the Indian past. But because these particular texts were given importance initially, their description of cyclic time came to be seen as the sole form of time reckoning in India. One can understand how James Mill dismissed Indian concepts of time as pretensions to remote antiquity, but it is more difficult to explain why H. H. Wilson did not recognize the linear pattern of time in, for example, the succession list in the *Vishnu Purana*, on which he worked at length and which he translated.

In relating the details of what happened in the Kali Yuga, the *Vishnu Purana* provides us with various categories of linear time. The Vamshanucharita section consists initially of genealogies and subsequently descent lists of dynasties. The genealogies are of the chiefs of clans, referred to as Kshatriyas and they cover about a hundred generations. They need not be taken as factual records but can be analysed as perceptions of the past. The word used for the descent group is vamsha, the name given to the bamboo or a plant of the cane family and an obviously appropriate symbol since the plant grows segment by segment, each segment from out of a node. The analogy with genealogical descent is most effective. The imagery emphasizes linearity that is expressed in what might be called 'generational time' seen as the flow of generations. This construction of the past as we have it today dates to the early centuries AD, and subsequently is known to be used to negotiate and manipulate the claims and statuses of later rulers through a variety of assumed links.

But the flow is not unbroken. There are time markers separating categories of generational time. The first time marker is the Great Flood, which enveloped the world and which separates the pre-genealogical period from the succession of generations of clan chiefs. Each of the rulers of the antediluvian time, known as Manus, ruled for many thousands of years. At the time of the flood, Vishnu in his incarnation as a fish, appears to the then ruling Manu, and instructs him to build a boat. This is tied to the horn of the god-fish, and is towed through the floodwaters and lodged safely on Mount Meru. When the flood subsides, Manu emerges from the boat and becomes the progenitor of those who are born as the ruling clans. The flood is first mentioned in a text of about the eighth century BC and is later elaborated upon in the *Puranas*. It has such close parallels with the Mesopotamian legend that it may well have been an adaptation from the same source as for the Biblical story of Noah's Ark.

Subsequent to the flood the supposed genealogies of the ancient heroes or the Kshatriyas are mapped. The succession of generations is divided into two groups named after the sun and the moon, a symbolism of both dichotomy and eternity, used frequently in myth, yoga, alchemy and on many other occasions. The solar and the lunar lines mark a different pattern of descent. The solar line or the Suryavamsha emphasizes primogeniture and claims to record the descent only of the eldest sons. The pattern of descent forms vertical parallels. In the *Ramayana* the families of status are of the solar line. The lunar line or the Chandravamsha is different. It is laid out in the form of a segmentary system and the lines of descent fan out since all the presumed sons and their sons are located in the system. The advantage of a system similar to the segmentary system, is that it can easily incorporate a variety of groups in a genealogy by latching them onto the existing ones. These constitute the structure of society in the other epic, the *Mahabharata*.

The solar line slowly peters out. But those belonging to the lunar line are brought together in the second time marker, the famous war said to have been fought at Kurukshetra when virtually every clan of that period was involved, as described in the *Mahabharata*. The war, we are told, terminated the glory of the ancient Kshatriya heroes. In the representation of the past, the war demarcates the age of heroes from the subsequent age, which was that of dynasties. A major indicator of change is that the narrative switches from the past tense to the future tense and reads as a prophecy. This invokes astrology, especially popular in court circles.

The narrative in this section of the *Vishnu Purana* is limited largely to the names of rulers with an occasional but minimum commentary. Regnal years are sometimes included, further highlighting a sense of linear time. The dynasties, unlike the Kshatriya families of the earlier section, had no kinship ties between them and were of the Brahmana or Shudra caste rather than Kshatriya. In practice, the profession of ruling seems to have been open to any caste, another example of the reversals of the Kali Yuga. The names of dynasties and rulers are sometimes corroborated in other sources such as inscriptions, which were now being issued in large number.

Genealogies incorporating generational time are within the framework of linear time. The texts included in what is called the ancient Indian historical tradition—the Itihasa Purana—make claims to representing the past 'as it was'. The flood seems to demarcate the time of myth from the time of history. There is a distinct beginning from after the flood and an equally distinct termination in the war. The arrow of time moves steadily through the generations and to the battlefield. That the lists may have much that is fabricated—as is the case with all such lists—is not so relevant as is the perception of the form of time, which is linear. This is further underlined in the next section of the *Vishnu Purana,* recording the dynasties ruling over a major part of northern India.

Thus the section in the *Puranas* describing the succession of those who ruled encapsulates three kinds of time. The prediluvian rulers, the Manus, are referred to in what could be called cosmological time, beyond even the purview of the great cycles. This is almost a form of reaching back to time before time. It is distant from the two more human time frames: genealogies and dynasties. With these, the presence of what is conventionally regarded as history begins to surface. This move in the direction of historical time may have been associated with another form of measuring time more closely linked to history, namely the creation of eras.

The use of a particular era, the samvat, related to historical chronology, probably grew out of a consciousness of enhanced political power with a focus on the royal court. The earliest inscriptions, those of the Mauryan emperor Ashoka who ruled in the third century BC, are dated in regnal years counted from the date of his accession. This may have provided an impetus for establishing an era that would be a commonly accepted base point for historical dates. But in Buddhist reckoning the preference would have been to take the date of the death of the Buddha—the Maha Parinirvana—as the starting point, as indeed was done for events in the narrative of the history of Buddhism. The start of the earliest, probably secular era was the much used Krita era of 58 BC, later to be called the Malava era but more popularly known as the Vikrama era. There has been much controversy regarding its origin. The current consensus associates it with a relatively unimportant king, Azes I. Its impressive continuity to the present suggests associations other than just the accession of a minor king, for eras are often abandoned when a dynasty declines. There might have been a connection with astronomy since the city of Ujjain, the meridian for calculating longitude, was located in the territory claimed by the Malavas.

Historical events become the rationale for starting eras subsequently, such as the Shaka era of AD 78, the Chedi era of 248–249, the Gupta era of 319–320, the Harsha era of 606, and so on—a virtual blossoming of eras. Many of those who started these eras were, in origin, small time rulers who had succeeded in establishing large kingdoms. As a status symbol, the Chalukya–Vikrama era of AD 1075 was not only a claim to supremacy by the Chalukya king Vikramaditya VI, but included the legitimizing of Vikramaditya's usurpation of the throne. The creating and abandoning of eras became an act of political choice. The continuity of an era is not just the continuity of a calendar but also of the associations linked to what the era commemorates. The ideology implicit in starting an era calls for historical attention.

Events related to dynastic history were not the only occasion for starting an era. Time reckoning based on the year of the death of the Buddha, the Maha Parinirvana became current in the Buddhist world. The date generally used was 486 or 483 BC. Recently, however, some scholars such as the German Indologist Heinz Bechert have questioned these dates and would prefer to bring the Maha Parinirvana forward by anything up to a century. Nevertheless, what is important is that events described in Buddhist texts such as religious councils, the establishing of monasteries, the accession of kings and such like, are generally dated from the death of the Buddha, which is calculated on the basis of a definitive date.

Buddhist chronicles demonstrate a concern with time and history in that they record and narrate what they regarded as historically important events: as, for example, the history of the Buddhist order or sangha starting with the historical founder Gautama Buddha; relations between the Buddhist order and the state; the founding of breakaway sects and the events which led up to these; records of gifts of land, property and investments;

and matters of monastic discipline. All these are tied to linear time in various ways. The Buddhist calendar was pegged to what were viewed as events in the life of the Buddha and the history of the order. The linear basis of Buddhist chronology was nevertheless juxtaposed with ideas of time cycles. These had their own complexities distinct from those of the *Puranas*. This was not specific only to Buddhism. Jaina centres from the first millennium AD maintained the same kind of records. This involved histories which, in order to be legitimate, had to cohere up to a point. Such histories were not always intended to be taken literally, and certainly cannot be so taken today. As with many texts that are used as historical sources, their historical elements have to be decoded through the prevalent social and cultural idiom.

Historical time is a requirement for what have come to be regarded as the annals of early Indian history. These are inscriptions issued by a variety of rulers, officials and others. They frequently narrate, even if briefly, the chronological and sequential history of a dynasty. Some were legal documents conferring rights on land and were proof of a title deed. Precision in dating gave greater authority and authenticity to a document. The granting of land or property to religious beneficiaries had to be made at an auspicious moment so as to carry the maximum merit for the donor. The auspicious moment was calculated by the astrologer in meticulous detail and was mentioned in the inscription recording the grant. Other categories of grants also carried precise dates. It is this precision which enables us to calculate the dates of the inscriptions in the equivalent date of the Gregorian calendar. Much of early Indian historical chronology is founded on the calculation of these dates carefully studied by Indologists. Yet, curiously, there was only a little effort to go beyond the bare bones of chronology and try to deduce the time concepts reflected in these dating systems.

Inscriptions recorded the official version of the events of a reign and were issued by almost every ruling family. The legitimizing of power, especially in a competitive situation, included a range of activities. Among them was the making of grants of land, particularly to religious beneficiaries who would then act as a network of support for the ruling family. This was the occasion for obscure families who had risen to rulership to claim a status equivalent to that of established ruling families, a claim which the beneficiaries were ready to substantiate. The document accompanying the grant had to be inscribed on imperishable material—copper or stone. Grants had to be impressive and often more generous than those of earlier times or of competing rulers.

In many instances the donations were carefully culled from the donor's income and given with a maximum of faith. But in some cases where the donations are virtual treasure troves, or the equivalent thereof, there is the suspicion that the demonstration effect of a substantial donation was more important than the act of giving. Such an action, as has been noticed for many other cultures, is to bring attention to a claim to status. It also brings to mind the anthropological theories of the cultures of the Pacific northwest, where the 'potlatch', the ritualized giving away of wealth in a spirit of competition, was the most effective form of claiming status. Obviously the rituals were not the same. Nevertheless, one has to look for meanings other than the most obvious in actions such as these.

From about the seventh century onwards there is an efflorescence of another category of historical texts that combine elements of linear time such as genealogies, dynastic histories and eras. These were biographies of kings or an occasional minister, what was called the Charita literature. The subject of the biography was a contemporary ruler, and the biography narrated the origins of his family and the history of his ancestors, particularly that which led the family to power. The central event of his reign, as assessed by the biographer and presumably the king as well, was described with appropriate literary elaboration, sometimes quite flamboyantly, and frankly eulogistic as is frequent in courtly literature. Often the intention was to defend the usurping of a throne and overturning the rule of primogeniture. Sometimes the intervention of a deity was required to justify the action of the king. And if the interventions became too frequent, the reader would understand that their intention was other than what was being related. Whatever the intentions of the biographies, they did describe and present some significant events of a king's reign in a linear succession.

Dynastic chronicles or regional histories also drew legitimacy from linear time. These were the vamshavalis, literally the path of succession. The most famous among these was the much quoted *Rajatarangini* of Kalhana, but similar although less impressive narratives come from many other parts of the subcontinent dating to about the mid-second millennium AD, such as Merutunga's *Prabandha-chintamani* and the *Gopalaraja-vamshavali* from Nepal. At the point when a region changed from being viewed as the territory of a chiefdom and came to be seen as the state claimed by a dynasty, the records of the past were collated, and a chronicle was put together. This was maintained as an up-to-date narrative of what were regarded as significant events. In their earlier sections such chronicles incorporate some of the genealogies of the ancient heroes of the *Puranas* to whom they link the local rulers. Writing the chronicle of a region became another form of recognizing the region as an entity and legitimizing its succession of rulers.

Time is linear in these texts and the assumptions of cyclic time may be implicit but remain distant. Cyclic time is not denied and is present in the larger reckoning. A longer continuity of time is assumed in the inscriptions recording grants of land, one that went beyond even the mahayuga. The formulaic phrase here reads that the grant should last 'as long as the moon and sun endure'. Clearly time was thought of at many levels. The simultaneous use of more than a single form of time and its layered representation, does point to some awareness that different segments of a society may view their past differently. For the historian to recognize this perception requires a certain sensitivity in seeing the past as being one of multiple perceptions within the intricacies of the use of time.

Deities and incarnations tend to be placed in the earlier cycles. But events relating to the human scale are more properly expressed as part of what was perhaps seen as the more functional linear time. This did not preclude a reference on occasion to cyclic time. A seventh-century inscription records an event in the Shaka era of AD 78 and includes for good measure a reference to the date of the Kali Yuga. Whereas a reference to something like the Kali Yuga might be added, what seems to have been required was a historical date.

In texts related to ritual the reference is often to the four ages. However, in the genealogies and inscriptions the immediate point of reference is linear time. Despite this intersection the function of each form is differentiated. The presence of more than one form of time in the same text is perhaps intended to point us towards different statements being made about each. In the *Vishnu Purana*, cyclic time is projected as part of the cosmology, whereas linear time is foundational to the historical sections that deal with lineages and dynasties. Within linear time there can be differentiation. Clans, lineages and their generations are recorded in a way that is not identical with the dynasties of kings, although the chronology of both is linear. The former precedes the latter. The linearity underlines continuity even if the forms change.

My intention has been to suggest that various forms of time reckoning were used in early India and that concepts of both linear and cyclic time were familiar. The choice was determined by the function of the particular form of time and those involved in using it, and the purpose for which it was being used.

◆

As part of history, time was tied into social and political functions and these can be seen either in the diverse authorship of some historical traditions or else in the compositions of the authors from the same social group using time for diverse purposes. It is stated that genealogies were originally compiled by the bards, and presumably incorporated the world view of the ruling clans and were intended to record their past. But when this compilation came to be edited by the Brahmanas, in order to use it for establishing the legitimacy and social claims of their patrons who could be upstart rulers, this past could have been taken away from the bards and appropriated by the Brahmana authors of the *Puranas*. The cyclic concept was comprehensive, although distant, and was more apposite to the ritual and other concerns of the Brahmana priests and their perceptions of the past, requiring as it did an emphasis on that which is beyond human control. The cyclic concept became a temporal frame within which any past could be incorporated. These two concepts of time, therefore, are also related to the particular interests of two socially distinct groups, but are linked less to Brahmana and Kshatriya caste groups and more to categories of societies, such as clan societies or kingdoms. Other theories arising from religious ideologies also influenced these concepts in some of their applications.

The past was sought to be captured. One way of doing this was to associate it with various projections of time. As the creators of cosmologies, the Brahmanas often refer to time in the cyclic form of the four ages. As keepers of the genealogies or composers of inscriptions or authors of royal biographies, the immediate point of reference is linear time. In spite of this intersection or encompassment, the function of each form is differentiated. The simultaneous use of more than a single form and its layered representation indicates some awareness that different segments of a society may view their past differently. For the historian to recognize this requires certain sensitivity in seeing the past as multiple perceptions within the intricacies of the use of time.

The presence of more than one form of time in the same text is perhaps intended to point us towards different statements being made about each. Within linear time there can also be differentiation. Genealogical time based on a succession of generations is always at the start of the record and precedes that which we would recognize as conventional history. This is evident from the succession lists in the *Puranas*, as also from the regional chronicles. This format underlines continuity. But it is also a way of differentiating two categories of the past with the deliberate and consistent placing of one before the other.

After the mid-first millennium AD, the past, where feasible, tended to be introduced into the construction of ancestry and claims to legitimacy, and in rights to property. This was likely to be more so where claims were being contested. The past involved multiple views of time. For many, the fourth age, although part of the great cycle of mahayuga encapsulated nevertheless the linear forms of the perceived history of heroes and kings. Eras became fashionable and necessary, precise dating systems came to be used in the epigraphic annals of the various dynasties, and regional societies were poised to patronize the writing of royal biographies and the chronicled histories of the past. A sense of history was perhaps embedded in some sources but was visible in others.

As I have pointed out, the insistence on Indian society having only a cyclical concept of time has been questioned. But even its rejection has not yet encouraged recognition of forms of history as evident in some early Indian texts. Such recognition is likely to be strengthened through a demonstration of the presence of linear time. Given that every society has an awareness of its past it is perhaps futile to construct a society which is said to deny history. This can only be an argument to support distinctive characteristics of 'Otherness' whether justified or not, and the lack of what is believed to be the norm from the perspective of European history.

◆

The two time concepts, cyclic and linear, do not exhaust the variations on time. In Indian texts alone time is portrayed in diverse images. Some maintain that time was the creator begetting the sky and the earth, the waters and the sun, the sacrifice and the ritual verses; and drove a horse with seven reins, was thousand-eyed and ageless. Or it was the imperishable deity through whom everything that has life, eventually dies. For others time was the ultimate cause lying between heaven and earth and weaving the past, present and future across space. Krishna in the *Bhagavad Gita* proclaims, Kalo'smi—I am Time.

Groups within a society visualize time in different ways often depending on how it is to be used. The creators of myths, the chroniclers of kings and the collectors of taxes subscribe to divergent images of time. Distinctions can be made between cosmological time and historical time. The first could be a fantasy on time although a conscious fantasy, carefully constructed and therefore reflective of its authors and their concerns. The second is based on the functions of measured time, also carefully constructed but reflecting concerns of a different kind. If time is to be seen as a metaphor of history, which is what I have been suggesting, then perhaps we need to explore the many more patterns of time and their intersections.

As I have pointed out throughout this chapter, in various guises, concepts of time become features of cultural articulation. Sometimes the forms intersect, at other times the one encompasses the other and at still other times they are distinct. The *Vishnu Purana* in one chapter describes at length the various ages of cyclic time. In another chapter it provides details of the genealogies of the heroes and the rulers of the dynasties in the Kali Age. The way in which time was envisaged and used in determining the pattern of living makes it an important ingredient in the formulating of the culture of either a segment of society or the entire society, depending on who follows the pattern.

4

SCIENCE AS CULTURE

Historians tend to view the history of science from two perspectives. One is the familiar linear projection of the evolution of particular disciplines regarded as scientific, such as astronomy or mathematics or medicine, a projection determined by our modern understanding of science. The emphasis is on isolating inventions and discoveries and focusing on that knowledge which is seen as strictly scientific. The other is the attempt to view science as culture and as part of the social formation of a society. This perspective is obviously much more recent, more wide-angled and takes in many facets involving interactions and osmosis, which bear on a particular body of knowledge. Whereas the first is frequently the close preserve of scientists, the second approach is the one in which the historian can intervene. Historians of India have tended to stay with the first. Hence science linked to cultures is a marginalized subject.

Both ideas relate closely to the way in which historians search for explanations. Two recent studies, among many others, have underlined the need to relate science more closely to its cultural and social context and to investigate the nature of scientific thinking as part of a historical context, with an added cultural and sociological dimension. Thomas S. Kuhn in his book on *The Structure of Scientific Revolutions* has argued that a shift in paradigm occurs when existing knowledge is questioned and a new explanation is found to be more apposite. The British scientist and historian Joseph Needham in his path-breaking study of science and civilization in China, used the phrase ecumenical science, referring to science having to include all the ways in which it has been studied in various civilizations. There is now the realization that scientific thinking needs to break away from just observing the study of science in Europe. It is necessary to study Chinese science, and for that matter of other cultures as well, and observe how it is treated as knowledge in its place of origin. The caveat, however, is that as in Needham's study of science in China, it has to be examined from both a scientific perspective and as a reflection of the cultures involved.

Many Indian scientists, competent in their fields of specialization, know less about science as a form of knowledge, or the kind of reasoning involved in the scientific method that can also be applied to other forms of knowledge. This might explain their surprising and tacit acceptance of some of the more ridiculous statements made by non-scientists on the fantasy-based claims pertaining to science as supposedly practised by our ancient ancestors. This reduces their ability to recognize the difference between the remarkably impressive knowledge of premodern Indian thinkers in some of the sciences, and the infantile fancies that are often projected in their name by those ignorant of science in both premodern and in current times. The reasons for doing the latter are more often political rather than due to any scientific assessment.

The onus is not only on the scientist but also on the historian. Not enough attention has been given by historians to integrating the ideas related to the sciences from earlier times to other aspects of culture. The historian's intervention from this perspective would require the re-crafting even of some historical formulations. This is being done for some other aspects in recent historical reinterpretations. One of these is the notion of 'civilization' as a somewhat fixed and continuing historical unit.

Used more casually in the earlier centuries to refer to the softening of manners and to artistic and literary achievements, it became a widely accepted unit of history from the nineteenth century, coinciding with colonial perceptions of history. The world was divided into discrete, geographically bounded areas each with a dominant culture, recognizably different in intellectual, aesthetic, technological and religious attainments, all of which were associated with urban centres, the use of scripts, the existence of a state and of an organized social order. In *A Study of History*, the British historian Arnold Toynbee counted twenty-six such civilizations, each rising in response to challenges and declining when the response was inadequate. More recently the count has been reduced to eight in Samuel P. Huntington's *The Clash of Civilizations and the Remaking of World Order*. As a spokesman of the American political right wing, his theory that the future of the world will revolve around the clash of civilizations inspired by religious identities seems to envisage conflicting civilizations as a replacement for the cold war.

Huntington's identification of these eight is, as is often the case, a confusion of various characteristics of religion, geography, dynasty, nation, race and ranking, and is generally unacceptable to serious historians. But more increasingly, the reaction it drew from critics indicates new parameters in the concept of civilization. Civilizations are not seen now as static or geographically bounded. Cultures, patterns of life and belief are not immutable and do not in themselves give rise to violent conflict, nor are civilizations necessarily defined by rationality as argued earlier by the German sociologist and philosopher Max Weber. Other schools of thought such as Marxist historiography as well as the rather different perspective of the Annales group in France have encouraged the reformulation of the notion of civilization focusing on explanations of historical change.

The more important components are cultures defined as patterns of living, deriving from economic factors, social divisions and belief systems. Variations in cultural forms within a geographical area tend to erode the monolithic character of earlier views of civilizations. Consequently, civilizations are characterized both by changes from an internal dynamic and by a constant borrowing, assimilating and interacting with others, which call for a continuous process of reordering and redefining. It is less the isolated uniqueness of each civilization and more the forms which societies take and the reasons for these, which have become the basis of comparative studies.

This in turn means that knowledge emerges from the combination of an indigenous genesis together with transmission from other coexisting cultures, a transmission that can involve some contestation and some negotiation. This process takes the form of cultural transactions, within a culture and between cultures. Knowledge, viewed either as a body of information or as theories of explanation, is part of this transaction. Questions of agency and of the exploitation of knowledge become central. This is as relevant to scientific knowledge as to philosophy and literature and requires that the former be integrated as part of culture. Where the history of science is written as technological innovation based on rational modes of thought, there the historiography of scientific knowledge frequently misses out on its being embedded in a particular kind of society.

Other aspects emerge from what I have mentioned so far. One is that scientific achievements can no longer be seen as the product of just one culture. A major breakthrough in science, or in proto-science as some prefer to call it, is more frequent when there is an intersection of ideas from various cultures. Understanding these points of departure is assisted when it is known which cultures were involved and how these cultures used the knowledge. The old nineteenth-century obsession with who got there first, and thus claiming superiority in scientific advance is no longer the concern of historians of science.

Even more pointless is the current fashion in India of proclaiming that the ancient Hindus were already familiar, many centuries ago, with what are now regarded as the achievements of modern science. Attempts to back such statements takes recourse to untenable statements such as that knowledge of plastic surgery is proved by the elephant head implanted on the child Ganesh. Minor grafting was known to many cultures but this was not plastic surgery. Equally ridiculous are the claims to the Pushpaka Vimana being an aeroplane despite the lack of studies of aerodynamics. The birth of the Kauravas from a hundred jars is said to be associated with the use of stem cell research but there is obviously no reference to this research in any text.

The answer to the statement that possibly such knowledge existed and that we do not know about it is that we do know and it didn't exist. Scientific inventions have a long gestation period and historians can trace the steps by which the theory and practice came together in an invention. These experimental ways of thinking are recorded in texts that inform us of the stage at which scientific thinking has arrived. If such documents are neither available nor referred to, then obviously even the theory about the invention is in doubt. Another test of the existence of such knowledge requires that the information given in a text should be demonstrable through observation and experiment. If the description of a Pushpaka Vimana, as given in the texts, can be used to construct a machine that can fly, only then can we call it an aeroplane. Attempts to do this have not met with any success.

Unreliable statements on ancient scientific knowledge demonstrate a fundamental lack of an understanding of the methodology of science. Trying to prove the existence of the end result without indicating the steps by which it was arrived at is not the way science proceeds. This attitude extends to the way in which science is taught as part of Indian school education. What matters are the formulae that are learnt like mantras, without questioning in detail the methods by which they are arrived at and extending the method to other branches of knowledge. In our definition of inherited culture we have also marginalized that which has to do with mathematics and astronomy, for instance, with little effort to teach what was known earlier and why it did not go beyond the known knowledge of a certain time. There is reference to what is fashionable in social circles these days such as yoga and Ayurvedic medicine but the analyses of the basic method involved in these studies is less well known, nor their applicability in contemporary knowledge. Early scientific ideas are rarely correlated with other current theories. For example, did Aryabhatta's geocentric theory of the earth rotating around the sun influence in any way the description of the universe as described in contemporary *Puranas*, and if not, why not? Did it have any impact on philosophical thought?

Histories of early India refer to these ideas in separate compartments. Historians continue to be guilty of maintaining this segregation. We have not thought of how ideas of a scientific kind may have affected other ideas or even activities that we regard as essential ingredients of culture. We describe the magnificence of temples and mosques and marvel at their architecture but do we correlate these forms with the knowledge of engineering that existed at the time, or examine whether a change of style may have arisen from a different calculation in the construction of the building? Despite the teaching and use of modern science in India for over a century we have not introduced the scientific method as a method of investigation, applicable in many areas of knowledge, nor do we debate its usefulness to our understanding of the world around us.

In the last few years the priority given to irrational explanations of various kinds has increased noticeably, frequently justified by statements that such explanations are in keeping with Indian cultural traditions. Those that use modern methods of analysis in their research are accused of relying on Western ways of thinking, yet what is virtually not discussed and given little attention is the tradition of logical thinking, rational argument and emphasis on causality that was prominent in premodern Indian thought. It was present in many philosophical schools. The question is why do we not give adequate representation to this tradition?

The question of the universality of science hinges on how we define 'universality'. Is there a difference between how it was viewed in premodern times and now? At the level of philosophy and science the area of communication would have been narrower and more specific. It also has to do with how we perceive change. Historians conveniently use the term 'revolution' for a process of qualitative and quantitative change, but the nature of revolutions differs. V. Gordon Childe referred to the transition of early societies from hunting-gathering and pastoralism to agriculture as the Neolithic Revolution. This was the change based on the cultivation of crops that became more possible with an improvement in technology, even if it was limited to stone tools. Historians also refer to the European Industrial Revolution of the late eighteenth and nineteenth centuries that, because it occurred in the historical context of capitalism and colonialism, spread rapidly. 'Revolution' is a convenient label for indexing societies. But the two revolutions referred to here are not identical, neither as a process nor as the universalizing of a process.

In the case of the Neolithic Revolution similar changes occur in unconnected societies as for example the Yangshao in China and Mehrgarh in Baluchistan. The changes have characteristic patterns of settlement, agriculture, pottery, artefacts, icons symbolizing fertility, and so on. They appear to be internal to each culture, therefore the diffusion and transmission of ideas was not the cause, although this has been debated. This may have been so where these cultures were in proximity to each other. However, subsequent to the Neolithic Revolution, there is a considerable interaction of peoples, even if the Neolithic societies took variant paths. The question that is asked is whether the internal change was predictable. And particularly if there were some characteristics such as a required technology that might act as determining factors. Does technology become a central focus? The oral transmission of technology is a major study in this kind of knowledge. But is technology alone what is required? It is a useful index in labelling a society but we have to go beyond technology in assessing how a culture understood and used it.

The Industrial Revolution has a horizontal universality when it cuts across various societies. Changes are encouraged partly by the internal dynamic of the society but perhaps more as a result of diffusion and transmission. The possibility increases in a historical situation where transmission occurs through trade and contacts, conquest and colonialism, media and communication, the market and globalization.

The change is frequently in two stages and this is significant in understanding the diffusion of scientific ideas. At first there is an imitation of the dominant culture and this presupposes an unequal relationship among and between societies. The dominant culture controls what is transmitted and thus controls knowledge through power. This, for example, is characteristic of colonialism where the colonizing power decodes that knowledge which is to be made available to the colonized. Subsequent to the colonial phase there is the internalization by the recently colonized of the knowledge arrived at via colonialism and later more independently.

A question that requires a comparative study is: why in the period subsequent to colonialism did some of the erstwhile colonized still cling to the framework of culture for the ex-colony in accordance with what the colonial power had projected. There is a hesitation in questioning this. A case in point is the political use of religious identities that in most ex-colonies remains rooted in colonial interpretations of its cultures. The current obsession among some Indians with the solely Aryan foundations of Indian culture, or the insistence that anything Islamic is alien to Indian culture and must be erased, even if this involves erasing historical facts, is rooted in colonial interpretations of Indian history and culture taken to a further extreme. Distance from the colonial period seems to increase the decibel count of those who subscribe to this view.

The Industrial Revolution as a widespread occurrence is linked to the scientific revolution and their emergence in turn is linked to the coming of capitalism and colonialism. The 'scientific revolution' cannot be clinically removed from this historical moment and treated as an isolated happening. To ask why the scientific revolution did not take place in China or India would require asking the prior question of why social change of a particular kind that evolved in Europe in the form of early capitalism did not develop on the same scale in these areas. Asia and Europe were at par in their economies up to the eve of colonialism, after which Asia dropped behind, easing the coming of colonialism. There has been a debate on whether the kind of capitalism that surfaced in Eurasia saw the beginnings of merchant capitalism, whereas the capitalism that supported the scientific revolution was industrial capitalism. This grew and was nurtured in Europe.

However active India and China may have been in the premodern period in terms of advancing science, the scientific revolution as experienced in Europe eluded them. Various reasons have been suggested. Was it that India and China lacked the turn to rational thinking to the same degree as Europe, this being necessary for the Enlightenment? Or was it that the scientific revolution required a particular conjunction of historical changes—capitalism, industrialization and colonialism—that were absent in Asian cultures. In *The Religion of India*, Max Weber has argued for an absence of economic rationality in Indian religion, as also that of a Protestant ethic as in Christian Europe, an ethic that he saw as contributing to the emergence of European capitalism. But as others have argued, the Protestant ethic may not have been the key factor in the scientific revolution in Europe.

We now have in India a healthy capitalist class studded with millionaires and some small degree of industrial development—both the earlier state capitalism and the current private capitalism.

Yet few among these capitalist sources invest in exploring scientific innovation. They are content to repeat the scientific models of the West. Some institutions suffer from government patronage that is stultifying, and others, dependent on private patronage, are reminded that a concern with acquiring more wealth is not to be ignored. Neither of these situations is conducive, for neither oneself nor for one's patron, to scientific ideas. The elephant in the room is of course colonialism. There need to be more detailed studies of the contribution of wealth from the colonies to advancing capitalism in Europe.

The leap, as it were, to a changed condition of science, rides on other historical changes within institutions that emerge as a result. Apart from industrialization and capitalism, with a counterpart in colonialism, there have been other changes that altered the contours of society. Among these has been the emergence of nation states. The nation state was a new kind of state, different from the previous feudal states and absolute monarchies. Nationalism takes shape at a particular point in history and does not exist in early societies. It coincides with the changes brought about by the Enlightenment, in the shape of capitalism and industrialization. Democracy and secularism are also linked to nationalist thinking, although not to what has come to be called religious nationalism. The change in nationalist thinking requires that the loyalty of people to their immediate communities be they based on religion, language, caste, ethnicity or whatever, should be subordinated to an overarching loyalty to, and identity with, the nation. This is the new community of citizens for whom the nation is pre-eminent.

New social classes in Europe supported the idea of the nation two centuries ago. These came to power with a new agenda. Some of them became patrons of new ways of applying science to industry and evolving new technologies. They tapped resources other than agriculture and created a new kind of wealth that strengthened capitalism. Many became patrons of science and technology of a particular kind, such as the use of coal and oil as energy. The old division between those who owned and controlled resources and those who worked them and laboured on them continued under capitalism although the resources changed. Political philosophers of the nineteenth and early twentieth centuries such as Karl Marx and Max Weber analysed the historical changes that had taken place in Europe. The question of the equality of human rights, of access to resources and of social justice became crucial issues of social concern.

Representation and democracy, together with demands of social equality, rational government and secularization, brought in ideas from sciences as, for instance, from Darwinism. However, these ideas were also used to divide peoples and societies into categories of race and ethnicity and such like, that were adverse to ideas of equality. It was thought that science could be viewed as being value-free or at least neutral, although in effect it can often be value-loaded in support of the agendas and patrons governing it. Like much of knowledge, those who control it generally set its social agenda.

It has been argued that among the technologies that extended the reach of the ideas of science and new ways of thought, was what has been called 'print capitalism'. This creates large communities since it marginalizes dialects and localized forms of the use of language, broadens the language of the mainstream and brings many groups together, as, for instance, in creating and propagating the idea of nationalism and the nation state. Print culture is certainly very different from manuscript culture since it is more democratic and can reach larger numbers. Accessibility to the understanding of science when it extends to larger numbers would bring about social change.

The history of science in India is characterized by many historiographical perspectives and, as with all historiography, has been influenced by events and ideas of its own time. Premodern science was seen as a set of separate studies defined by modern disciplines, resulting in a concern with evaluating the degree to which they approximated to European science. In the race to determine both the most ancient and the most superior civilization, discoveries in technology and subsequent inventions were also assessed in terms of who got there first. Non-European sciences were regarded as having ceased at a point in time, for only Europe experienced the scientific revolution.

The study of scientific inventions or innovations of premodern India are generally treated as isolated from other aspects of life. A more interdisciplinary approach would be an improvement. Varahamihira's *Brihat Samhita* is consulted by historians for nuggets of information. What would we learn from it if we examine it as a text reflecting social attitudes and cultures? The same question could be asked of the *Lilavati* of Bhaskara. To what degree were philosophical ideas, so essential to concepts of 'high' culture and civilization, in dialogue with scientific ideas? This would be crucial to the understanding of each.

Astronomy and mathematics, as we have seen, were linked in the conceptualization of time, and this was in turn used by some for astrology. The latter was far more influential in the premodern world than we are willing to concede. This was so not only among people by and large but even more so in the decisions taken in royal courts. Inasmuch as astrology governed the life of a person, it was also tied to alchemy with its obsessive search for longevity and immortality. This had a logical connection with medicine that controlled the well being of the body. At one level, each is an abstract search for knowledge, at another their connection points to a concern with the human condition.

The binary separation of the rational from the irrational, astronomy from aspects of astrology, for instance, is necessary to the analysis of scientific knowledge, but the irrational cannot be entirely dismissed as a subject of historical study. Its presence has to be explained. It too has to be assessed, whether as an alternative, as is fashionable these days, or as peripheral, if indeed it was so. It was a system within itself confronting the rational, or, in the form of superstition, acting, as a parasite eating into rational analyses.

The search for the rational and for positive sciences was, and is, in part, the claim to parity with the West. There was a determination to disprove the singularity of what was often referred to as 'the Greek miracle': that the Greeks alone of all the ancient civilizations provided the foundation for modern thought. Taken to the point where the search for the rational appropriates the irrational, it ceases to be only the recovery of the self in postcolonial times. Instead it supports the distortion of history as we have recently witnessed in the arbitrary claim that 'Vedic mathematics' is superior to other mathematics.

A scientific revolution, in any case, requires more than just rational thought that might advance certain categories of knowledge. It also requires patronage and finance of a kind that will motivate technological change, frequently to enhance the profits of those supporting it. Thus, repeatability and standardization in technology was basic to industrialization and dissimilar to the individualism of the craftsman and artisan. That the scientific revolution occurred in the colonizing societies is not an accident.

Since Indian civilization was earlier defined as Hindu civilization, its science was described as Hindu science, even though the more active proponents of this science were people who could be socially degraded by Brahmanical orthodoxy. Because it was viewed as Hindu science, the texts read were limited to Sanskrit and the Indian languages. Even if mention was made of interest evoked in any of these sciences in China or the Arab world, such as the interest in Indian alchemy in China, or in Indian mathematics in the Arab world, there was little extended attempt to discover which aspects of these sciences appealed to other cultures and whether there was a transmission back from the scholars who were translating Sanskrit texts into Arabic and Chinese. There would, therefore, be much to be learnt even about Indian science through consulting texts in these languages, as indeed much was learnt about the condition and status of Buddhism in India in the late first millennium AD from the accounts of Chinese Buddhist scholars who visited India at the time.

Detailed information is available on Arab interest in these sciences from the eighth century onwards, especially at the court of Harun al-Rashid, where Indian scholars were resident and Sanskrit texts were being translated. Arab interest in the trade routes of the Indian Ocean also acted as a nexus between China, India and West Asia. The overland trade through Central Asia was yet another route for the merging of ideas. Arab scholars added the knowledge from these sources to translations from Greek texts and together they form a remarkable intellectual transmission eventually transmuted into early European science.

The Sung period in China saw a flow of Indian texts coming to China, and resident Indian scholars who arrived either as Buddhist monks or in their company, together with Indian merchants. Some are said to have brought longevity medicines and others are believed to have changed ordinary stones into lapis lazuli, which then became so common that lapis lazuli failed to fetch a high price in the market. Alchemists clearly had no head for business. The imprint of Buddhist interests would have determined the kind of knowledge that was more readily transmitted. But much of this points to an essential feature of the times, namely to encourage a free flow of knowledge, people and artefacts, from one place to another.

Because the study of premodern science was separated, as it were, from other studies, and isolated from its link to historical change, little attention was given to locating it as an idiom of culture at any time. The absence of a scientific revolution in colonial societies fuelled disparity, viewing the colonial as hegemonic and the colonized as marginal. For the colonized, modern European science has come to be seen as neither neutral nor universal but largely a mechanism of control. Its practice is said to induce alienation. Indigenous science in contrast is visualized as holistic. However, this rejection allows the setting aside of scientific knowledge, even in premodern societies, and negates its return to the wider culture.

◆

What then do we mean by science as culture? Joseph Needham saw it as integral to the economic, social and intellectual history of the culture from which it was generated. This is not a determinist view but one that also investigates the concerns and sensibilities of a society. Let me touch briefly on this with reference to medicine and alchemy in early India.

The earliest evidence of medicine are references to those who heal through herbs, incantations and chants—the bhishaja. It is said that herbs gather around such a person like chiefs gathering around a king. They were not doctors and were more likely shamans, who functioned as healers in most societies and claimed to destroy the demons of disease. But the healer had an ambiguous status in a socially hierarchical society. He was excluded from the ritual of sacrifice—a major expression of religious belief and practice—because he was regarded as impure.

At the turn of the Christian era, medical knowledge and practice changed with the writing of medical treatises such as those of Charaka and Sushruta. The fact that they were written in Sanskrit, and therefore by scholars, gave a superior status to the information that they contained although they described the basic practices of healing and medicine. The medical man was now more frequently called the chikitsaka. Still later, he was called the vaidya—the learned man. It is stated that experience and knowledge based on skilful examination, together with rational diagnosis, would explain the cause of an ailment or the effect of medication. Chants and incantations were subordinated to diagnoses, at least in some recorded cases, although it is likely that practices of a shamanistic kind continued as they still are. The new knowledge circulated among those who could understand it and afford it. The bhishaja remained a permanent feature among the less well-established strata. With the formulation of knowledge as part of a discourse, the more random practitioners were relegated to the ranks of heretics—the disciples of the Shudras with no knowledge of the Shastras, as the *Maitri Upanishad* describes them.

The change was from experience to experiment, and analyses were based on precedent and also on anatomical and other knowledge derived from autopsy. While experience drew from customary and subjective knowledge, experiment was linked to theoretical knowledge. The theory drew in part on precedent and this required recording and availability, which in those days meant the writing of a text. This change has been described as a shift from therapy dependent on the supernatural, to therapy dependent on rational application. The shift may not have been quite so marked but is nevertheless apparent.

The medical texts were written in Sanskrit, the language of high culture, and have become essential to the Ayurvedic tradition of medicine. At the same time, the Brahmanical norms of social hierarchy would, in theory, place physicians in a low social category, their handling of diseased bodies and corpses making them polluted, unless the actual handling was done by another person of low caste. Nevertheless, this medical knowledge not only survived, but encouraged a variety of other medical interests. Buddhist monks, for instance, were in theory less squeamish about disease, and monasteries had to ensure the health of their monks. Royal courts patronized the veterinary sciences, pertaining particularly to the health of horses and elephants, so essential to the army. Because of its utility, medical knowledge had an ambiguous relationship with the dominant orthodoxy. Investigating the history of medicine therefore requires more than an analysis of the available texts. Even the dialogue between the healer and the physician, or the intervention of a physician, which may frequently have to be deduced from various texts, becomes important information. The intention was not to control nature, but the intervention became an attempt to assert control. It would be worth investigating whether medical knowledge and practice moved from the healer to the professional physician, or whether they worked in unison, or whether they handled different aspects of medical knowledge.

The period from about the mid-first millennium BC to the mid-first millennium AD saw the classification of various fields of knowledge in the form of texts. These included grammar, geometry, ritual—both domestic and public—social codes of ordering society, political economy and medicine. Some clearly were meant to enhance the dominance of those who formed the ruling groups and to provide them with a structured model. But such classifications also occur when there is the availability of new information. There appears to have been at the time the opening up of Indian cultures to other neighbouring cultures, particularly of the west Asian and Hellenistic world. On the Greek side, Theophrastus's work on plants suggests information on new sources and species coming from Asia. New information needs systematizing and leads to the redefining of existing knowledge. Such an exercise is also carried out when there are contending theories, some of which may eventually be subverted.

Analysing the nature and function of texts, apart from the information they contain, becomes central to investigation. How do texts organize information and formulate arguments? Does their language relate to the segments of society that they are addressing? How do they observe the world and represent what they see? How do they reflect the relations between cultures and classes, or provide the characteristics of what we like to recognize as Indian? When an alchemical text on mercury takes the form of a dialogue between the deities Shiva and Parvati, it is surely telling us something other than providing information on mercury. These are questions that might illumine science as culture and would require the interaction of history and science.

The pattern of alchemy is a little different. The body is again one of the arenas of experimentation, with attempts at longevity and immortality. The other arena was investigating minerals where the changing of base metal into gold brought wealth. Alchemy, therefore, became secret knowledge, and alchemists—as everywhere else—were part of the underground. Alchemy, of course, provides one of the best examples of a truly ecumenical science, namely that it has been studied as a feature of virtually every civilization. There are similarities across Eurasia of the applications of the knowledge it claims to control, and we are told of the attitudes of the people among whom the alchemists lived.

In India, it was also extensively interwoven with the more esoteric Tantric practices and beliefs. Again, at a certain point, in the late first millennium AD, it ceased to be only practical experimentation and came to be textualized knowledge as well. Initially there is a distancing by the established religious elite. Association with Tantrism was linked to heterodoxy; the search for immortality probably became more central than the belief in transmigration and rebirth that was by now a fundamental ideology for asserting dominance; and those who carried out the experiments associated with Tantrism were of high and low castes, since caste was not central to this ritual. Yet the texts when they came to be written were in the language of the learned and were part of the cultural exports to West Asia eliciting intense interest on the part of Arab scholars. The textualizing of this knowledge appears to have coincided, even in India, with royal and courtly interest in its many possible uses. The text then plays a dual role: it is both a body of knowledge and a statement of claims.

One of the more intriguing transmissions involved astronomers and mathematicians and the authors of the early *Puranas*—texts incorporating legends, myths and some history, and were composed from the early Christian era. The dialogue included concepts of time. As we have seen in the chapter on time, astronomers used enormous figures for their calculations, figures that are in many instances identical with those in Puranic cosmology. Did the astronomers borrow these figures or did the Pauranika authors take their cue from the astronomers? Not only are the figures for the cycles of time the same but the concept of the four ages, although simplistic, is mathematically ordered. However, whereas the astronomers later came to argue about the authenticity of the measurements of time, the Pauranikas held to the original construction. Astronomy and mathematics also involved dialogues with counterparts in the Hellenistic world and later China. Possibly the authors of the *Puranas*, in constructing their cosmology, were peppering it with items from what were regarded as superior branches of knowledge, intending thereby to associate their construction with the authenticity attributed to astronomy and mathematics.

That explanations are of the essence in determining rationality may again be illustrated by some activities of the earlier past. Avoidance of disasters appears to have been one of the aims of premodern science, whether they were crises in the life of an individual or catastrophes of a larger kind. This sometimes resulted in a particular study being deviated towards irrationality. There are records of astronomers calculating and predicting eclipses. At the same time there are also records of astrologers encouraging royalty to indulge in expensive rituals and gift-giving to fend off the evil effects of an eclipse. Needless to say, the astrologers were generally the recipients of the gifts. The credibility of scientific knowledge lies not merely in invoking the rational but in ensuring that the rational is not converted into the irrational. This distinction seems not to have been always observed.

Transmission of knowledge is a cultural transaction and raises questions about who does the transmitting and in what form. A theory may be expounded, texts may be translated and experiments may be demonstrated. Or, the transmission may be through a process of osmosis in a juxtaposition of cultures. Each of these undergoes its own evolution and change and what is transmitted may be at some variance with the original. We are familiar with the vicissitudes of translation in terms of what actually gets transmitted and whether the concepts have the same meaning in different cultures and different languages. The act of transmission would move the transmitted knowledge to a central role even if earlier it had been at the periphery. There is also the question of why all societies do not treat transmitted knowledge in an identical way. For instance, people in the ancient world used plane geometry in different ways. When the culture of a society is imprinted on a technology, then the analysis of the imprint is as significant as the technology, when assessing the historical role of the technology.

The question has been posed as to whether such knowledge from premodern societies should be called science or whether it would be better to differentiate it as proto-science. Are we privileging it by calling it science and do we then expect to find that it was also said to be based on rationality and therefore approximating truth, as has been attributed to modern science? The locating of those who controlled such knowledge becomes a crucial historical investigation and has a bearing on the nature of what is regarded as true. This has sometimes been tied to issues of nationalism and transnationalism, in the argument that proto-science is again a term which separates the scientific achievements of Europe from the efforts of the other civilizations which did not appropriate science in the same way. Much of what is called proto-science is actually the predecessor to science and much of science in the period of the Enlightenment is based on what went before. To call it science rather than proto-science seems to me to be more appropriate, especially if we can locate it in the larger conceptions of cultures.

In the construction of a national identity, a tradition can be invented through choosing from the past that which is most effective in creating the required identity. Historical reconstruction is central and there is a drawing on images of the past. This requires collating varieties of knowledge, and because science is seen as the crucial variable, it gets to be privileged. Science is perceived as a historical category. If the history of science is tied to nationalist ideology, and it may be nationalism of any kind, it cannot be treated as universal. Categories such as Hindu science and Islamic science or for that matter even premodern European science, disallow universality to science.

The privileging of science permits it to become a measure of progress and progress is an important concept in nationalism. It is also central to some theories that explain social change that is said to be implicitly moving in a particular direction, that has a particular teleology. This could be one explanation for the attempt to co-opt modern science by Hindutva nationalism in its claims that such science existed in the early past. This can also be seen as an attempt to advance the viability of its ideology. The claim that there were space flights from India some millennia ago would certainly boost the scientific achievements of ancient India and make it an extraordinary civilization for those times. Science also can be used by those in authority to assert dominance—an echo of the colonial pattern, as well as admiration for knowledge that is not fully understood but is regarded as bestowing authority on its practitioners. It would be interesting to analyse particular achievements of modern science that are claimed for ancient India. They might well have a resonance with contemporary aspirations, although flavoured with fantasy.

We are now experiencing that which claims to be beyond nationalism and calls itself transnationalism—a synonym for globalization, enticing us to the siren call of the international market. But its curious feature is the insulation that follows globalization, leading to the imagined past being invoked as a beacon of hope for the future.

The ecumenical nature of science, whether premodern or modern, lies in the fact that it is not limited to a single culture and more so in contemporary times. Its roots not only lie in multiple cultures, but also in what these cultures do with the knowledge they gather, and which takes varied forms. This multiplicity of origins and aftermaths has to be understood and recognized. Inevitably this requires assessing the ideas implicit in or expressed in this knowledge, and in the context of diverse cultures. This makes comparative studies more meaningful. Needham's investigation of science in Chinese civilization should not be studied only as an aspect of the Chinese past. Such investigations are required for other parts of the world as well, and especially in the cultures that have so far been set aside as not conforming to the accepted exemplar.

Al-Biruni visiting India in the eleventh century is generally admiring, but he does comment sarcastically that Indian astronomical and mathematical literature was a mixture of pearls and dung. He adds that both are equal in the eyes of Indians since they cannot raise themselves to the methods of a strictly scientific deduction. Al-Biruni was not a spokesman of the European scientific revolution, yet some recent debates would echo this statement. But the assessment of knowledge requires an understanding of the genesis of that knowledge, its function in society, the nature of its transmission, especially in the context of variant world views, and of course historical change that both generates and is generated by such knowledge. This brings us to a complex historical process, involving more than just historians and scientists, but a process that is inevitable and unavoidable. One is reminded of what Joseph Needham said, almost half a century ago, when he first set out on his quest for science in China:

> For better or worse, the die is now cast, the world is one. The citizen of the world has to live with his fellow-citizens, at the ever-narrowing range of the aerofoil and the radio-wave. He can only give them the understanding and appreciation which they deserve if he knows the achievements of the sages and precursors of their culture as well as of his own.

5

WOMEN DECODING CULTURES

The definition of the culture of societies is no longer restricted to the activities of the upper castes and elites. The focus is changing to commenting on the pattern of living of many levels of a society and therefore refers to various social categories. What was once referred to as the single category of 'women' is no longer viable, since women, like men, perform a variety of social functions. These conform to the section of society to which they belong, determining much of their activity and their articulation, both of which are now seen as a crucial aspect of the larger pattern of living.

Caste, for example, requires the investigation of how rules of marriage affect the role of women, since control over caste is associated with the assertion of patriarchy. This is one of the reasons why inter-caste or inter-religious marriages are being claimed as a threat to some aspects of conventional Indian culture. The mother goddess when worshipped as a deity linked to fertility is common to every part of the country, yet there are many areas where women are forbidden from drawing the plough or turning the potter's wheel. This is not just some mystical ritual tradition as it is rooted again in keeping women subordinated.

When we refer to the culture that we have inherited, our focus is more frequently on the achievements of men, either individually or in a group. Women remain shadows in the wings. A few are picked out and mentioned to prove that they were not all outside the cultural framework but these are often treated more as tokens than as making significant differences. When nationalism in the early twentieth century required the participation of women an interest began to be taken in the category referred to as 'women'. Little distinction was made in terms of their varied functions in society but a few books came to be written on the status of women in past times. Nationalist politics demanded that women participate fully by wearing handwoven cloth rather than the cloth made in the mills that contributed to British industrialization. To this end they were encouraged to campaign against the mill-made cloth; and were also encouraged to picket liquor shops. Women participants were lauded and it was said that they were playing the significant role that they had always done in Indian society.

Yet the depiction of their role in history is misleading. They are portrayed as seamlessly accepting what was expected of them in the *Dharmashastras*, even when this was not always the case, as we shall see a little later in this chapter. Differentiations of caste, economic status or religious commitments, tended to be glossed over within a broad category labelled as 'the status of women'.

For quite some time, the history of what was often described as 'women in ancient India', was a reiteration of what was said about the role of women in society, in the *Dharmashastras*. These were heavily male-oriented and not much attention was given to women other than underlining their subservience to men. Occasionally there was an attempt at a somewhat more positive gloss.

Historians assumed initially that these texts were largely descriptions of how society functioned without investigating the implication of what was being stated. There were some more positive statements about how women should act but these came from literary texts and were given less weightage. The *Dharmashastras*, both before and after the code of Manu, being social codes had greater importance since they were attempts at systematizing the rules for men and women. The centrality of Manu's code in modern times is possibly because it has a wider spectrum than most of the others, and was given more prestige in early medieval times, judging by references to it in the commentaries. That the authorship of these social codes was Brahmana and therefore likely to be conservative, and with a particular perspective, was not taken into account.

In recent decades, historians have come to see these codes more as normative than descriptive texts, and that the Brahmanical perspective was not as prevalent in society as it was once thought. Its prevalence varied in time and degree in relation to particular sections of societies. When non-Brahmanical sources and more secular literature were found to contradict the Brahmanical codes, the acceptance of the codes as descriptive became problematic.

I shall be commenting on the period mainly from the Maurya to the Gupta, the fourth century BC to the fourth century AD, with a few extensions. The sources for this period tend to bifurcate. Some adhere to the Brahmanical perspective and others to the Shramanic—primarily Buddhist and Jaina. They are not so far apart in time yet they present different perspectives. This is particularly so in the visibility they give to the perception of women. They can be viewed chronologically and the differences observed, but I would also like to comment on what is being said about women and their activities from a nuanced perspective.

I would like to view the theme from a perspective somewhat different from the usual of the largely conservative Brahmanical texts. It might invoke a different perception if viewed initially from the Shramanic sources, and from the special category of women present only in Shramanic tradition. From this I shall then move to looking at the categories mentioned in the other sources.

One of the prisms through which I intend to view the difference is what we refer to as renunciation, prevalent in different ways in Brahmanic and Shramanic traditions, with the latter allowing it as a special concession to women. This introduces the difference between the two traditions on the question of whether women can be renouncers. This might throw up some interesting questions, as for instance, why this concession and its visibility is prominent in Shramanic thinking and less so in the other.

The concept and role of renouncers came early to Indian society. The more extreme form of samnyasa or asceticism, was differentiated from the gentler version of renunciation, which by its logic of continuing to associate with society, was less distanced from it. The ascetic was expected to live in isolation altogether removed from society. The renouncer, apart from his concern with his own freedom from rebirth and nirvana, was expected to live with other renouncers and their concern was to project an alternate and more ethical society with the assumption that it might lead people to act in better ways. This may well have enabled some influence on social change—as indeed was the intention of a few renunciatory sects. Renouncers of the Shramanic tradition joined orders of monks and nuns, lived segregated in monasteries and nunneries, but had to visit the settlement to get food as alms and to preach. Hence the continuing link with society but in a distinctly different capacity from that which existed before their renunciation.

My focus is on women who renounced what we think of as the conventional social code. Some chose to join the Buddhist sangha discarding the *Dharmashastras* as definitive social codes. Such women may be seen as contesting these social codes in becoming renouncers. Nevertheless one has to ask why they did so and how should their social attitudes be assessed. Forms of what I like to call 'opting out of society' did not sever men and women from all social norms.

A few decades ago when I first wrote on renunciation in early India, I questioned the idea of its being a life-negating principle, as argued by the French anthropologist Louis Dumont. On the contrary, apart from its being viewed as a path to nirvana (enlightenment), or moksha (liberation from rebirth), it also led to exploring other aspects of life. Some categories of renouncers, for this and other reasons, became authoritative figures within the society. The person who labours (shram), to gain enlightenment acquires moral authority through this labour, and liberates not only himself or herself from rebirth but others as well through the teaching. The question remains whether those that lived lives different from the code of Manu, were actually edged out of society as advised by the code, or were on the contrary, respected as indeed many sources suggest.

Renouncers seeking nirvana were neither negating life, nor intending to make revolutionary changes in society. They were attempting to establish an alternative space and a system that would make moksha more accessible and social orthodoxy more flexible. Inevitably, theirs was a dissenting voice, discarding the mores of orthodoxy. Movements for change can depart radically from existing systems or else take the form of a kind of osmosis, where ideas governing a new mode of social living are practised by small groups. Ideas are thereby inducted into influencing the larger society. If the small, alternate society cannot be sustained then the group becomes marginal or fades away. The history of renouncers in India seems to suggest that renunciation nurtured the counterculture as a parallel society although limited in place and time.

Renouncers remained part of the social landscape. They are not isolated ascetics who live in inaccessible areas, single-mindedly focused on their own liberation, rather than the creation of a changed or a parallel society. That death rites are performed for the Brahmana ascetic when he decides to take samnyasa, is a telling difference. Such asceticism is known but is not that frequently practised. Asceticism, therefore, is distinct from renunciation.

If we argue that opting out of a conservative social system, as envisaged in the *Dharmashastras*, is intended to encourage a parallel society, then we have to consider how the constituents of society were related to each other. It also requires us to explain that even when certain central orthodox beliefs and social codes were renounced by some sects of renouncers, these sects were nevertheless accommodated in society and in some instances respected as figures of authority. Social mores, of course, can only be made functional if they are accepted by or imposed upon women. This explains in part Manu's insistence on not giving women a voice lest they protest. It is in the nature of social codes to treat defiant groups as somehow removed from society, or only to be referred to indirectly.

Caste rules do not apply if one renounces one's role in society. If one's status is anyway regarded as inferior, as is that of women, then breaking the code is perhaps not such an outrageous crime, except for better-placed upper caste women. It is not surprising that elements of renunciation become more visible in the activities of women than of men. Subordinated groups when they break their subordination attract attention.

I would like to look first at the Buddhist sources. These are relatively more descriptive than normative, although they too can give an ideological veneer to what they say, as, for instance, in observing the rules of membership of the Buddhist order, the sangha.

Furthermore, women occupied different levels of society and cannot be arbitrarily treated as one category, other than the category of gender. When viewed from the perspective of women's activities, they constitute at least three broad occupational groups that were not unconnected. Within each of these, were women of status as well as women of less or no status, the latter being more invisible in the sources. I shall try and present these categories first horizontally across society, identified with their distinctive occupations, and then vertically within each group identified by approximately similar occupations.

The most eminent and visible category, and the one referred to most frequently perhaps, was that of the grihapatni, the wife of the householder. In a general sense, households as described tended to be those of persons of authority: members of the ruling clans in the gana-sanghas (chiefships), royal families in kingdoms, and wealthy merchants residing in urban centres. These being persons of substance their wives were treated as ladies of consequence and not just as any housewife. The senior wife, often the first, married in accordance with the rules of patriarchy, bore the children that would inherit the wealth and the status. The girls in this category would have access to their mother's inheritance—the stridhana. In the early history of Buddhism, women from this space, the grihapatnis and their daughters, were the group from which the nuns of that period came. Permission to take orders had to be given by husbands and fathers, and occasionally even the men followed suit—if the Buddhist texts are to be believed.

If the better off grihapatni complained of the problems of being a co-wife or the pain in giving birth to a child, the compensation was that she did have a comfortable life and also the option of becoming a nun, provided her husband agreed. It is another matter as to how many actually became nuns. This was because these grihapatnis were not working outside their homes in order to increase the income for the family. The earners of such incomes were the women of peasant and artisan households where in some occupations the women had to share the work with their husbands. Such women, therefore, hardly had the choice of opting out. The poorer grihapatni dreamed of release from the pestle, the husband and the water-pot and the general discomfort of her life, where the option was that she could become a nun. However, it was not so easy to get permission to leave the household.

At a much lower level, but essential to the relatively well-off household, was the Dasi, the woman who fetched water, shopped, kept the home clean, washed clothes, ground rice, cooked, and attended to the lady of the house. She was the essential cog in the household machine. If need be, she also had to offer her services to the master or to male guests. This latter requirement is confirmed from other sources as well, such as the *Brihadaranyaka Upanishad*, that mentions Satyakama Jabala who was unclear about his caste as his mother worked as a Dasi in a household, and was unable to identify his father. There is also the reference in the Vedic corpus to the curious anomaly of what are called the Dasiputra Brahmanas (Brahmanas who were sons of Dasis). Reviled at first by regular Brahmanas they were subsequently eagerly recruited when their supernatural powers were revealed. When dismissed by the regular Brahmanas, they were followed by the sacred Sarasvati River, making it clear as to who were the exalted ones. According to the *Aitareya Brahmana*, what mattered was the caste of the father therefore the mother could well be a Dasi.

The Dasi was unfree and had no inheritance to fall back on. She could be freed either if she bore the master of the household a child, or if the master agreed to her manumission. Her life was virtually in the hands of the man who claimed ownership over her. The Dasi did not have the freedom to join the sangha, without the consent of the master. Judging by the limited numbers of those that did join, permission may often have been withheld. Dasis would, of course, bring little social status to the institution. In the context of the household the grihapatni and the Dasi represent the two extremes of relative freedom and unfreedom.

I would like to turn now to women involved perhaps in a more direct but contradictory way of 'opting out', in part revolving around their sexuality. Two categories that transgressed Manu's code were nuns and courtesans. Their contestation, however, was based on diametrically opposite premises and requirements. For those that became nuns, renunciation was a form of distancing from society, but the courtesan reasserted an involvement in society, although contesting accepted norms.

Joining the sangha meant becoming a bhikkhuni, a nun, a condition directly opposed to that of the grihapatni, but the ties seem not to have been severed. The bhikkhuni was no longer a housewife as she lived in a collective. She had no family to care for since she could not marry or, if already married, have normal access to her husband. She could meet her immediate family of children, if any, of siblings and relatives if so required. That she made donations to the sangha is suggestive of some continuing ties with the family and possible access to wealth, even if it was limited. It is quite noticeable that of the votive inscriptions at the Bharhut and Sanchi stupas, a fair number are donations from women and of these there are quite a few nuns.

Women could become nuns and establish their lives in nunneries. It meant leaving the comfort of home to live in a rather austere monastery; to be shorn of their hair; to dress in rough, uniform clothes; to eat whatever came by way of alms from the nearby village or town, observing no rules of commensality; to be strictly celibate; to spend time in prayer and meditation; and where necessary to help other women in distress. Joining the order was in itself an act of breaking the social code as dictated for women in the normative Brahmanical texts and acting contrary to the rules of caste and patriarchy. But it also meant submitting to the alternate code, that of the sangha.

The initial hesitation in recruiting women to the Buddhist sangha did not last for long. But the bhikkhuni had always to be subservient to the monk. There are narratives about those women who were well versed in the teachings of the Buddha and respected for this. Women teachers and philosophers are associated in Indian traditions with asking penetrating questions, but none establish schools of thought. Gargi and Maitreyi asked questions and so did Gotami and others, but these are not the questions that are quoted for instance, when reference is made to the origins of new schools of thought. Whereas the term Arya, meaning the respected one, was used for monks, such a title was not given to the nuns.

Older nuns knew the doctrine equally well since they ordained the new nuns. The nun Sanghamitta, said to be the daughter of Ashoka Maurya, travelled to Sri Lanka it is said in order to ordain the queen and the women of the Sinhala royal family. It has been suggested that the *Dipavamsa*—the earlier chronicle of the Mahavihara Monastery in Sri Lanka—may have been written by nuns, since it has much on the activities of nuns. This would suggest, not surprisingly, that scholarship could be part of the curriculum in nunneries. Some nuns such as Bhadda Kundalakesa were said to be skilled debaters. She could only be eventually defeated in debate by Sariputta, a senior disciple of the Buddha. A particularly accomplished nun could claim a long ancestry going back to the time of an earlier Buddha. But however well she may have known the doctrine, she did not depart from the teaching. This, the monks could do up to a point, and establish a new sect, as happened after discussions in the various councils.

In the lower register of the declared supporters of Buddhism were the women who were the lay followers, the upasikas. These were generally women of the household who performed the required rituals, made donations to the sangha and went on pilgrimages. Their activities are recorded in votive inscriptions at stupa sites. They may not have had access to great wealth but seem to have had some control over household finances that enabled them to make donations. Lay followers often identify themselves by associating their family with the donation.

An altogether different category was of women whose activity was diametrically opposed both to that of the women of the household and of nuns. These were the women who became ganikas or courtesans and are essentially a part of the urban scene. They have a continuity of occupation that can be traced through the centuries, although the forms vary somewhat. In terms of continuities one could say that the courtesan had the apsara as her ancestress, and in post-Gupta times the ganika, in turn, was a partial ancestress to the later Devadasis. Similarity also lies in the occasional references to the ganika being the daughter of a ganika, an idea that is repeated in the *Manimekhalai*. Some have suggested that this is characteristic of a matrilineal system, but a distinctive kinship system is not associated with the ganikas, even though they deviated from the patriarchal household.

There is again a need to make a distinction even in this

category, between the courtesan and the women at the lowest level of this hierarchy—the prostitute or sex worker. The terms used in the texts do not consistently demarcate between them but there is a considerable difference in social perception and practice. The courtesan had to be trained in music, dance and the arts, qualifications required of her before she could set herself up in her profession.

Her accomplishments and her physical beauty led the citizens of her city to respect her. She upheld a particular culture. Historians have compared the ganikas with the hetaera of the Greek city states. There is a similarity of function but the hetaera was often from another city. Indian cities of this period seem to have had a strong sense of being cultural centres apart from their other urban requirements. Association with particular cities was therefore prized. The much-quoted courtesan, Ambapali, was adopted by the city of Vaishali.

The courtesan was generally without a family, a child often being accidental. Caste rules were repeatedly broken in her dealings with her clients even if she had the freedom to choose her clients. Her actions discounted patriarchy in her giving priority to the erotic, over and above social codes.

The prostitute at the lowest level in this category, referred to as vesya or rupajivi, was also part of the urban scene. She was untrained in any of the arts, had no status other than what was viewed as rather routine sexual work. The prostitute's services were open to all whereas the courtesan could choose her clients and generally chose from among the wealthiest. For the prostitute, her work brought employment and income, whereas for the courtesan it presumably brought enjoyment as well as substantial wealth. The latter offered both pleasure and companionship. The difference between the two lies, as it has been said, in asking as to what is being treated as a commodity.

There is nothing new in all that I have said so far. I have summarized the scene just to remind you of what we know.

When differentiating between categories of women it is useful to see what, if any, are the social connections or demarcations among them. One of the ways of doing this is to note the binary opposition implicit in their social locations, both between the categories I have listed and within each category. Such binary oppositions do not have sharply demarcated boundaries. In some situations there is a fuzziness at the edges that confirms the reality of what is being described.

We have then what might be called one differentiated perspective at the horizontal level. These would be the groups of women regarded as being in the more defined segments of society, some of which are in opposition and some in conformity. The established status of the housewife in her husband's household is counter to the other two categories of the nun and the courtesan. The nun lives in the collective of the nunnery and is celibate. The courtesan exploits her erotic abilities, but her sexuality is not intended for the procreation of children. So the grihapatni is, in a sense, contrapuntal to both the nun and the courtesan, and the latter two are contrapuntal to each other. The horizontal perspectives at the lower social level are less rigid and more fluid. The upasika may stand in contra-distinction to the Dasi and the vesya, but at the same time she can be in part a grihapatni and has more freedom than the other two.

The vertical binaries within each category are at the upper and lower end of each. The grihapatni is socially respected. At the other end of the household is the Dasi treated as inferior but it is her labour that keeps the household going. She was often treated as mere chattel. Manu lists her together with animals when referring to the wealth of the household. In the Buddhist category, the upasika as the lay worshipper is among those that bring donations to the sangha and thus strengthens the institution, but it is of course the bhikkhuni who propagates Buddhism. In the other category among employed women, the vesya caters to the demand in urban centres for sex workers, but it is the accomplished ganika who receives the accolades from the city dwellers.

These binaries reflect relationships among women but their reading is also dependent on the perceptions of men. The grihapatni keeps the household and the family together around the fulcrum of her husband, the grihapati. The nuns, however respected they may have been, had always to obey the decisions of the monk. This was conditional to their ordination as nuns. Some upasikas made individual donations but quite a few were donations on behalf of the family. The courtesan was dependent on male clients, but of her choice. The sex worker had to service all that came since she had no status.

When viewed from this perspective, the separation between the categories is clear although not insurmountable. The nun could have earlier been the wife, daughter or widow of a householder or come from the courtesan's establishment. A courtesan could marry a client and set up a household but would then have to cease being a courtesan. It was less likely that a nun would leave the sangha and start a family. Apostate nuns are not mentioned, presumably also because it would be bad publicity for the sangha.

There were some links across the three categories. There were also connections of various kinds within each category. The Dasi was unfree as was the sex worker, and both were at the lower levels. There are references to both seeking the freedom of joining the sangha but the frequency of this was limited.

The question that now needs asking is whether the other tradition, the Brahmanical, despite its difference with the Shramanic, reflects these categories both as an idea and in institutional form. The grihapatni and Dasi are common to both. Whereas the Dasi receives the same treatment in both traditions, the grihapatni in the Brahmanical codes is a more subservient woman. Would she, for instance, have tried to persuade her husband to become a monk as did some of the women in Buddhist texts? Even where royal women make endowments to the sangha in the early centuries, as for instance among the Ikshvaku royalty, their husbands continue to perform Vedic sacrifices. Admittedly this may have been politically expedient.

Brahmanical sects treated monks and nuns as alien categories. Teaching the *Vedas* to women was anyway forbidden. The occasional mendicant, male or female, is referred to in the *Dharmashastras* and is known from other sources. However the female mendicant, bhikshuni, is mentioned in the *Arthashastra*, together with the somewhat degraded professions of actors, bards and other wanderers. She is differentiated from the shaven-headed Shudra woman ascetic—presumably the nun, who is mentioned in passing. She has a prominent role as a spy for the government, a role that is so heavily emphasized that it almost appears to be the definition of a female mendicant.

Female donors, barring the royal family, are not so well defined as is the upasika in Buddhist sources, and do not receive much publicity. The Brahmanical tradition had little space for female donors in the early centuries, barring members of the royal family. Even when temples became conspicuous on the landscape, in the latter part of the first millennium AD, a range of donors was rarely recorded, as compared, for instance, with the votive inscriptions at Buddhist sacred sites. In the triangle of connections that I have suggested, it is almost as if nuns in Brahmanical sources were expunged, with goddesses replacing them as among those that nurtured religion.

The category of the courtesan and prostitute finds prominent mention in the *Arthashastra*. Here they have a clear-cut role. They provide income for the state exchequer. The state pays 24,000 panas to acquire a courtesan—the same amount as is paid to the upper bureaucracy as salary. It also provides an endowment of 1,000 panas for her to set up her establishment. Her earnings are taxed by the state and she is obviously seen as a good investment. The condition and work of the courtesans is controlled by a state official, the ganikadhyaksha. An entire chapter in the *Arthashastra* is devoted to his work. For a society that should ideally be functioning according to the rules of Manu's code in the Brahmanical tradition, this does seem a rather cynical attitude to human relations. It differs in spirit from the admiration for the accomplished ganika in Buddhist texts, who is free to donate her property to the sangha, as some do.

Prostitutes are not in state service but all the same have to pay a monthly tax to the state. This is the equivalent of twice their one-time fee. It would seem that the state had no inhibitions in treating sex work on a par with the normal roster of taxable occupations, and additionally in utilizing sex workers as spies. Manu does not describe the courtesan. He only refers to prostitutes as ganikas (by which time the meaning of the word may have changed in common usage) and treats them with contempt. The *Arthashastra* and Manu take rather different positions from each other and from the Buddhist texts.

Given all this complexity it does become incumbent on historians when speaking about women in various traditions to consider which category and status is being discussed and by whom and when. The women in the top half of the categories claim status as patrons, donors and qualified persons whereas those in the lower half keep the essentials going in a different way. They each have different support systems—husbands, employers, the sangha, the family, their own establishment and state protection.

Keeping body and soul together is not central to the renouncer but at the same time cannot be ignored. The household was at the core of production. It drew its wealth either from cultivable land owned by the householder, or from artisanal and commercial enterprises that he may have controlled, or in some cases, both. When monasteries began receiving grants of land and instituted what Max Weber called 'monastic landlordism', the agricultural wealth was immense. No less was the wealth that came from domestic and cross-continental trade. Recent scholarship informs us that the monasteries were also directly involved in commerce, both as staging points along trade routes and as investors. Traders and monks carried cargo and religion to distant places.

This might partially explain the hostility towards the Shramanic sects in Brahmanical texts, apart from their strong ideological differences. The Shramanas are described as nastikas (non-believers), vedanindaka (reviling the *Vedas*), pashandas (fraudulent), and mahamoha (great deceivers). The two streams of dharma, the Brahmana and the Shramana, as mentioned in Sanskrit texts point to an antagonistic duality.

In terms of social differentiation there was expectedly an emphasis on caste and sectarian diversities. The *Puranas* deny freedom from rebirth to men and women belonging to the Shramana sects, and Manu ostracized them. Religion and caste intersected and religions that were open to all were automatically demoted in social ranking. But nirvana had no social boundaries. Nuns, who when they claim some degree of enlightenment, speak of having split open the mass of mental darkness, and describe themselves as having become free.

The nun carries a reminder of the autonomy of the woman. This is contrary to a code where the woman is, according to Manu, completely dependent on father, husband and son, at various stages of her life, and is not allowed a will of her own. Although mendicants of various sects do wander around, there are no orders of monks and nuns except among the Shramanas. Renunciation is ideally an individual act of separation from society. As such it does not occur with great frequency in Brahmanical sects, where the renouncer as an individual was separated from society, and in early history did not join an organized order. What is surprising is that the Brahmanical code, when speaking of women, gives little space to a nun of any dharma. Was this because the *Dharmashastras* were meant for only limited upper caste usage, focusing on what men should be doing, as a result of which nuns had to be invisible? Yet it was from the upper castes that women initially joined nunneries, or so it was suggested.

We have to remember that although in theory all religions had a place for renouncers, few maintained institutions for them such as monasteries and nunneries. It is not my intention to discuss the religious and social reasons for this, but suffice it to say that well-defined orders of monks and nuns with clear social functions, are found more frequently in Christianity, Buddhism and Jainism.

Renunciation in Christianity began with a literal resort to isolation as, for example, when Simeon Stylites, sat on top of a pillar in the Egyptian desert. When people gathered around Stylites and other such 'desert fathers', they were the nucleus of a new community. But by medieval times in Europe renunciates largely belonged to well-established monasteries and nunneries. Wealth came from various sources. The British historian Eileen Power in her brilliant study of medieval European society, *Medieval People*, provides some pointers. Fathers, when they dedicated their daughters to the Church, often had to give a dowry as well. Nuns could not inherit land so daughters likely to receive such inheritance were pushed in the direction of becoming nuns by their brothers. But institutions took advantage of this and some endowment accompanied the nun-to-be. Girls from poor families, therefore, had problems being accepted by convents.

Since everyone was born of original sin, according to Saint Augustine, much of the nun's time was spent in prayer, praying not just for her life after death but for others as well. The nun is often referred to as the bride of Christ and this can be interpreted as a metaphor at many levels. The nuns practised what were called 'feminine crafts' such as spinning, weaving and embroidery. But they were also taught Latin together with the art of illuminating manuscripts. Inevitably, some texts were read and discussed. This explains the emergence in the twelfth century of Hildegard von Bingen who, confined to a Benedictine convent, nevertheless wrote on theology and contributed compositions to early church music. Since she suffered from severe migraines she had amazing visions that she relied upon to explain the Bible! But visions apart, nuns contributed in some small degree to the configuring of a few European cultural forms.

Why are women like these less known among Buddhist nuns? Music of any complicated kind, as were the Catholic chants, may not have been a major part of the early Buddhist ritual, although it was introduced in later times. The initial absence of deities perhaps reduced the need for visions but not necessarily so. The copying of manuscripts and commenting on them should have opened up other possibilities.

Puranic Hinduism, from the late first millennium AD, as distinct from the earlier Vedic Brahmanism, did finally recognize, perhaps a little grudgingly, the legitimacy of women propagating their religious ideas. But orders of nuns were not established. These were not the women mendicants who were paid to spy for the state, that I have mentioned earlier, but were independent women devotees, included in the Bhakti tradition—independent women of intense religious belief. They contributed substantially to giving form to the Bhakti manifestation of Hinduism, often defying conservative belief and practice. The considerable literary quality and religious content of the compositions of some among them are now recognized. This form of articulating religious sentiments in admirable literary forms, began in the south through poems and hymns in local languages, from the later first millennium AD. Initially, it was men and women that wandered through town and village that taught these new religious ideas and preached new forms of devotion to the deity. Among them Andal and Akka Mahadevi have been and are frequently quoted. Andal's poetic compositions became central to Vaishnavite worship and Akka Mahadevi's worship focused on Shiva. Much is made of the assertions of some that they were married to the deity they worshipped. Was this a rejection of a human husband and of implicit sexuality? One is reminded of the Christian nun being the bride of Christ.

In north India this form of worship became more familiar later, in the second millennium AD. Two of the more popular women devotees in the north were Lallesvari, popularly known as Lal Ded in Kashmir, and Mirabai in Rajasthan, both of the mid-second millennium AD. They were upper-caste women and had problems with their conservative families, whom they finally left. Accepted popularly as among the highest devotees, they used the commonly understood language rather than the language of the learned. Their religion was, therefore, quite distinct from the religion that was being constructed in the mathas of the Brahmanas. Some mathas that cultivated new religious thought organized an informal order of monks for propagating these ideas. Was this in imitation of the Buddhists and Jainas to whom they were otherwise opposed? Or possibly even a Brahmanical assertion to counter the popularity of some of the Bhakti teachers, although their audiences were different. But, of course, there was no Brahmanical order of nuns in earlier times.

Nevertheless, the lifestyle of the women preaching Bhakti broke the social code of the *Dharmashastras*. They were no longer grihapatnis, nor did they observe the rules of commensality, and they led nomadic lives. The woman devotee, even if tenuously associated with Puranic Hinduism, did not belong to an institution as did the Buddhist and Jaina nuns. These women were sustained by a small following. Their caste status probably gave them some leeway in disregarding caste rules.

The nuns had been recruited into an alternate, parallel society and had institutional support. They underwent formal training, were literate and learnt the texts required for their ordination. The institution had its own hierarchy of office from novice to superior and its own regulations about dress, appearance and the routine of daily life. Nuns were not entirely cut off from their family nor from receiving family gifts. Such institutionalized support was almost necessary for the survival of the nunneries. This is evident by the manner in which they declined when patronage was discontinued by the early second millennium AD, and Buddhism itself was fading out in many parts of India.

To sum up the ideas discussed in this chapter, both nuns and women Bhakti devotees, discarded the code of Manu in rejecting the centrality of being a dutiful daughter, a subservient wife and an uncomplaining widow. In societies conforming to the Shramanic tradition, the emphasis was less on the binary of conformity and non-conformity vis-à-vis caste codes. They looked for a legitimate alternate space for those that wished to be renouncers. The Brahmanical tradition was more severe on nonconformists who were contesting orthodox caste norms, and for which there were penalties. Mirabai would not have been accused of being immoral had she joined a nunnery. But then there were only the Jaina convents by then and the very occasional ones of a Bhakti sect, such as the Mahanubhava. The alternate society of the Buddhist sangha had provided protection from oppressive norms. But it also required that nuns obey the rules of the sangha, the nuns having voluntarily chosen to join it. These were rules the nuns could not change on their own. In some ways this forecloses the freedom of renunciation in that even if one breaks caste rules one has to take on the rules of the sangha.

I would like to think that we have reached a point in research on the history of women, where we might investigate the awareness of countercultures among the women of earlier times. These range from renunciation in order to join a religious order, to renouncing social conventions in order to discover individual self-expression. The Shramanic traditions provided accessible opportunities for the first via the institution of the sangha, whereas the Bhakti and the Shakta traditions seem to follow the second.

The category on which we have little information are the women who lived with their families in the ghettoized outskirts of settlements—the areas inhabited by the Avarnas, those outside caste, who were regarded as Asprishya, untouchable. It is likely that their social codes would have differed from the ones I have discussed, as they would be more directly involved in the professions of their husbands. As such they may have had more freedom, but at the same time this would have been circumscribed by the overall excluded status of the Avarna.

The significance of such studies would be of two kinds. One is that we have not given much attention to the fact that some categories of women did contest patriarchy in their own way and to a reasonable degree if not at every level. The silence of the later *Dharmashastras* on those that defied the code could have been an attempt to ignore the unpalatable, and pretending that such people did not exist, or else were only worth condemning in passing. Such studies would also strengthen the various movements organized by groups of women in the past century. These have confronted patriarchy in a direct manner by calling it a form of extreme injustice, and have argued for replacing the existing shallow attempts to give Indian society a more equitable turn in terms of gender justice. There were groups of women in the past who stood up against such injustice, not necessarily in a flamboyant way but in a purposeful way. This would be enough of a heritage to help discard the idea that traditional Indian culture required women to be subservient, and therefore for women to show their independence is contrary to Indian tradition. The assertion of a woman as an autonomous person today would be the continuation of an assertion that goes back to early times, and an inheritance from our past cultures.

6

THE CULTURE OF DISCRIMINATION

Observing exclusion and claiming identity to justify it, have been inherent in almost all societies since earliest times, and continue to be. What is not inherent are the reasons for this, the degree to which they prevail in a society, or for that matter the role that they play in giving form to the society. The reasons could provide pointers to the ethics, ideologies and values that govern a society and even what we call civilizations. We have tended to brush them aside or have not always found plausible explanations. But historical explanations today do try and answer such questions.

Social exclusion, common to most societies, is of different kinds. A power-wielding group excludes others dismissing them as inferior or deviant. The power can be based on anything ranging from physical force to superstition. Deprivations of various kinds become forms of discrimination, controlled by the conditions under which they are practised. Access to resources of livelihood can be restricted or even denied, the justification for this given a religious gloss or the claim that it was the command of deity, or even just an assertion of power.

Exclusion, is a demarcation and by its own logic those excluding and those being excluded, require an identity. Emphasis on one presumes an emphasis on the other. This is often a label that imprints the demarcation. Thus for example, those included in caste society are identified as the Savarna (included among the varnas), and the Avarna (those outside and excluded from varna identity).

Information on these practices comes to us from ancient texts. As I have pointed out earlier, in the ancient past, these texts were generally written by the elite and reflected their views. They provide an image of how society was envisaged by those in authority and incidentally also provide some clues, probably unintended, as to how it actually functioned. The norms for how society should function did not necessarily hold—as they seldom do. Where there is repeated insistence on a rule it could be due to its being observed infrequently or casually. For instance, does Ashoka Maurya repeatedly advising his subjects to honour the sect of the other person imply that this was not the norm? What is of interest to historians is the manner in which the difference between norm and practice was recognized, and then negotiated and adjusted. In theory, the norm was said to continue, in effect, it may have changed. However, rules could be subverted in subtle or even brazen ways, as we shall see.

It is thought that rules governing caste or what is referred to as varna-ashrama-dharma, determined all social relations. This was the regulation of the code of behaviour applicable to all varnas, or what might be called an ideal pattern in which caste society functioned; and ashrama, in this context, referred to the four stages of the life span of generally an upper-caste man—namely, being a student, then a householder, then leaving home, and finally becoming an ascetic.

However, a close inspection shows deviance. Activities actually practised could change what was permitted to a varna but not in an obvious manner. The claim of observing new norms could hide new occupations, rituals, and custom, differing in practice from the rules of dharma, but negotiated so as to allow the person to retain his varna status. In theory it encapsulated a continuing pattern of hierarchy and occupation but there were disjunctures. There were also large numbers outside the varna-jati system that had diverse rules of functioning. Among this majority were the segregated category of people, immutable in their segregation and referred to as the Avarna.

Exclusion and identity are more deeply imprinted when defined, as they frequently are, by differences in social practices, language, or belief. What is of historical interest is why some concepts die out with historical change, but others persist. My attempt is far more limited in addressing this question. My focus is on the form of discrimination that differentiated Indian society from others, namely the carefully worked out theory of varna-ashrama-dharma that was thought necessary to the idea of the Savarna society, followed by the creation of the category that was to be kept outside the Avarna.

Caste was not a rigid system of organizing society that was defined once and continued to conform to the definition without change. It registered changes in the history of its use over time. Of the early texts the Vedic corpus mentions varna, and occasionally jati. Other early texts in their references to Indian society make only a passing reference or none at all. For example, Megasthenes, a visitor to India from the Hellenistic world in the Mauryan period (fourth century BC), lists seven social categories, largely occupational. The inscriptions of Ashoka mention the subjects of the kingdom, the praja (literally children). They also refer to other categories of people such as pasamdas (religious sects) and to atavikas (forest dwellers). There is however, no mention of caste as either varna or jati.

Six hundred years later, the Chinese Buddhist Faxian travelling in India gives an example of extreme exclusion. He mentions in his account *A Record of Buddhistic Kingdoms* that the Chandalas, as Avarnas living outside the town, have to strike a wooden clapper when they enter the town so that people can move away from them since they are regarded as impure and permanently polluted and therefore untouchable. Caste was by now well established and those that were identified as Avarna were treated as polluting, so they had to live outside the settlement. This was a substantial social change from Mauryan times and registers a devaluation of some categories of people. Yet this was also the same Gupta period that was assessed in modern times as the utopian golden age of Indian civilization.

Let me begin with the earliest mention of varna in the *Rigveda* and continue to later times. I shall be discussing the opposed duality of the more frequently mentioned aspects of the exclusion, such as the Arya-Dasa varnas, the Arya-Mlecchas differences, the four-fold varna that we refer to as caste, the exclusion of the Adivasis, and the establishment of the category called Asprishya (literally untouchable). I will not be discussing exclusions based on religious beliefs and on gender. Both are beyond the scope of this book, although I have touched upon some aspects of how women were discriminated against in the previous chapter.

The earliest mention of varna in the *Rigveda*, is the two-fold Arya and Dasa varna. The authors of the text see themselves as Aryas and see those that differ from them as the Dasas, as the 'Other'—the ones to be excluded from the identity of the Arya. The Dasas were equal or more in number to the Aryas. The term Arya is not used in a racial sense but marks a linguistic and cultural differentiation. They are the Aryan-speaking people, who are respected for their distinctive culture, all of which allows them to presume superiority over the Dasas.

Speech is an important marker. The Dasas either do not speak the Aryan language or speak it incorrectly. There are references to Mridhra-vac as incorrect speech. But language is not insurmountable. The *Mahabharata* narrates the activities of the central superior lineage of Puru. Yet in the Vedic texts his speech is said to be defective—Mridhra-vac—and his ancestry was of an asura-rakshasa. Are we seeing a contradiction here or the inclusion of the Other? In Buddhist texts the Mlecchas are sometimes said to speak their own language and some among them are associated with the southern region. Living in proximity to each other the cultures of the Aryas and the Mlecchas would have mixed and would have constantly changed. References are made to their speech—Mleccha bhasha—and lands where it is spoken are not located but merely cordoned off from Sanskrit-speaking areas. Where the language is entirely unfamiliar, there the speakers are said to be making unintelligible sounds—barabara karoti. But the linguistic demarcation slowly declines.

Elsewhere, an example of Mleccha speech is a replacing of the 'r' sound with 'l'—therefore saying 'ali' instead of 'ari'. This was characteristic of the language of the middle Gangetic plain, where in later times Ashoka's inscriptions refer to him as 'laja' instead of 'raja'. Mleccha, as meaning socially inferior, is also used to mean 'different'. Thus, when a Hindu merchant praising Sultan Muhammad bin Tughlaq, refers to him as Mleccha, the reference is not uncomplimentary. This is another instance of using an exclusionary term but not intending it to mean inferiority. Like Dasa, Mleccha also changes its meaning, but unlike Dasa not invariably for the worse.

The concept of varna has its own history. The literal meaning is colour, or in some senses, cover. It is also used to describe the colours of the day and the night. It could well be symbolic of two moieties where colour is a symbolic separator. Its meaning as colour drew on the reference to the Dasa as being tvacam-krishnam (dark-skinned). Interestingly the medieval commentator, Sayana, does not suggest skin colour, but maintains that it refers to the skin of a demon named Krishna. Some physical differences are mentioned but are the subject of scholarly debate. Does 'anas' mean 'without a nose' i.e., snub-nosed, or does it mean 'without a mouth,' i.e., speaking another language. The Dasas have their own clans (vish) and some of their chiefs are mentioned. They are rich in cattle wealth and are therefore raided by the Arya chiefs. They have different rituals and customs, worship the phallus and are niggardly and unfriendly.

Gradually the words changed their meaning in accordance with social usage. The meaning of both Arya and Dasa changed. Arya referred largely to those who spoke the Aryan language, and it became a term of respect. In this capacity it came to include more categories of people. Buddhist monks were addressed as Ayya or Arya irrespective of their social origins. Whereas initially there were a larger number of upper caste monks, their caste composition came to include lower castes as well. There are stories of the Buddha ordaining such persons to monkhood and they would then have been addressed as Arya. Royal families even of uncertain ancestry use the honorific form of Aryaputra. The territory designated as the land of the Aryas, Aryavarta—shifted from the western Gangetic plain eastwards. By the time of Manu it covered northern India down to the Vindhyas, but interestingly not further south.

The use of 'arya' was not exclusive to India. The ancient Iranians also used the term to identify themselves. Where two groups of people use the same identity, it would suggest some connection. There are parallels between what is said in the *Rigveda* and in the early sections of the *Avesta*, the text composed in Old Iranian in northeastern Iran. This has been much commented on, suggesting at least a geographical proximity of the speakers. The languages were cognates therefore similar, as were many of their important deities and social forms, despite some inversion. The dual division of the ariia and daha is said to be the equivalent of Arya and Dasa. The Achaemenid king Darius, of the mid-first millennium BC, refers in the Behistun inscription to the Aryan language and to being Arya. The identity was not limited to India and included sections of the ancient Iranian people.

The Other who were seen as different, the Dasa, slowly acquired the meaning of those who were subordinated, and in some instances reduced to slavery. However, this did not apply uniformly as some members of the Dasa community were incorporated into the Arya varna. But not so the Dasi. We have noted that the Dasi is frequently the slave woman who does the household chores. She can be gifted together with other forms of chattel as is evident from the *Vedas* and the *Mahabharata*. The inscriptions of Ashoka distinguish between Dasa and Bhritakas, slaves and servants. Domestic slavery was however more commonly referred to than the use of slaves as agricultural and artisanal labour. This change took its course and later texts such as the *Jataka* refer to the price paid for slaves and to unpaid labour. Because the Dasa now became unfree, he could not be ordained as a monk. No concession is made to the status of the Dasa who invariably remains a slave unless manumitted. However, the Dasas could work in the homes of the wealthy because they were not a category regarded as polluted.

The Arya-Mlechha duality was, however, not as central as other differentiations that were to emerge. A possible reason for this change may have been the parallel reorientation of the structure of society in the form of caste—in other words, the new formulation, that of varna and jati, gradually became more important. The *Rigveda* has one late hymn that mentions the god Prajapati creating four groups of people—the Brahmanas, Kshatriyas, Vaishyas and Shudras, in a hierarchical order, but the word varna is not used in this context until in the later texts of the corpus. The attribution of divine creation to these categories gave the highest sanction to a scheme that was put together by a society of humans. Interestingly, the four varnas emerge from the human body. Essentially a Brahmanical theory, it is formulated as the varna-ashrama-dharma in the *Dharmasutras* and *Dharmashastras*. It is reiterated in the *Bhagavad Gita*, but here it is stated Krishna claims to have created the four varnas. The origin of the theory therefore varies but is of divine origin. Complex regulations are worked out exemplifying the social behaviour of each category. Non-Brahmanical views did on occasion change the hierarchy. The Buddhists placed the Kshatriya at the highest level and referred more frequently to jati.

What was involved in this process of change? To oversimplify the argument, let's say that the basic unit of early society was the extended family—the kula. It would seem that families came together to form a larger and more efficient unit, that of the clan—the vish or the jana. This probably became one of the factors in the division of society later into jatis. I would argue that this was necessary to giving some organizational structure to society, given the intermixture of peoples and their cultures that was taking place in the first millennium BC. The jati as a caste is a different unit of society from the jana (clan), but many of its characteristics suggest some continuity from the clan. Identity is through birth into a jati as in a clan. Marriage rules of endogamy and exogamy—whom one can or cannot marry—are prevalent both in clan and jati. These were so organized as to make the woman the negotiable unit and allow a patriarchal ordering of society. Occupations came to be associated with the jatis and these were then arranged in a hierarchy. It was enjoined on each jati as a religious duty to maintain the rituals and customary laws that are essential to its identity.

As jatis expanded they became complex organizations. Each jati had its own hierarchy with variations in the rituals and codes for upper and lower levels. They were not subdivisions of varna, but could be grouped on the basis of occupation and such like into categories that were given some varna affiliation. This could have been just to give some legitimacy to the organization. New communities could be inducted into a jati or more often assumed a rank in the overall structure as a jati. Rules of commensality reinforced hierarchy. Slotting in a new jati was probably easier in this system than converting people individually. Where conversions did take place, caste hierarchies were frequently grafted into the converting religion. Such new identities could more easily be fitted into jati ordering than varna. Mixed religious groups tended to become sects sometimes with jati affiliations.

Varna is suggestive of an organizing principle giving a manageable structure to the range of social divisions. It was more a model with norms than a practising code, but with those in authority insisting on overt conformity. Defined by a Brahmanical perspective it was clear about upper-caste norms, codified in the *Dharmashastras*. The Shudras and those lower down that formed the larger number were left to their own devices, except for distancing them from the dvija (twice-born). The rules for them were not strictly uniform. Even their rules of endogamy differed from text to text.

The centrality of varna is that it becomes the normative ideology that controls the functioning of jatis, often through their assigned status through varnas. The control is legitimized through the claim that the varna-ashrama-dharma had divine origins, and that it was based on theories of pollution and purity—all familiar to us from many ancient societies. Except that caste was fixed by birth, controlled by strict rules of marriage, was said to condition one's life, and in theory disallowed a change of occupation and status. Notwithstanding this, the acceptance of the structure was enabled through those at the upper levels controlling the resources that supported the society, and those at the lower levels ensuring through their work that the resources remained productive for those that controlled them. It presumed that inequality was the norm in every activity, be it political, social or religious.

The question we need to ask is whether societies in India observed the varna model as is claimed in the textual codes. The mainstream castes claim that this was so but the more marginalized are ambivalent. Was there a divergence from the model in its actual working? What were the concessions made in the norms to accommodate deviance? Did this dilute the rules? I would like to consider a few examples of such deviance. Were there elements of a duality even between jati and varna, such that each had to make concessions to the other? For the jati to make a concession would perhaps be easier since it would require adopting new rituals and customs, and more likely these were claims to a higher status. But did the normative model of varna have to make concessions and negotiations that would dilute its own rules?

This becomes significant if we examine the difference between the theory of the *Dharmashastras* and the reality on the ground. In theory, wherever the Aryas were in a majority, the four varnas prevailed in the established hierarchical order. And yet, as I have remarked earlier in this book, in many parts of the subcontinent the dominant caste was actually not the Brahmana. Where those claiming to be Aryas were well established for centuries, as in the period prior to colonial rule, even though the varna hierarchy was said to prevail, there were discrepancies in the dvija varnas. Some who claimed a particular varna status need not have been of that status and may well have acquired it in various ways. This is fairly common for instance among those who claim Kshatriya or royal status through their myths of origin and their genealogies linking them with ancient clans. In this the Indian experience is similar to that of other societies.

The ordering of society was seen less in terms of varna and more as other local jatis who actually formed the dominant castes—Khatris, Rajputs, Marathas, Patedars, Vokkaligas, Reddys, Kayasthas, Vellalars, Nairs, and such like. The variations were substantial, their origins were often as owners or controllers of land, and their relationship with the Brahmanas altered with time and place, since they were all—the Brahmanas included—competing for power and economic resources. Even where the Brahmanas controlled the economy, the routine functioning of the society was in the hands of the jatis. Some among the latter picked up the trappings of a varna status if they chose to, others did not bother as long as they had the authority and controlled the economy. The one area where they did make concessions to the Brahmanas was in the performance of rituals. In this the force of superstition required that rituals be performed and the priests were the ones that received the tangible gifts as dakshina, the fee for performing the ritual. Who patronized and who performed the rituals was also a mark of social demarcation. This raises the question of what was happening behind the façade of maintaining the theory of varna society?

The varna scheme differentiated between three components drawing on degrees of exclusion. The first were the Brahmanas claiming the maximum superiority on the basis of ritual purity, acquired from divine sources or from performing rituals; and as custodians of knowledge and learning. Their distinctive rules separated them from the rest. To begin with, they were conceded the status of being dvija at birth and at initiation. But gradually this epithet came to be used for other upper castes. The second component consisted of the non-Brahmana varnas—the Kshatriyas, Vaishyas and Shudras, each in turn becoming more open-ended about occupation and ritual activities, and lower in status. These four categories constituted the Savarnas—those included in varna society, although the Shudra varna became a compendium in which all kinds of people were listed. Their low status was attributed to their supposedly mixed varna parentage and described as varna-sankara or sankirna jati. Attributing a low caste status did not necessary reflect a careful assessment of social origins since it could be used just to put down those trying to claim a higher status.

The third component was that of the Avarna, those that were altogether excluded from society. This group was vague to begin with but became clearly marked later in time. It included those called Chandalas in the earlier sources as well as what later came to be called Asprishya, literally untouchable. Their habitat was beyond the settlement and segregated from the others. These were in effect ghettos. This civic pattern took shape in the early first millennium AD. It has been argued that it was brought to a head with the increasing claim of the ritual purity of the Brahmana that had as its counterweight the impurity of the Asprishya. Therefore the latter had to be demarcated as being polluted, and to make the point it was treated as a genetic pollution as it were. Such persons were born to polluted persons therefore were automatically polluted themselves. One may well ask whether this was the only historical reason.

Essential to caste society was categorization by exclusion. Who was included and who was excluded? The degrees of exclusion strengthened hierarchy. The basis of exclusion were more frequently socio-economic factors, but sought to be legitimized by resort to sacred sanction. How closely were the rules of varna system followed? When it was flouted then who were the ones to do so? One would have thought that the Brahmanas who had the maximum advantages in the system would insist on staying close to the rules and demanding the same from the others. Demand they certainly did, but how effectively, is another matter. As far as the lower castes and the Avarnas were concerned the leash was tight, but relations with the upper castes were open to negotiation in some situations.

The Brahmanas claimed to be a category apart that had access to the deities, therefore maintained maximum purity through special rituals and strict rules of marriage and gotra functions, as well as acceptance of types of food. Their profession was restricted to their being ritual specialists and extended to scholarship. Yet there is mention of a few strange categories of Brahmanas with curious origins. The Vedic texts mention, by name, an exceptional category called the Dasiputra Brahmanas, almost an oxymoron, whom I have touched upon earlier. As the name implies they were sons of Dasis.

A much-respected Brahmana Kavasha Ailusha, the son of the Dasi, Ilusha, is said to be a purohita. They tend to take their mother's name which was perhaps an assertion of their Dasa identity. Kavasha tried to join the sacrificial ritual but the Brahmanas drove him away to the desert because of his Dasi birth. There he recited a hymn to the waters and the Sarasvati River came and enveloped him. So the Brahmanas conceded that he was known to the gods, took him back and acknowledged that he was the best among them. Equally revered was Kakshivant Aushija, the son of the Dasi Ushija.

The *Upanishads* relate the story of Jabala who came to the

rishis seeking knowledge. They asked if he was a Brahmana and he replied that his mother was a Dasi employed in a household who had to be available to the men who visited, so she did not know who was his father. The rishis replied that since he had told the truth he must be a Brahmana and took him on as a student.

Gradually the occupations associated with Brahmanas took another turn. Their pre-eminence as ritual specialists lasted as long as elaborate sacrificial rituals were performed. It began to recede later when Vedic Brahmanism gave way to the more popular Puranic Hinduism in the first millennium AD. Vedic rituals were then performed largely for royalty on special occasions, and ostensibly as heritage from past times still regarded as effective. The patrons of such rituals were more often those who were claiming Kshatriya status, and Brahmana specialists could be called upon to legitimize their status.

Later when temples began to be built, Brahmanas became temple priests. This was a departure from Vedic rituals. Prior to the Gupta period—the fourth century AD—there were of course no temples and the placing of icons in temples to be worshipped also came later. The Vedic gods Indra and Agni gave way to Shiva and Vishnu as the premier deities. The ritual changed from the vast open-air yajna to the more restricted puja in the enclosed sanctum where the image was kept. Not surprisingly medieval period commentaries on the *Dharmashastras* argue over who is superior in status, the Vedic Shrotriya Brahmana or the temple priest. This became problematic when multiple new kingdoms were established. As a result, some local cults and their priests were inducted into Puranic Hinduism. Did they also, as with the Dasiputra, automatically acquire purity and become high status Brahmanas?

But this was also the period when the occupations of Brahmanas proliferated. They had been employed as ministers to kings, as was Kautilya, and managed the administration of the monarchies together with a few upper-caste non-Brahmana administrators. From the Gupta period onwards they became the managers of the vast estates that they received from royalty as land grants, also in some instances, huge herds of cattle. In some cases and over a few generations, they were even acknowledged as rulers of small principalities.

Others had to administer the estates and finances of the many wealthy temples that were established in the late first and second millennium AD. They were well experienced in this from being administrators in the kingdoms. The accumulation of wealth in the temples, and especially in the larger ones in the second millennium AD, was by any standards most impressive—as it continues to be, judging by what pours out from the vaults of the major temples of today in every part of the country. Having to record and safeguard such wealth would convert the temple priest into a proficient administrator and accountant. Inscriptions from all over the country refer to these new roles of the Brahmanas and they are described with the appropriate qualifying label. The competition was to come later with the rise of the Kayastha caste, scribes and competent administrators, said to be partly Brahmana in origin.

Yet another departure from the norm was Brahmanas controlling extensive commercial institutions. Some were so successful, as in the highly lucrative horse trade with Central Asia, that they are recorded as substantial donors to temples in northern India.

The second carefully described varna was that of the Kshatriyas. They were said to have descended from ancient lineages labelled pre-eminently as the solar and lunar lines, and were warriors, and often constituted the royalty of early India—the heroes and the kings. There is general agreement that the janapadas (territories of the early period), were frequently ruled by clans identified as Kshatriya such as the Kurus, Pandavas, Vrishnis and so on. But when it comes to the early dynasties, we are told in Brahmanical sources that the rulers were not Kshatriyas. The earliest and much respected *Vishnu Purana* provides a list of dynasties for the period approximately from 500 BC to AD 300. The Nanda dynasty and their successors were said to be Shudra. This is probably because in this period many dynasties had Buddhist and Jaina affiliations rather than Brahmanical. Such affiliations from the Brahmana perspective would make them low caste Shudra. This included the Mauryas. But the Buddhist texts state without any doubt that the Mauryas were Kshatriya. After them came the Kanvas and Shungas who were Brahmana and were followed by a series of non-Kshatriyas including the Guptas. Varna identities could change according to the author's preference. Clearly the theory of varna-ashrama-dharma was running into problems.

Another category associated with the Kshatriya was the Yavana, also referred to as the Yona. Originally the name for the Greeks of Ionia in Asia Minor, Yavana gradually came to be used for the Hellenistic Greeks and various people coming to India from the general western direction. Their overall culture was different and yet they made attempts to adjust to northwest Indian culture. Some were rulers with a base either in northwestern India or in Central Asia, and some were traders. The rulers had to be given status so they were slotted into the Kshatriya varna but as vratya—degenerate or inferior Kshatriyas, a grudging concession.

The addition of vratya was probably because the Brahmanas did not take too kindly to the Yavanas whose preferential patronage seems to have been to the Buddhists. The Buddhists referred to Yavanas without what was then an offensive qualifier. Some Yavanas were donors at Buddhist sacred places, and a few were Vaishnavas. A lengthy dialogue between the Indo-Greek king, Menander, and the Buddhist monk, Nagasena, as recorded in the *Milinda-panha*, points to attempts being made to convert people of status to Buddhism. We do not have the same mention of dialogues in Brahmanical texts, yet we know that they took place since the mathematician-astronomer Varahamihira remarks in his work, the *Brihat Samhita*, on how knowledgeable the Yavanas were despite their being Mleccha—outside the pale.

The same *Vishnu Purana* that provides a list of dynasties, states that subsequent to the Guptas, new Kshatriyas would be made. They would be people of low status—vratyas of various kinds and upstarts (advija-vratya, udita-odita-vamsha). Ironically this is precisely when many ruling families claim genealogical links to ancient Kshatriya lineages, such as the Suryavamsha and the Chandravamsha, or the freshly invented Agnikula, and the even more recent Nagabansi. They recorded their claims in inscriptions from the late millennium onwards and in later bardic poems. What then were the actual origins of those claiming to be Kshatriya royalty? How was Kshatriya status acquired? Some of the rulers listed are quite clearly Shudra or even lower by Brahmanical standards. Historical origins are not necessarily what they claim to be and sometimes the myth associated with the origin provides clues, not as historical statements but as hints of what might have been the actual story. Tracking the fabrication of lineages can be a fascinating historical pastime.

A striking feature of the culture of local heroes, who died defending the cattle of the village from raiders or the village itself, was shown on their memorial stones as being carried by apsaras directly to heaven. It would seem that their death in this manner exempted them from rebirth. The theory of karma and samsara appears not to have been universally applied, and it would be worth analysing the groups that were exempted and why.

The use of varna as a formal identity increases in the post-Gupta period. This is also the period when sizeable land grants became a way of rewarding supporters and extending agrarian resources at the same time. Sizeable land grants of cultivated or wasteland were given to Brahmanas who had performed rituals for the new Kshatriyas—legitimizing their status, or diverting the ill-effects of an eclipse or averting the evil eye. A smaller number were given to officers of the administration either in lieu of salaries or for services rendered. As the land-owning elite, some of these claimed the status of a split varna, the Brahma-Kshatra.

Sometimes the land so granted included areas of forest that had to be cleared. This involved a new relationship with existing Adivasi communities leading to the process by which a few Adivasis were converted to jatis, and on occasion given a varna status as well, or alternatively could even be treated as outcastes. Some texts refer to them as Atavikas, or else as Mleccha-jatis. The reason for the differentiation is unclear. Can it be taken as a form of what has been called statecraft becoming a project of internal colonization?

Banabhatta's *Harshacharita*, the seventh century biography of Harshavardhana of Kanauj, describes the Shabara tribes living in the depths of the forests. They were not treated as Asprishya. They are said to be remarkably knowledgeable about the forest. The difference in their physical appearance is encapsulated in describing them as dark like a cloud of antimony, with bloodshot eyes, high cheekbones and thick lips. Such descriptions become conventional and are reminiscent of those of the rakshasas in Sanskrit literature. Other Adivasis inhabited villages that were in the process of mutating into the rural settlements of the kingdom. But interestingly there are references later to the curious label, Shabara Brahmanas.

Given that such concessions could be made to mediate in, or even alter the rules of varna, we may well ask what then was the extent to which varna was negotiable in order to accommodate facets of social change? To what extent did the theory of varna-ashrama-dharma mould Indian society in its actual functioning? Or was it a seeming observance for the larger society whereas the other socio-economic divisions may have been applied more rigorously? Jati was not the same as varna so the nineteenth century European view that caste as varna overwhelmed Indian society needs to be re-examined. Could social requirements take precedence over caste rules although not always in a transparent way? The usual reference to an unchanging observance of varna rules would not be tenable.

The new occupations regularized for Brahmanas fanned out in many secular directions. The slow fading of Buddhism in the late first millennium AD seems to coincide with Puranic Hinduism coming to the forefront. There was even a change in the structure of that segment of society that drew upon the model Brahmana of the *Vedas*. With extensive royal patronage and the acquisition of wealth through royal grants, a section of the Brahmanas set up an alternative society, part authoritarian and part renunciatory. Brahmanas with claims to learning—and some were indeed very learned—organized their lives in mathas. These institutions had a different curriculum and function from ashramas. The focus was on scholarship, much of which was religious and philosophical discourse. It has been said that the Buddhist monastery, the vihara, may have suggested the idea of the matha. The inhabitants of the mathas were however not celibate and had their families living with them. They were not centrally concerned with popular religion therefore the Bhakti sants did not inhabit the mathas. A few established their own separately. The head of the matha would ideally observe a distance from public life, but even then as now, the attraction of exercising secular authority through the façade of a religious form, was extremely tempting. The heads of mathas would certainly have had political relations with royal authority.

The mathas were thought of as isolated, autonomous institutions segregated from the settlement, with their own independent resources and organization. This gave them a charisma through which they asserted their authority. The parallel with the Buddhist vihara is noticeable. Scholarship in the mathas focused on texts of Vedic and classical Sanskrit and often took the form of commentaries on these, apart from new writing. Debates with scholars of other traditions on logic, methods of reasoning, mathematics, astronomy and medicine, were held and recorded. There may also have been some trickling in of ideas from other traditions such as those of the Bhaktas and the Sufis. This needs investigation. The last thousand years were rich in its dialogues between scholars and teachers of various sects of religious and philosophical thought, with new ideas emerging from this thinking. This encouraged the creation of new religious sects of every persuasion and more so in the span of sects linked to the Hindu religion.

Some of the new sects such as the followers of Kabir, Dadu, Ravidas and a few others, propagated a liberal social code, especially with reference to the lower castes. The lives of those at the lower and lowest levels was unenviable and had been so since early times. The exclusion of the Avarna groups seems to have been viewed as the normal condition of the society. I mentioned earlier that the counterweight to the assertion of purity by the Brahmanas was the demarcation of the excluded groups that were not only outside the four varnas but also characterized by norms that contradicted those of the four. This component was jointly referred to as the Avarna, or often as the Asprishya, the untouchable. This had been in the making over a period of time but seems to have taken shape in the early first millennium AD. What brought it to a head was ostensibly the notion of pollution, but was this the only historical reason?

Notions of the ritual purity of the Brahmana go back to the Brahmana as the Vedic ritual specialist. As I have mentioned earlier, Vedic Brahmanism had been less prominent with the rise of Puranic Hinduism. But there was a revival of Vedic rituals, legitimizing rulers in the multiple kingdoms that emerged in the post-Gupta period. This assertion of Vedic Brahmanism was initially limited to a small elite, but it grew both in numbers and in claims to extraordinary status.

The exclusion of the Avarna took the form of arguing that some communities were Asprishya, a term that came into use at this time. This dates to the early to mid centuries of the first millennium AD. But let me try and trace the evolution of what might have gone into the making of this idea, although the explanation remains historically incomplete. This is partly because social historians have not as yet focused on studying the Avarna in early Indian society. The ghettoized communities were not educated, so they have left no written records. They have to be studied by combing through the records of literate groups. If exclusion and discrimination is specifically explained and juxtaposed with whatever descriptions we have, then it might be possible to retrieve some idea of the functioning and values of this ghettoized Avarna society.

Another possible reason for the emphasis on purity and pollution at this point, could be that the requirement of legitimizing rulers in the multiple kingdoms that emerged in the post-Gupta period, may have revived to some extent, the ritual role of the Brahmana, required to perform rites of legitimation for the new royalty. Did this revival reinvigorate the theory of the maximum purity of the Brahmana, at least among the Brahmanas? Did this then require as a counterweight, the more extreme identity of the Asprishya? Exclusions of various kinds and degrees are not unknown to other societies in other parts of the world, but untouchability, as it came to be established in India, is virtually inhuman, and not resorted to by any other society. Not only is the touch of the person polluting and therefore physical contact with the person is forbidden, but what is even worse is that the pollution is inherent, is of genetic origin, since the kinsfolk are also polluted and the person is polluted from birth.

A number of communities are listed as being at the lowest levels of society and the lists differ. But the one that invariably figures is the Chandala. Vedic texts mention the Chandala as one of impure birth and a victim of a sacrificial ritual. He is not quite an untouchable since in this context he is linked to the ritual but becomes so in time. Some social codes describe him as being of mixed caste. Punishment for having sexual relations with such a one, or eating with a Chandala are severe, so apparently it was not entirely unthinkable. The Buddha had a far more humane and rational view and is reported to have said that one becomes a Chandala by one's actions and by evil thoughts and not by birth. Buddhist narratives such as the *Jataka* however do reflect discrimination against Chandalas. There is also a linguistic barrier since mention is made of a Chandala-bhasha or language specific to the Chandalas and different from the generally spoken one. The *Arthashastra* sharpens the difference between Chandalas and other low castes and locates the habitat of the former as close to the cremation ground. The grammarians Panini and Patanjali differentiate between those Shudras that live in the settlement (anirvasita), and those that live outside (nirvasita), and the Chandala is among the latter.

Manu speaks of their descent from a mixed marriage between a Shudra father and a Brahmana mother—the worst form of hypogamy. It reads as if it was also intended as a putting down of women, in keeping with much else in Manu. It was said that the Chandala receives leftover food, wears clothes taken off corpses, and can only have iron ornaments. Only in dire hunger should food be accepted from a Chandala. This is precisely the discussion in a late chapter of the *Mahabharata*, which had an angular relationship with the *Dharmashastras*. In this episode the Sage Vishvamitra has a discussion with a Chandala during a severe famine, on the kind of meat permitted to a Brahmana, and whether it is legitimate to eat what is forbidden simply to keep the body alive. Although the Chandala tries to dissuade the sage from breaking the taboo (which Vishvamitra is about to do to assuage his hunger) he does not succeed. It is interesting that the Chandala seems to know so much about the Brahmana dharma and one wonders if this is meant as a sarcastic comment. The other explanation could be that this episode belongs to an earlier period when the social distancing between them was not so rigid and the taboos on eating forbidden food were not so severely maintained.

By the mid-first millennium AD the exclusion of the Chandala and others that formed the lowest jatis was well established. Buddhist texts state that other communities generally listed as excluded tended to be Adivasis—such as Nishadas, Pukkasas, or in low occupations such as Venas and Rathakaras. Little is said about why they are low jatis. Forcing communities to live outside the settlement immediately marks them out as excluded. Had this not have been required they may over time have merged into the general population of not so low jatis.

Gradually two characteristics came to be embedded in the identity of those thought of as polluted. One was that of impurity. This increased when they were required to not only maintain the cremation grounds since a dead body was thought to be polluting, but also do the scavenging in the settlement. Curiously, the cremation ground was also the location for certain Shaiva and Tantric rituals involving corpses, and in which the upper castes participated. Did people not think about the social implication of such rituals? As for scavenging, unfortunately, the excellent system of drains that was a striking feature of Harappan cities, is not found in later cities, so scavenging became a necessity. Scavenging would not have been required in rural areas but was necessary in cities. The insistence on this category of people being polluted was partly tied into the work they were expected to do.

The inclusion of those of Adivasi origin in this group could suggest that when new areas were opened up the existing small communities from these areas were either left isolated or else were inducted as low jatis. Some recruitment would be required to maintain numbers. Because such communities were regarded as polluting they had to live outside the settlement hence their names have qualifiers such as antya and bahya and such like, meaning outside. Living outside the settlement further segregated them. The sense of there being two different societies took root—one which was regarded as polluted and therefore lived outside the settlement, and the other which lived in the settlement and was thought of as unpolluted. Some might have seen those living outside as the fifth varna but the *Dharmashastras* kept them distinctly separate from the categories of varnas. The society that claimed to be unpolluted and lived in the settlements has been studied in much depth but not so the other society that lives beyond the settlement.

There were at least three pointed features of this definition of Otherness that differentiated the Asprishya from all the other categories of excluded groups. One was that this group had a distinct and separate physical location. As in many premodern cities the world over, there was a tendency for those in the same profession to cluster together and these came to be demarcated as the locations of those professions. But the Asprishya were not allowed to live in the city since they were regarded as polluted and because their profession was polluting. Their pollution was underlined repeatedly as their occupations were scavenging, carrying away dead animals, executing criminals and maintaining the cremation ground. This was a distinctly separate and physically segregated society associated with what were regarded as the impurities of death and dirt. According to some, it developed its own hierarchy of virtual jatis, as if it were an isolated clone of caste society. Why some other professions were also regarded as polluting is not explained in the texts. It is simply stated.

A second feature was the constant underlining of their being permanently impure and polluted, since they had to handle what was regarded as polluting objects as viewed from the Brahmanical perspective. Pollution was not an issue with the other categories of exclusion. In this case it is not so evident in the early texts but gradually intensifies. Curiously the references to maximally polluted groups seem to coincide with the period of a revival of Brahmanical claims to being maximally pure.

It is worth noting that when Megasthenes, the Greek visitor, writes about Mauryan India in the late fourth century BC, there is only a garbled description of what might have been a vague reference to caste, and no hint of anything like an untouchable category. As I have mentioned earlier, when Faxian visits in the fourth century AD, he describes how untouchables have to strike a clapper on entering the town, to indicate their presence so that the others can move away. This is in the so-called 'golden age' of the Guptas that the presence of the untouchable is heavily marked and emphatically defined. This was the age that has been taken for the last century, and still is, as the high point of Indian culture with a spectacular civilizational stamp. The achievements of the period especially pertaining to cultural items are frequently mentioned. But curiously the other side of the coin, the presence of the Asprishya, is ignored when describing the 'golden age'.

The Avarnas were of mixed origin, spoke a different language in some places, and inevitably had different social customs and belief systems. Given their large numbers it can be asked whether they developed their own hierarchy of virtual jatis and whether this was a rigid or flexible structure. Was it a clone of caste society? Was it an inverted mirror image or was the inversion more important than the mirror? That the Avarna society has its own subdivisions and its own priests, perhaps from earlier times, suggests a possibly dissimilar society in earlier times.

The third feature is that the pollution is permanent. Virtually every society of the ancient world practised temporary periods of impurity especially in the context of performing rituals. Even ritual specialists could be impure for a specific time but this was not the same as being permanently untouchable. Purity was claimed by Brahmanas who were ritual specialists. But to commit people to a permanent state of pollution and impurity is unique to India and calls for far greater investigation than has been done so far. The Asprishya cannot change his jati or his varna status or work in professions other than those stipulated in the *Dharmashastras*. His is a distinctly separate society and he can only move along the hierarchy of his own society. This is again different from the other categories where, as we have seen, some concessions were made and varna status could be adjusted. Permanency also meant that the features of separation never changed nor were they reapplied as in the case of the Arya, the Mleccha, the Yavana and the varna. Pollution was not a temporary condition or one that could be shed by the next generation. It was permanent and was inherited because birth was from parents also regarded as polluted. This genetic factor makes it different from other categories of pollution.

Permanent pollution as a demarcation had not been linked with other excluded groups. Could the need for such permanency been a revival of claims to maximum purity by ritual specialists of a particular kind who were now figures of authority, as for example those performing legitimizing rituals for the new Kshatriyas, or were such activities too limited for such a major change? It has been pointed out that this was also the period when the demand for cow protection was more frequently mentioned in the texts and may have been linked to the enormous number of cows gifted to Brahmanas as listed in contemporary inscriptions. Together with this came a spurt in cattle raid hero stones dedicated to local heroes who had died defending the cattle of the village. Cattle breeding was clearly vital to the rural economy. But more numbers of cattle required more scavenging to clear the bovine carcasses. Prevention of the slaughter of cows, presumably addressed to the upper castes, finds more mention now. This would have affected the nutrition pattern of the lower castes and the outcastes.

To ascribe genetic impurity to a set of communities calls for the investigation of this ascription. Why was the concept so widely accepted, questioned by only a handful of Bhakti sants and a few others? It reflects on the mores and values of the larger society that accepted and imposed this belief and practice. What was the ethical foundation of this thinking? If it is not apparent then it would be troubling since some other aspects of upper caste culture of these times are rightly regarded as deserving of admiration. How could such a contradiction of the ethical and the aesthetic with the unethical be acceptable to the same society?

As we have seen, it has for long been held that the culture of the mid-first millennium AD and its continuation was the golden age of Indian civilization, the utopia of past times. This evaluation has been contested by historians who argue that the material culture of the Gupta age as available from excavations of settlements, was unimpressive. Nevertheless, this period saw the articulation of sophisticated philosophical schools, the high literary quality of Kalidasa and other poets, the aesthetic of Gupta sculpture and the Ajanta murals, the coming of temple architecture as well as the impressive advances in mathematics and astronomy made by Indian scholars. Some of this had started taking shape in earlier centuries and then grew to maturity when it crystallized into what is regarded as the Indian aesthetic as well as the growth of knowledge. It is worth reiterating the point I made earlier. How could this same society have internalized the idea of Asprishya and been so immune to its treatment of the men and women whom it categorized as Avarna? To declare such people to be physically so impure that they could not be touched, and not only them individually, but their entire community and its descendants, is a belief and practice that inheres to Indian society alone.

One may well ask how such a severe degradation of the human person can be reconciled to such an impressive aesthetic and pursuit of thought? Surely at some point the aesthetic must touch the notion of the ethical? Are these the contradictions of a culture? Was the ethic so abstract that it did not connect with the human condition? The trite answer often heard is that it was tied into the theodicy of karma and samsara—as you act in this life so shall you reap in the next birth. This does not answer the question as it is limited to justifying the existing condition. Where did the idea of a genetically impure person come from and why did it take root? There were men and women in various traditions who rejected the segregation and did so quite forcefully in their teachings, but to little effect in terms of social regulations. Why were those who propagated an unethical discrimination in society permitted to control both religious and social functioning and that too for centuries? Is this a legitimate articulation of a utopia, the implications of which did not disturb the ethical conscience of our ancestors? Our descriptions of our golden ages of the past will have to be more realistic than they have been so far. Or, is this an example of early societies being unconcerned with questions of social equality, a concern that emerges as a feature of social thought only in modern times? That social segregation existed can be explained, but the particular justification for it is incomprehensible if not inexcusable.

Later in the second millennium AD there were conversions of some Avarnas to religions that maintained the equality of all in the eyes of God. Yet so deeply embedded was the notion and practice of untouchability that even God in these religions had to make room for accommodating it. Why were these religions thwarting the ethic associated with their God? The concept and its practice had converted Islam, Christianity and Sikhism to accepting the permanent pollution and social exclusion of the Avarnas, even though it went against their fundamental tenets. In other words, either the condition goes beyond its association with the Hindu religion, or else these religions did not wish to challenge the authority of the Hindu religion. Islam and Christianity did not introduce it for West Asia and Europe. It has been asked whether it is rooted in religion or more so in socio-economic requirements, although it is sought to be legitimized by resort to religion.

The claim to being the legitimizers of the system comes from those associated with a range of factors: the maximum assertion of purity coinciding with its legitimizers having direct access to wealth; a mystique of the innate superiority and power of the legitimizers; an assertion that the system has divine sanction and was divinely created; and the notion of the maximum purity of one group requiring the counterweight of the maximum impurity of another.

As a social structure, caste society has evolved on the basis of social and economic requirements. These aspects are historically conditioned and can therefore be mutated or even changed without resort to any divine sanction. The Brahmanical mode of Hinduism was the prime legitimizer of caste society and untouchability as is evident in the disjuncture between Savarna and Avarna society. As has been rightly said religion can be the resistance of the oppressed but it can equally be the oppression by the elite.

It would seem that on the issue of untouchability social ethics were marginalized by religions in India. If that was so then we have to examine the socio-economic requirements of Indian society that ensured the continuity of the Avarna communities. Apart from the occupations associated with them and regarded as polluting, it has been argued that an additional historical reason was the growing requirement for landless, unfree agricultural labour, a requirement crucial to the agrarian economy of that period. The segregated settlement provided a source of such labour whose permanency was insured by the stigma of pollution and who had no future other than that of reproducing itself. Unlike China where peasant revolts took place, protest in India in earlier times took the form of peasants migrating to neighbouring kingdoms. But those said to be permanently polluted could not migrate nor find employment elsewhere. As Avarnas they would have problems settling in new places and it would be impossible if they were, in addition, bonded labour.

Expansion in agriculture associated with the post-Gupta period and continuing into the second millennium AD, required a larger labour force than in earlier times. Were the outcast communities also diverted into becoming landless labour and kept tied to working the lands and living where they were initially located? Coercion would have been one way of achieving this but the additional way was to prevent migration. Vishti and begar were sources of forced labour. Whether this labour came in the main from the Avarna category needs investigation.

As has been noted, groups have been excluded and discriminated against since early times in virtually every part of the world. Some societies impose short periods of impurity on certain members for ritual reasons, such as women after childbirth or at menstruation. Those among the Avarnas more generally subordinated were used as labour and some converted into slaves. The latter worked either in agricultural or artisanal production or in the household. The former lived in communities segregated from the mainstream as the helots in Sparta, or the blacks on plantations in the American south. African slaves were regarded as genetically inferior in the race science of the nineteenth century, but even they were never treated as genetically polluting.

Deliberately ghettoized societies from the past to the present call for deeper study. Why was there resort to this extreme form of exclusion and distancing and why were those that were thus set apart given such a degrading identity? These are questions that are intrinsic to evaluating cultures.

We need to know why such systems were created and the effect of the distortions that resulted. The dialogue between the Chandala and Vishvamitra was not just a casual chat. It has a meaning that we need to fathom. The ideas of those who critiqued the institution of caste directly or indirectly should be more visible in the narrative of the past since our heritage is not one-sided. We should know more of the ideas of the Charvakas, Buddhists and Shramanic teachers, and some such as Chokhamela and Ravidas as well as some Sufi teachers on the society they lived in. The Charvakas are dismissed because they questioned religion and with the others their social concerns are rarely discussed except in a general way. The *Dharmashastra* literature is concerned with the well being of only a small part of society. We need to know the thinking of those who disagreed with it so as to have an idea of what was discussed in the dialogues of past time. Alternate ideologies of dissent are significant facets of our culture and we have to understand them.

Early historical texts come to us largely from the upper castes. They have to be sieved meticulously for evidence on the lives of those who have not left records. For more recent centuries there are oral traditions, even from the ghettoized societies, that need careful examination. Oral history is now a recognized branch of historical exploration. It ranges from what the Incas thought of the Spanish conquest in Latin America, what has been called 'the vision of the vanquished', to the reconstruction of Sub-Saharan African history from Bantu oral sources. The Bantu peoples inhabited central and southern Africa, spoke Bantu languages, and these oral compositions are now being studied analytically. Similar methods may reveal something of the past of Indian communities that only have oral traditions.

History may tell us why the exclusion came to be, but the question—as was famously said —is how to change it. This concern is not only of our time. People in past centuries have spoken against the inequities of Indian society but were unable to change it. We have to ask why. Perhaps with a greater exploration of the reasons for its becoming so rooted we may have better ideas about how to uproot it. This may tell us what we need to do apart from affirmative action, since this latter is not a permanent solution. It is already being hijacked by some influential dominant castes claiming to be OBC (Other Backward Castes) in order to appropriate the advantages. Two more permanent and effective efforts that are obvious would be in the educational curriculum and in civil law.

The mindset that continues to view society through the kind of optics that we have had, now needs to be discarded. In this, education can contribute to creating an ethically more responsible society. But this requires the content of school and college education to be changed to explain and endorse social ethics, apart from the need to improve the quality of education. This I will touch on in the next chapter. Inequities and disadvantages cannot be wiped out in a hurry. It needs both a more pointed economy directed towards decreasing disparities and disadvantages, which unfortunately is not the direction in which the current economic change is moving. It also needs the endorsing of social values aimed at altering the mindset so that notions of genetic pollution can be expunged.

Then there are our civil laws enmeshed not only in a range of religious traditions but also drawing from colonial readings that further complicate the laws. Here again the purpose and content of the laws pertaining to marriage and inheritance need to be assessed. It may be more to the point if we cleared away the multiple laws of majority and minority religious codes and drafted an entirely fresh secular code applicable to all Indian citizens alike. That may bring back the ethical in our thinking.

I have tried to argue that the Savarna society was specific to the time when it was constructed. When historical change required an adjustment this was made in accordance with social and economic needs, although the claim to an unchanging façade was maintained. Where groups in power wished to assert a high status this was conceded often with a legitimation of the appropriate status. The upper castes did not maintain a rigid, unchanging system of caste identity among themselves. However, once the Avarna was created by the upper castes it remained distinctively different as the exceptional, permanently excluded set of communities, their permanent exclusion being irrationally explained as due to genetic impurity. In their case there were no adjustments or concessions, only additions of numbers.

Exclusion can be of different kinds. Some are excluded by those in authority so that the latter can assert authority and set aside others as subordinate. Exclusion also often requires deprivation and this is then given a specific identity to demarcate it as excluded and the deprivation is maintained. The most frequent counterpoint is that authority comes to those that control resources and against those that labour on the resources for those that own them, or do services for them, and are therefore treated as excluded. They are denied rights and obligations. In the worst possible case they are declared genetically polluted.

If we are to understand ourselves as a society, should we not analyse what went into the including of some communities as the mainstream, and the excluding of others. How in historical times did these earlier evolved positions change? Equally important is the question of why the exclusion has taken such an extreme form. Questioning exclusions and identities will explain how and why they came about, their contribution to the making of what we call our civilization and our ethical values. It might also lead us to effectively annul that part of our heritage that denies social justice and is ethically unacceptable.

7

KNOWLEDGE AS HERITAGE

It is repeatedly said that education is critical to the making of a civilization. In its different forms through the centuries it has been and is central to our understanding of the world in which we live, and in some ways, how we experience it. This in turn inculcates in us the values necessary to all human interaction. For all our talk about having inherited a great civilization, we are the least concerned with giving priority to quality education that leads us to enquiry and encourages us to think outside the mould, which was precisely what had contributed to the making of our past achievements.

This chapter on education is divided into two parts. The first part looks at what is lacking in the content of education at present, and why educational institutions play a miniscule role as agencies of culture. They have neither been able to perform with success, their expected task of educating the public to make them responsible citizens, nor have they encouraged the non-conservative quality of thinking that advances knowledge and explores theories of explanation that is so central to understanding ourselves and our requirements. Among those that have marginally succeeded in doing the latter some are being currently barred in various ways, not least with state support, from continuing to do so. Of the population barely half can claim to be educated, and many of these minimally so. In this first part of the chapter I shall comment briefly on education and knowledge that existed in India in premodern times to the present day, and suggest what needs to be done to systematically improve the quality of current education.

The second part of the chapter is more personal and has to do with my involvement with Jawaharlal Nehru University (JNU) or rather more specifically with what those of us who were part of the founding team of the Centre for Historical Studies (CHS) were trying to do, in order to institute a place where historical knowledge could be known and advanced. This was encompassed by the wider vision of JNU as an agency of education. What JNU stood for, in our minds, was part of the effort to encourage universities to become catalysts to develop new ways of thinking. Universities in India have tended to be clones of a single model, inherited from colonial times, rather than institutions that have been shaped by their contribution to the growth of knowledge. JNU was intended to be different and I will go into this in some detail in the second part of the chapter.

I

Educational institutions are not static. They change when societies change. The minimum that is required of them is that those they educate should be trained to understand the world they live in through the knowledge they receive; to have the confidence to question this knowledge where such questioning is needed; and to be aware of claiming their rights as citizens of a reasonably well-ordered society. Democracy is meant to enable people to change from being subjects of the state, to becoming citizens of the state, with rights and obligations. Citizenship in a democracy should mean equal access to social justice and to human rights, given unanimously and universally. No category of citizen has priority over others. What we have today is a citizenry of which almost 50 per cent, for no fault of their own, remain effectively without education. This lack and its general acceptability is a reflection on how poorly we define our democracy.

Cloning the existing institutions in larger and larger numbers is not a solution. We need to return again to two themes that have cropped up in past times. They remain undecided and therefore prevent the shaping of the programme for education. One is the question of relating the content of education to its purpose and function; and the other is the tangled but connected question of the language of instruction at various levels. In order to discover the potential from hitherto uneducated sections of society, obviously there has to be universal education that goes beyond the lowest common denominator. That this is not happening makes one wonder whether political parties feel threatened by the possibility of an educated electorate. It is also not happening because the content of education is not directed towards encouraging new thinking and the language of education is inadequate.

We treat the purpose and function of education rather casually. Its budget is paltry to begin with, nevertheless it meets with constant cuts, education being thought of as dispensable. Efforts to educate being so casual it is not surprising that only less than half the population can claim to be educated, and even among these only half again acquire an education that is of some use. In most schools where science is taught without conducting experiments, or geography is taught without maps, such teaching has little value other than providing cursory information. Yet if quality education were to be available to larger numbers it would result in many more competent people facilitating even the basic simple programmes of economic development, or the application of new technologies, and would understand the need for social change, hopefully moving towards the society we aspire to. I am making a distinction here between merely imitating a technology currently used in technologically advanced countries, such as digitization, and adopting it after investigating the kind of change that it will bring about not only in our economy, but also in our society. In order to prepare for the much more intensive impact of this technology on the form of social relations that will result from it, we have to understand and foresee this result. We have superficially adopted the idea with little understanding of, and preparation for, the consequences.

Every government claims to be concerned about the poor quality and dismal reach of our educational institutions but little effective change is made. It seems to me that no government to date has been seriously committed to a systematic agenda of establishing and improving education. Are we caught between what we have inherited which requires reassessment and the current populist ideological drives that are pushing us away from quality education? Quoting the increase in the number of schools, colleges and universities, doesn't tell us much about the criteria that go into the making of education. Improvement would lie in providing every Indian with some degree of comprehension of the world that he or she lives in.

Part of the problem is also the increasing interference from non-professionals in the content of education. Disallowing inquisitive enquiry can easily undermine the purpose of education as can diluting or even falsifying the content of what is taught. Neither of these are unknown today in schools. This becomes evident from the poor training that teachers receive—if at all—and the quality of the textbooks from which they teach. Administrators often look upon educational institutions as stepping stones to personal ambitions and the institution suffers. Political and religious organizations have demanded deletions in the content of syllabi, reading lists and textbooks, and at another level, they intervene in appointments of teachers. Proximity to a particular ideology becomes the driving force of activity. This was barely visible four decades ago but has accelerated to a far greater extent in recent times. Unfortunately many academics, even if they are aware of it, are hesitant to resist it.

A violent agitation by a group of students in Delhi University, claiming that an item in a syllabus hurt their religious sentiments, resulted in the Academic Council removing the item despite its importance to teaching the subject. The university recognizes the threat from groups with political backing but does it also understand the intellectual damage of conceding to such demands? This is precisely where decision through debate is called for. In much earlier times the better vice chancellors tackled these problems, and found ways of disallowing such interference. But in recent years, vice chancellors and administrative heads, in some cases, are themselves a part of this problem.

Universities have four components—teachers, students, administration and financier. In the best universities of the world, the financier—whether the state or a private organization—is disallowed from intervening in academic matters. But since the roots of our university system lie in colonial governance, we have become accustomed to allowing interference by those who claim to be in authority or have the ear of authority. This was warned against by our first president Sarvepalli Radhakrishnan who had stated, 'Higher education is undoubtedly an obligation of the state, but state aid is not to be confused with state control over academic policies and practices.' University administration should ideally be the function of keeping the machinery working, but not claiming primacy in academic matters, irrespective of whether it is the vice chancellor or any other who in the administration tries to assert this primacy.

The crucial core of the university, then, should be those who teach and those who learn. This core is meant to be concerned with what is taught as required information, and with learning how to explore knowledge through new ideas and methods. At the broadest level the intention was, and is, as I have said at the outset, to produce an educated public and therefore responsible citizens; and at a more specific level to contribute to the advance of knowledge. To provoke new thinking and where necessary to dissent from conventional thinking, is axiomatic to this process. It is foundational to a university that it be the required space that nurtures freedom of thought. This has been the essential condition of the best universities anywhere resulting in research that has advanced our understanding and knowledge of the world, and in every field. Autonomy is of the essence in the functioning of universities, and they have to protect their right as being places where there is freedom to think, to speak and to debate. This is what we were trying to do in JNU as I shall explain later.

Whether in the primary and secondary schools that lay the foundations of education, or in tertiary education, the planning and funding of education in the country could have been far more adequate and focused. State universities struggle with paucity of funds and facilities. It is thought that the alternative could be private colleges and universities. But for some private investors education has become an industry. Colleges and universities are sometimes run more as factories than faculties, and the central concern of the financiers is investment and profit. Financial ambition takes over and many such places are seldom open to the most meritorious unless they can rustle up the enormous fees required. Are these alternatives giving us qualified specialists and responsible citizens? And in advertisements what is often promised is not so much learning and knowledge, but success—and the meaning of success is clear to all.

◆

After all these years we remain among the countries with the lowest rate of literacy. Yet even literacy is not the test of an educated population as it is only the initial step. There are other components of education of which I shall discuss two as essential. To put it simply, one is access to knowledge and the other is the communication of that knowledge.

Access to knowledge requires up-to-date information on the subject taught, and demands the questioning of existing knowledge to ascertain whether it is still valid or has been replaced by new knowledge. This could begin with knowing about the world we live in and how we relate to the cultures of our neighbours.

Creating curiosity is a major step. But we show scant interest even in what is being discussed by our neighbours. To take the simplest example, when did we last make a serious study of curricula in schools and universities in neighbouring countries? Yet what is taught in these countries would tell us about their self-perception, and their attitudes to neighbours, of which we are one. Our neighbours also experience controversies on what should be included in textbooks and why—controversies that should be of great interest to us since they parallel ours. A study of educational programmes would tell us much about how we see ourselves and how others see us.

The quality of education is not determined only by the amount of information acquired by students. More important is whether they have been taught to think critically. Are students familiar with the process of critical enquiry so essential to every form of education? It applies to each subject of study and to virtually every human activity. It begins with asking questions, the answers to which are statements on the subject being enquired into; these in turn can be questioned and analysed. A simple explanation of what is a logical statement and what is not, can be a start. This does mean of course that teachers themselves must understand what is meant by critical enquiry.

A more purposive beginning may be made by first teaching the teachers. And who better than knowledgeable teachers to do this training. This does not require an extensive financial outlay, which is always the pat excuse. Teachers have in any case to be trained and textbooks written for teaching. The teacher can be trained to ask questions, to think critically, and be familiar with methods of enquiry instead of stopping at merely providing information, and in some cases even misinformation; and textbooks should both inform and encourage students to ask questions about what they are learning. Textbooks are amongst the most difficult pedagogic tools to write and yet it is amazing how we allow all kinds of nonsense to pass as textbooks. This would require an extensive and transparent commitment to conveying knowledge and to also explaining its social value on the part of those advancing education. Better-trained teachers would be better appreciated by parents and others and thereby receive more respect than they are currently given.

What do I mean by critical enquiry and why do I think that it is the essence of education? Learning and the acquisition of knowledge are incomplete unless there is an awareness of the method of enquiry that is used to prise out knowledge. This has to be taught as a process of thinking and one that is relevant to all subjects. It assumes the freedom to ask questions, and to direct questions that enhance the enquiry. Such training helps in another way. Every enquiry involves assessing the validity of suggested explanations. All explanations do not have equal validity. Giving priority to some involves a selection and an explanation of why some are selected and others rejected. This involves critical enquiry.

The method draws on common sense. It starts with collecting data and ascertaining its reliability. Some fantasy may intervene in this process but fantasy has to be differentiated from evidence. Causal connections necessary to theories of explanation draw largely on logical argument and rational thought, but perhaps the occasional leap of imagination may be permitted if it illumines the argument. New discoveries both of information and of new methods of analysing it are happening continuously. Consequently the range of sources of knowledge expands. As a result existing information has to contend with the new and if necessary be revised.

Let me try and demonstrate this from my own specialization in ancient history. There was a time when a source consisted of what was said in a text. Herodotus, dated to the fifth century BC, popularly described as the father of history, was accused by a few of his contemporaries of replacing history with gossip in some instances. They accused him of using hearsay as evidence, and hearsay—as we all know—is not evidence. The same accusation was made of some of the chronicles of Indian royal courts, both of the earlier kingdoms and of the sultanates. Nevertheless, until a couple of centuries ago, narratives from these sources were retold and described as history. Today's historians have to investigate these texts and their contents for reliability before treating their narratives as history. This means checking the text with other sources. If these are limited we resort to the technique of Agatha Christie's detective, Hercule Poirot, of trying to piece together a hypothesis, in the expectation of finding a solution.

The historian therefore has to cross-question the text and, in retrospect, the author. What was the social and intellectual background of the author—caste, occupation, family, religion, location, learning and so on? Did his background influence what he wrote? What was his intellectual predisposition? What was the historical context of the text? Who read it and why? What was the intention of the text—both covert and overt?

In past times it was enough just to know the language of a text to use it as a source of information. Now we have to know more than the language. Specialists in linguistics tell us about the various dimensions of a language, such as, does one language carry the imprint of another that may have been used in its proximity. For example, some argue that Vedic Sanskrit has elements of Dravidian. This leads to new questions about the cultural interface of the speakers of the two languages. Another source is archaeology that can involve the comparison between objects described in the text with those excavated from sites of a similar date. Wine amphorae from the Mediterranean found at sites such as Pattanam in Kerala can be compared with descriptions of them in Greek and Tamil sources referring to the Red Sea trade. Archaeological finds are now examined by using various scientific techniques so the archaeologist is forced to be familiar with the relevant science. For example, the archaeologist tracking settlements on the banks of the river Sutlej has to consult hydrologists, since the river changed its course more than once. Where population migrations in history are being studied, their DNA analyses and genetics are becoming part of the argument. Maritime trade cannot be explained in detail without technical information on shipping and navigation in past times.

Apart from such methods of obtaining information, history is now interpreted with the aid of theories explaining the organization and functioning of societies. Historians, therefore, are in dialogue with other social scientists. The public perception of history has yet to be made aware of the fact that the divide today is between historians trained in interdisciplinary research and techniques of investigation, and an array of amateurs, quite untrained, who claim to be historians. Education based on critical enquiry would enable the non-specialist to differentiate between arguments based on reasoning or on myth.

Methods of critically examining texts can sometimes lead to new departures in disciplines. This is how, over the years, the importance of oral history emerged as a sub-discipline of history and literature, adding another dimension to the understanding of the past. For example, oral records were once dismissed as fiction, but now techniques of investigation have been developed that require a meticulous examination of the oral composition that can result in obtaining some historical information. What is said in the composition cannot be taken directly at face value but the methods of analyses can provide some historical clues. Some of the latter that were worked out for modern oral epics, for instance, have yielded interesting results when applied to the epic literature of the past.

Inevitably, when new theories are proposed controversies abound. They can only be resolved by academic debates or the discovery of fresh evidence. Controversy between scholars and polemicists are frequent in the public space and some are linked to political ideologies. In India, controversy hinging on historical interpretation is often tied to defining a national identity, which can be a secular identity or one given to upholding religious extremism.

In the USSR, the claim to alter genes by agrobiologist Trofim Lysenko was linked to genetics, and was projected as a possible way of thinking about social change. In the USA, the Scopes Monkey Trial involved attacks on Darwin's theory of evolution, which was seen as opposing what was said in the Bible about God creating man. In such situations textbooks are the victims. Ideally they should be left to professionals. But instead, all kinds of people intervene in determining the contents of textbooks. Most people are ignorant of the new knowledge in the discipline. Their only purpose is to push an ideological agenda.

In recent decades general elections have brought different political parties with dissimilar ideologies to form the government. Some advocate interference in the content of education, where the aim is not searching for knowledge but ideological reasons for controlling what people think. So when the political party governing India changes, the history textbooks used in central state schools also change. This has happened with alternating UPA and NDA governments. As I have mentioned, an array of non-historians, among whom are politicians, bureaucrats and their hangers-on, as well as diverse religious enterprises that have nothing to do with historical research, demand the inclusion of their views in the textbooks. One wishes that they would stay within their own jurisdiction of marketing religions and garnering votes, and leave the control over the contents of education to those professionally qualified to do so. This is why many of us argued twelve years ago that the National Council for Education Research and Training (NCERT) that produces textbooks, or the councils of research in various disciplines, should cease to be institutions controlled by the central government and instead should be autonomous organizations under the control of academics specializing in the specific subject. But not surprisingly, no one in authority responded to this suggestion. Politicians are loath to give up their access to patronage.

We have to take a decision as to whether the content of what is taught in school and college is to be the promotion of the ideology of a political party, or whether it should be up-to-date knowledge on the subject concerned. This is a choice that so far has been critical for the social sciences but not for the sciences. Recognizing the intervention of ideology in the sciences has so far been of marginal interest to scientists, not because there is no such intervention but because most scientists regard their research as being value-free and altogether unconnected to ideology. A few have tried to show the connection, but the majority remain unconcerned. Is this because science is still largely treated as a technology rather than a body of knowledge inherent to social change?

◆

In a seemingly contradictory manner the past, as we envision it, is often sought to give shape to the present. Political ideologies seeking to establish particular identities resort to interpreting knowledge to support the identity. This is then linked to their reading of nation and nationalism, of democracy and of a secular society—all of which are central to our public life. We have therefore, to understand these concepts by analysing and debating them and not treating them as slogans. Fundamental to such discussion are the right to information and the right to question.

Rights are what nurture citizenship. The right to information is crucial to public life. Questions have to be asked to obtain information. Raising questions therefore is not anti-national as is being maintained by some contemporary politicians. Questioning is at the root of the process of thinking. It was the questions of Socrates that initiated Greek philosophical discourse. It was the questions of the Buddha, the Charvaka thinkers and some of the rishis in the *Upanishads*, and questions by many others that provoked Indian philosophical thought. There were parks in the towns where people gathered and debated ideas. These were called the kutuhala-shalas (literally, places for raising curiosity).

Buddhist and Jaina viharas and later the Brahmana mathas and the Sufi khanqahs were places for discussion and debate covering a range of theories. We acclaim what emerged from the thought but give little recognition to the inherent process of questioning.

It is often said that there is a distinction between premodern and modern education and that questioning what is written in the texts was alien to premodern education. This is a generalization stemming from only the orthodox traditions that discouraged new questions. Established institutions propagating a particular religion socialized the young into that religion. They did not always encourage the questioning of existing knowledge. Their preferred form of teaching was one where predetermined questions were given predetermined answers and both were memorized. Questions were confined to the learned few. The appropriate religious body of each religion—Hindu, Buddhist, Jaina, Muslim, Sikh, Christian—controlled the content of education in its institutions. Deviations or alternate enquiries were not encouraged. Yet critical enquiry can suggest new ways of exploring ideas, even those relating to religion and society, and they may be more apposite to our times or to our requirements.

However, despite the authoritative conventional beliefs of the upper castes and elite, there was no shortage of breakaway sects and persons that questioned the beliefs. They were interested in new aspects of knowledge, and proclaimed alternate avenues to social organization. Various Shramanic groups—of Buddhists, Jainas, Ajivikas, Charvakas and such like—questioned Brahmanical beliefs. These groups were, therefore, dismissed by the more orthodox as nastika or non-believers. The accusation of preaching false doctrines at the popular level, was repeatedly exchanged between the two, the Brahmana and the Shramana dharmas, although the philosophical debates between them on, for instance, the meaning of categories such as 'doubt', or the use of logic, was of a high intellectual order.

This duality of the Brahmana and Shramana dharmas is on

record for 1,500 years and may have continued until longer. It is referred to in many texts until the early second millennium AD, and is regarded as characteristic of Indian religion and thought, as is also the antagonism between the two as dharmas. Despite the frequent description, at the popular level, of the last thousand years being a period of Hindu victimization, historical facts contradict this. It is actually a period particularly rich in the growth of religious and philosophical sects and their beliefs, and especially in the direction that their compositions and texts gave to religions such as Hinduism and Islam. As I have noted elsewhere in the book, the founders of the sects ranged across the social and religious spectrum and included people of learning and scholarship, as well as composers of popular religious verses. These also included women, Dalits and other lower castes, who had been excluded from upper caste religious articulation. Some sects were dedicated to a particular deity. Most others broke the boundaries of the formal religions and illuminated the overlapping areas between them and their big followings. In the interstices, were Muslim devotees of Krishna, among whom was Ras Khan whose verses are sung to this day in Hindustani classical music. The teachers of the last thousand years enriched existing religions, by creating new foci of faith, that often drew in those who had been distanced before. These activities expanded earlier conventional knowledge.

The questioning was not necessarily a critical enquiry as we understand it today, but more of a probing into conventional knowledge and suggesting alternatives. We tend to project these sects merely as manifestations of a single religion. We ignore the fact that, as late as the fourteenth century, a compendium of Indian philosophical schools—the *Sarva-darshana-samgraha*—begins with a chapter on the Charvaka or Lokayata school. This was an earlier school of free thought drawing on arguments based on reason, which despite the opposition from conventional sources, continued into much later times. Histories of philosophy written in the last century tend to give it short shrift. Yet the author of the compendium, Madhavacharya, states that although he personally did not subscribe to the Lokayata philosophy, others did, and so it had to be given recognition. This attitude to the world of the intellect is sparsely observed these days in India, and more so by some in positions of power. The freedom to speak or write and defend one's views with transparent evidence and logical argument, is often difficult to demand and protect, but is an essential characteristic of a civilized society.

Scholars have pointed to the existence of a long tradition of rational thinking and enquiry in India. This was to be expected as such traditions are always present in cultures with strong centres of philosophical thought. We need to see this tradition in its historical context and use it in educational curricula. It is a heritage from the past that points to thought-provoking perspectives, some of which challenge the ones that we constantly quote.

It also illustrates what I mean by the content of education having to be defined by professionals and scholars in respective fields. Few non-professionals are aware of this philosophical tradition of logic and rationality in the early Indian past. Even if they are, they hesitate to make it a part of an intellectual stream. We have been imprinted with the idea that traditional Indian thought was largely resistant to the rational. Therefore now there will be those who would oppose incorporating logic, rationality and enquiry into the educational curriculum, describing it as alien to the Indian tradition of thought, as much as there are others keen to pursue it. And, above all, bringing in the stream of rational thought would be so pertinent to interpreting the world around us.

We now come to an issue I raised earlier. A concern with the content of education means giving serious consideration to communicating through the most effective language of instruction—the language used for this purpose must be conducive to the discussion of knowledge. Whatever the official policy may be, the practice is that in most parts of the country the regional language is increasingly being used as the medium of instruction. More ambitious students and their parents, however, prefer the medium to be English both as a valuable qualification for employment and for its expansive intellectual world usage. We end up mainly using the regional language. English is generally used in such a way that it hardly provides any intellectual appetite, except of course in elite schools. This condition could be changed given that we have always used more than one language, and each in different ways.

Looked at historically, the variation is interesting. The language of the Harappa culture is so far unknown but it would have been used in northwestern India. A millennium later, there were three languages concurrently in use. Two were from the Indo-Aryan group. One of these was Vedic Sanskrit that Panini differentiates from the Sanskrit used in non-Vedic texts and in speech. Grammatical and linguistic works and etymologies of great brilliance were written in Sanskrit from the first millennium BC onwards. The need for such specialized texts points to the fact that languages other than Sanskrit were also in use at the time. Even the normal change that any language undergoes over a long period requires a revised grammar and etymology. The writing of such detailed grammars further suggests that Sanskrit was diversifying, probably due to the presence of other languages, and needed rules to embed its structure; and that it had to be taught to non-Sanskrit speakers.

The other Indo-Aryan language was the far more widely spoken Prakrit. As has been noted, Buddhist and Jaina texts were composed in Pali and Prakrit, both languages of the Indo-Aryan family but different from Sanskrit. Prakrit was used extensively in inscriptions as in those of Ashoka and other rulers. It was also the language used by women—some of the upper castes—and by Shudras and other lower castes. These together formed the majority of the population. Sanskrit became the language of governance particularly with the coming of dynasties from Central Asia around the Christian era, such as the Shakas, Kshatrapas and Kushanas, some of whom issued inscriptions in Sanskrit rather than Prakrit. Subsequent to this it became the court language, the language of administration, and the language associated with upper caste males. It remained so for a millennium. Inevitably, it was the main language of learning. Texts of the Brahmanical religion were composed in Sanskrit, as also on secular subjects, ranging from mathematics, astronomy and medicine to philosophy, aesthetics, literature, and an array of commentaries on the social codes, epics and other subjects. Buddhist and Jaina authors also began writing their texts in Sanskrit. When Persian and the regional languages began to be used in the royal courts, the use of Sanskrit as the court language, declined.

Parallel to Indo-Aryan was Dravidian, the second language group, and current in peninsula India. That there were languages other than Sanskrit even in northern India is clear from references in Sanskrit texts to people who speak their own language; references such as *Shatapatha Brahmana* (III.2.1.24) portrayed those who didn't speak Sanskrit in derogatory terms such as speakers of the incomprehensible Chandala-bhasha, and the Mlecchas, who could not speak Sanskrit correctly. Tamil was important in south India from the latter part of the first millennium BC, and some Prakrit was known. Sanskrit was a later arrival here. If the Adivasi presence went back to this period then languages such as Munda would also have been spoken, and would have formed another group of languages.

What has recently been described as the Sanskrit cosmopolis, other languages notwithstanding, was established in the mid-first millennium AD. The other languages were the associated Prakrits, and still later the evolving Apabrahmsha, not to mention the Dravidian languages of the peninsula. The primacy of Tamil in the south, and the emergence of Telugu and Kannada took form in the Dravidian language areas. In north India the derivatives of Indo-Aryan were also diversifying into a variety of languages by the early second millennium AD (and in some cases even a little earlier), which we now refer to as regional languages. Much cited Sanskrit texts, such as the popular versions of the narratives of Rama, were adapted into new forms and in various languages, among which the Tamil, Hindi and Bengali have received much attention. The Sufis of north India and the Mughals wrote in Hindi, apart from other languages such as Persian, and that was the language of the learned and of the court. At the Mughal court there was active collaboration between Brahmana and Jaina Sanskrit scholars supervising the translation of major Sanskrit texts into Persian. Braj Bhasha was common to some northern courts and to popular culture in the northern region.

Then came European trading companies bringing Portuguese, French and English. Portuguese continued to be used in the colonies of Portugal in India. French declined since the colonies of France gradually became insignificant. English became the major European language introduced by British colonialism. English as the language of governance and power was also used by the emergent middle classes, together with their regional languages. If occupation was one factor in the segregation of castes, English education had a similar role in segregating classes. As the language of communication it reached out to larger numbers than had Sanskrit, since lower castes, Avarnas and women were learning English. Specialized knowledge in the sciences, philosophy and the early social sciences was taught in English. Soon the literary articulation of the middle class both in poetry and prose was to include English, in addition to the regional language. The language of knowledge, therefore, changed from Prakrit to Sanskrit to Persian and then to English.

What then would be the most felicitous use of languages in educating Indians? Implicit in this question is the future of English or what some call Indian-English, and its relationship to the regional languages? The need for English in the world of today is linked to the fact that it is the language of knowledge.

At another level it is also the language of the international market to which the Indian economy is now connected. If English is linked to the advance of knowledge then it has to be known and known well. The correct and precise use of a language is crucial to research in all branches of learning.

Knowledge of the language in which a particular subject was being researched was necessary to research even in past times. Advances in mathematics and astronomy, for instance, were possible because scholars in these fields were familiar with works in Arabic and Sanskrit. Arab scholars had translated Greek texts and they also acknowledged the expertise of Indian scholars in mathematics. They were doubtless familiar with Sanskrit texts apart from the language of signs used, as for instance, in algebra as part of mathematics. Working with contemporary knowledge means knowing its language. This applies to the social sciences as much as to the other sciences.

In the Indian subcontinent no language had the monopoly of being the only one used at any time for all purposes. There was always diffusion in the function of various languages. Left to itself that is what is likely to happen now. But it can be made more effective if a properly worked out system is adopted.

So what should be the language of instruction? To know three languages sufficiently to make even impolite conversation is not a problem. To know each well enough to use it in fundamental research is problematic. Generally one is the preferred language. I would argue that a student should know two languages really well. Initially it has to be the language of his/her socialization into the family and society. Subsequently comes the language of knowledge. One language may not fit all.

It might therefore make some sense if we were to opt for a modified bilingual formula: we begin with the language of socialization at primary school—the regional language—the language of childhood, imagination, poetry and much else. English could be introduced towards the end of primary school as the additional medium together with the first language. If some subjects are taught bilingually they might be better understood by the student. That would certainly strengthen both languages. By the end of secondary school a student should be able to use both languages with relative ease.

Education today is increasingly given in the regional language with little emphasis on training in English, even if just as an additional language. Knowledge is being reduced to what is available in only one local language. This is fine for developing a facility in using that language but its ability to communicate up-to-date knowledge may not be adequate. To merely repeat knowledge that is no longer of much use defeats the purpose of education. Translation seldom keeps up with new knowledge. The danger is that communication between Indians may also decrease.

As I have said earlier in the chapter, in recent years we have had market forces edging out the humanities in favour of disciplines linked to the market economy and its technologies. This is a problem facing the best universities the world over. Giving priority is understandable but utilitarian value should not be the chief or sole criterion of education.

If the Indian genius expressed itself in grammatical works, this was partly because language was not an obstacle but was used creatively. Many languages coexisted. Emanating from different social strata and regions, they were used for different activities, and were communicated through osmosis in the proximity of two or more languages. I can recollect the ease with which my grandparents and parents moved between both the written and spoken forms of Punjabi, Hindi, Urdu and English. Each language seemed to be attuned to a specific function. The advantage of a bilingual education is that both languages borrow concepts from each other and thereby take on extended functions.

◆

Many of these basic problems of school and university education remain and will continue to do so unless we deliberately and consciously decide to improve the content and accessibility of education. Let me restate some of these problems, both the obvious ones of physical infrastructure and the more subtle ones of the content of education. The initial pressure of larger numbers of students is spiralling out uncontrollably with little back up of qualified teachers and faculty. The hub of a university is a well-equipped library and up-to-date laboratories, yet priority is always given to the administration buildings. Adequately furnished and properly run hostels provide an addition to university culture and this is generally not recognized. Building more and more substandard institutions and filling them with unqualified students and teachers is not the answer. Knowledge is not a game of numbers although we have reduced it to that.

Despite this dismal scene, there are nevertheless, almost in defiance, pockets of excellence. A tiny percentage of bright students and teachers become prized professionals. Given the natural potential the percentage could be much higher if properly tapped. But on the contrary the advance in thinking is being mowed down by a preference for a larger percentage of pedestrian or even regressive actions and thought. Most students these days are expected to grapple with grades rather than ideas. Relatively less and less is being done to peg schooling to decent, leave alone high standards. If that could be done then the students admitted to colleges would be more prepared for the tertiary level. We could move well beyond the colonial inheritance and reformulate our educational needs in accordance with our aspirations to social improvement and the appropriation of knowledge. Instead of learning from the good institutions and replicating them, there seems to be a wish to tear down the good institutions so that only the lowest common denominator prevails.

◆

I would like to conclude this section by reiterating what I have been arguing for: that the content of education has to give priority to critical enquiry. By this I mean teaching students to feel liberated enough to ask questions about the world they live in; and to question knowledge in a systematic, logical, reasoned manner that might well give them new insights into their world. This may release the potential of not only those that are first generation learners, but also of others having to learn out-of-date knowledge that they, in any case, are not permitted to question. A different kind of education may well lead to the discovery of new knowledge. It is only then that education can help in changing mindsets for the better. Values have to be experienced and nurtured. Where values are imposed, they tend to wither away. And if a bilingual education can also be implemented through using both the language of socialization and the language of knowledge, then there can be a greater comprehension of the world and why we live the way we do. The world will open up to many more than just the few. And that surely is what education, a crucial component of our culture, is all about.

II

The ideas that I have discussed above were some that a few of us had when we joined JNU in its foundation year of 1970–1971. We were able to make of it a leading university in India. Its students in turn are teaching in India and in other parts of the world in the best universities. Some have manned a variety of jobs in India, ranging from senior positions in the administration to ambassadorships to politburo members of the Communist Party (Marxist). The success of JNU was that we knew what was essential to a good university and were not willing to compromise on this, whatever might have been the academic and political inducements to doing so. Today, there is an attempt to systematically dismantle JNU and other centres of advanced research in the social sciences, largely because the powers that be prefer it that institutions encouraging critical enquiry and freedom of expression be snuffed out, or at best be converted into what seem like nursery schools for adult students.

I would like to describe my experience in helping to found the Centre for Historical Studies in JNU that in a sense encapsulates much of what went into the making of JNU. The focus on critical enquiry was central as was also the concern that students of history must be familiar with the methods of investigating the past. What did this mean? It meant that as a first step the student had to read the major writing on a subject and work out tentative questions that might be relevant to an enquiry. It meant that students had to be made aware of the fact that studying any aspect of history required bringing together as many of the known sources as possible, assessing their reliability, analysing them by asking pertinent questions, establishing causal explanations, and ensuring that the generalizations that emerged drew on a logical and well-reasoned argument. This was a new experience for the students who came to us.

The readings for such an approach meant consulting books not just on the specific subject but also on the theories of explanation in the social sciences that could be used to ask broader questions of the sources and relate them to their context, which is not done so often. The debates on these themes were in books written in English and required a more than basic knowledge of the language. This was less of a problem for students who came from metropolitan areas and from what we now call elite schools, but it was that much more problematic for those who came from schools and colleges that had the regional language as the medium. The problem of familiarity with English had to be a special concern in the teaching programme. Nor was it only a matter of language. The larger problem lay in the comprehension of concepts. Nevertheless we were determined to work with the students to ensure that the quality of the learning they acquired was high.

The university had further decided that students from economically backward regions would be assisted to get admission.

So we were teaching at various levels in the first semester, but what was most impressive was how quickly the less equipped students came up to the required levels in subsequent semesters. My explanation for this is that it was a highly personalized form of teaching with much discussion in class, and a heavy emphasis on library reading and tutorials, the grades for which went into the final mark. Timetables were adhered to but so much extra time went into informal, worthwhile discussion. Since JNU was not a school, attendance was never compulsory, nevertheless classes were fully attended.

I joined JNU in November 1970 and was among the first few appointed. We started teaching in 1971, so we had time to prepare syllabi, courses and the pattern of teaching. I came from Delhi University where I had taught in the history department for seven years. I left there because the courses had been drawn up some thirty years earlier and changing these had become problematic. The focus was on political and diplomatic history—quite legitimate—but with minimal attention to other aspects of the past. History was a narrative of the politics of the elite. But history as a discipline had begun to change with new methods of analysing sources, and a wider range of explanations of what happened in the past, and why. History was undergoing a metamorphosis from being a subject in Indology and providing useful information, to a discipline of the social sciences. I thought, therefore, that JNU might provide an opportunity to work with a new approach to the past.

In the late 1960s, this new history was taking shape. It was being extensively discussed elsewhere, although in India this was restricted to a handful of historians. This was the time of the teach-ins associated with the Dialectics of Liberation meeting in London in 1967, and similar events in universities in France and the United States. New ideas emerged from wide-ranging debates as also some protests about what was being taught and how. A less audible echo of this could be heard at Delhi and

Calcutta universities, and a few other places, but only at the edges. Nevertheless, this was a time of optimism, the coming of a better world and of intellectually vibrant universities.

Theories explaining the historical basis of societies, were taking on a new legitimacy. There was immense interest in the challenges of contesting theories and the insistence on free discussion. Debates ranged over ideas emanating from Marxists, anti-Marxists, Neo-Marxists, extending to other theories that were later to evolve into subaltern studies, postmodernism, and still later, postcolonialism and the literary turn, and the variety continues. If some used Marxism to explain the functioning of the society under study, others criticized them, not by abusing them as is the fashion among Hindutva ideologues in India today, but by putting up counterarguments based not on hearsay or fantasy but on research. New ways of using Marxist analysis led to Neo-Marxist theories especially in the social sciences. These debates suggested other theories of explanation some of which were closely tied to studies of literary texts, searching for further ways of analysing texts, as argued in Postmodernism and Postcolonialism—the literary turn. It was a new way of understanding text and context and raised many intellectual controversies. Whatever might be the intellectual stance of the participant, pro- or anti-current theories, it was not just sloganeering. It was rooted in reading and thinking about what was being discussed. This was the intellectual ambience when JNU was founded. Discussions in parliament on the university focused on the ideas of the man after whom it was eventually named. That was the starting point, but intellectually JNU debated much else that had been thought and written about since then.

The founding vice chancellor was G. Parthasarathi, known to everyone as GP. Although his career had been in diplomacy rather than academia, he turned out to be a better VC than many academics have been. Vice chancellors in India, as we all know, have to be carefully chosen, as they can make or break a university. We have not got to the point where the conventions of a university in its functioning, hammered out through experience, are always honoured by the vice chancellors, as they should be. Some tend to foist their personal ambitions onto university functioning and this can be disastrous.

GP was a liberal, and well aware that what makes a fine university is the exploring of knowledge and ideas through teaching and research, as well as a concern with the welfare of students and faculty. For him, JNU had to be a university of quality, a path-breaker in the pursuit of knowledge, which brought this knowledge within reach of students from every segment of society. To achieve this he asserted the autonomy of the university and was not dictated to by the Education Ministry or as it was later called the Ministry of Human Resource Development. The support of academic opinion mattered more to him than that of politicians or bureaucrats. A university, after all, is a place where academic knowledge is advanced among bureaucrats and politicians.

Since we were starting from scratch we needed time to work out courses and syllabi. So we were given a few months off to do this and also to recruit more faculty. The initial faculty of the Centre for Historical Studies consisted of Professors Satish Chandra, Sarvepalli Gopal, Bipan Chandra and myself. Our specializations covered the range of Indian history and we recruited other faculty. Satish left shortly after, to become chairman of the University Grants Commission (UGC). It needs to be said that if Bipan Chandra brought in the radical element (radical as in the radicalism of those times), Sarvepalli Gopal was the quintessential liberal. The combination of the two invested the CHS with an appropriate ambience. Small things made a difference, such as the insistence that we address each other by our first names, which in those days was a break in convention. It did not eliminate the sense of hierarchy but did noticeably reduce it.

We gathered a small faculty and discussions on what was to be taught became a manageable exercise. Our courses were not a repetition of the MA History courses of any other university, and they were interdisciplinary, adding to the quality of our own discipline. GP, to his credit, made no attempt to control whom we recruited nor what we taught and who taught what. We had complete independence and a heavy emphasis on professional responsibility. This is essential to the intellectual life of any university and to the quality it hopes to achieve.

We were concerned with teaching courses that would enhance the understanding of Indian society. Imitating courses of the best universities in the West, some still being colonial in their orientation, was not how we saw the new history. There was an ongoing debate among historians of modern India, between the CHS and what was referred to as the Cambridge School on the interpretation of the colonial period. Sensitivity to the world around us led to an effort to teach some courses that raised issues around questions of social inequality, control of resources and categories of labour, or the articulation of cultures in various forms, or religion as a social enterprise. Added to this was the significance of understanding points of historical change or transitions as essential aspects of understanding the structure of society—its changes and the cultural patterns that emerged. Our effort was to create an independent space for thinking and producing new knowledge, making research a primary activity.

The semester system encouraged smaller courses that were introductions to themes and to sources, or could illustrate the use of concepts. These courses were central and self-contained and could be completed in a period of four months. The insistence on tutorials as a system of evaluation resulted in students learning how to analyse sources and understand concepts. This was necessary to the kind of history we were teaching. The requirement of reading for a tutorial was dependent on a well-equipped library. Writing the essay and discussing it formally, was an innovation in methods of teaching at Indian universities. In most universities the system of focusing only on information was declining into learning by rote.

The tutorial system also brought about a greater communication between the tutor and the student. However, given our hierarchical society, the implicit hierarchy did not disappear. Another obstacle was the arbitrary increase in student numbers without a parallel increase in qualified faculty and in the availability of books. The quality of education suffers the most when this happens.

The tutorial system as the contact between student and tutor, sometimes had a curious side. A student whom I got to know through tutorials came to me with an emotional problem and after we had discussed it at length she said it would help her if she could talk with a psychiatrist. So I made an appointment for her at the All India Institute of Medical Sciences (AIIMS). She insisted I go with her. This I did for a few times but then stopped because a friend rang me from AIIMS and said that my visits had been noticed, and did I have a serious problem that made me visit the psychiatrist so often?

The system of tutorials and exams was dependent on the availability of the recommended books in the library. This, the faculty had to ensure. There was much rushing around in those years to buy books, and even look out for private libraries on sale, such as that of D. D. Kosambi, that we gladly acquired. The bonus in this case was getting to read some of his acerbic or amusing comments scribbled on the margins of the page.

There was initially a debate on internal assessment at the MA level. Our courses were different from other universities, and taught in a manner that was unfamiliar to faculty and students elsewhere. Some argued that external examiners ensured rigour. Ultimately it was decided to keep evaluation internal at the MA level. The faculty would be required to maintain standards, because the reputation of the university depended on the quality of the students that were given its degrees. This was another way of emphasizing professional responsibility. Inevitably, there were sometimes small differences of opinion on grades, but by and large it worked well. Mechanisms of redressal came into use and continue. The reverse procedure of student evaluation of those who teach them, has never taken root in Indian institutions, perhaps for obvious reasons. For a guru to be evaluated by the shishya would require turning the Indian mindset upside down.

The admission policy of JNU was discussed at length. There were arguments over having a written entrance exam, an interview, the number of deprivation points for various categories of people, and so on. Contentions over admission policy, or other aspects of university administration, took the form of occasional gheraos of the VC or the chairperson of the centre. The gherao had other uses. Sometimes it became the occasion for a chairperson of a centre to join the captive VC, since this allowed for a long, uninterrupted and generally useful dialogue on the problems of the centre concerned. In the case of the chairperson being gheraoed, (I do recall one such occasion in which I was involved as chairperson) it finished up with my doing a kind of extended tutorial discussion with some of those gheraoing me.

We had to engage with the idea that students when taught to think independently will protest about many things. Protests need to be talked over. The university needs to have all its component parts participating in this conversation. Such discussions took place in the classroom or in open meetings. It is a pity that there are not more teach-ins on campuses, as they can be a useful form of extracurricular conversations on a variety of questions.

The contention over admissions led to the introduction of the entrance exam together with an interview. Many exam centres were set up and JNU drew students from an all-India range, unlike most other universities that tend to be parochial. This enhanced the national character of JNU and that in turn meant a greater mingling of students from different parts of the country. Our system of deprivation points—giving a few extra points to students from economically underprivileged backgrounds—at the time of admission, brought in students from social classes that normally do not easily get admission to universities. First generation learners from lesser-known colleges mingled with those from metropolitan backgrounds. Most of our students came from the humanities stream but some were from science. We had to devise a syllabus that would in the initial stage convey to them not only a sense of what history was about, but also train them to think in a manner that grew out of critical enquiry. Asking questions is vital and one has to learn how to ask questions that yield answers, whatever the answers may be.

Widening the catchment area brought in student interests pertaining to their own regions. This inevitably extended the geographical range covered in research. Similarly the diversity of social backgrounds also alerted us to the need for expanding the themes that we included and more so at the MPhil level. For those that had some difficulty in following the analytical methods that we were teaching, we worked out a one-year 'catch-up' course on language training and methodology. Any student wishing to be better prepared could take this course prior to the two-year MA course. But the students rejected the idea, arguing that they could not extend the MA for another year, even if given a grant to do so. This has been at the crux of many problematic conditions over the years, and has intensified in recent times. It needs to be considered more seriously by many universities if school education continues to be as pathetic as it is these days.

If the general level of education in schools and colleges cannot be immensely improved, such interventions will become increasingly necessary to maintain even the minimum standards. This is a problem faced elsewhere too. A college in Oxford has very recently started providing for such a preparatory year for students from underprivileged backgrounds. It has the advantage that the quality of education does not have to be lowered and students get a bonus year of being trained to handle what may appear initially to be unfamiliar courses.

The MA consisted of sixteen courses, most in history and some in associated social science disciplines, to be taught over two years. There was an additional language course, other than in the student's mother tongue, and chosen to relate to the textual sources he or she may be required to use. This was debated at great length as some thought it might be an extra burden on the student. It was thought to be more difficult for medieval and ancient history students who had to learn Persian or Sanskrit. But some of us felt that a working knowledge of Sanskrit was essential for students studying ancient India. JNU was about the only university in India where a degree in ancient history required a credit in Sanskrit. We were fortunate in having a linguist in the CHS, K. Meenakshi, who specialized in both Dravidian and Indo-Aryan linguistics, and taught both Sanskrit and Tamil.

Of the total of sixteen courses taught over a two-year MA, we decided that four would be compulsory for all students. These would be the courses in which we would focus on two aspects of history. One would be on the methods of research and the interpretation of history. The assumption was that all social sciences have a method of investigation, especially for research. In history, the purpose is to get information on the past, and to explain what happened in the past and why. This means recognizing and analysing the possible range of sources, and checking their reliability as a first step. The second equally important aspect is to ask questions of the sources in order to explain what happened in the past. Existing knowledge gets to be checked for having advanced in various ways. We thought comparative history would help, not just as more information on other societies, but in seeing how historical concepts are used in the study of these. Were such analyses relevant to our history?

The four compulsory courses were Historical Method, Ancient Society, Feudalism, and Capitalism and Colonialism. These four courses were the most innovative in our syllabus and were its backbone. They were unheard of in other universities, until more recently. The maximum brainstorming went into fashioning them. These early years were intellectually the most stimulating for us as faculty, since they forced us to think critically about what we were intending to teach, and how we were going to justify courses that were so different from the usual.

The brainstorming in the CHS was occasionally contentious but ultimately useful, with differences usually being ironed out through much discussion. Kind friends from Delhi University teased us about the new syllabus, declaring that we would never get any bright students, since why would they waste their time on such way-out courses. Yet not only were our students among the brightest, and excited by our courses, which they found to be different and more relevant to understanding the past, but we noticed that slowly some of these courses were finding their way into the syllabi of a few other universities.

There was amongst us at that time a strong sense of a shared social commitment, underlying both what we were teaching, and in the stands that most of us took on public issues. There were plenty of public issues given that history is the chosen battlefield for what is described as religious nationalism of an extreme variety. When the question of the historicity of the Ramjanmabhoomi became a public debate, there was initially a clear divide between historians who questioned the historicity of a location designated as the birthplace of Rama, and those that were not historians but had other reasons to support the idea that the Babri Masjid was built on the site of a temple that marked the Ramjanmabhoomi, the temple having been destroyed to build the mosque. Some of us put out a brief essay giving historical reasons to doubt the location. This was supported by most of us in the CHS yet some disagreed, not with the historical facts but with the form of debate. Since there was no compulsion in the matter it remained an individual option. When the Emergency was declared in 1975 many of the faculty in the CHS were opposed to it, and defended the opposition of other faculty and students.

For quite a few of us historical research was a way of understanding the past not just in itself but also as a way of illuminating the continuity or the discontinuity of that past into the present, and subsequently, as the manner in which the present shapes and uses the past. Explaining the past is in many ways the purpose of researching it, but since the past is so closely linked to the present for a variety of intentions, historians have also to understand this aspect of history. Apart from this, it has been pointed out that history is an essential ingredient in a variety of nationalisms. This also makes it necessary to be aware of the use of history for political mobilization.

There was a time when it was said that the purpose of history was to try and discover the truth about the past. This claim is rarely made these days. The truth about the past cannot be known by any method because the past has disappeared and cannot be reconstructed or conjured up. What we are concerned with now is how to explain what happened in the past by using the sources at our disposal. This is why the causal links that we make in order to explain the past should draw on well-reasoned and logical connections. The final statement, if based on a cogent explanation, becomes that much more firm.

But should some new knowledge come our way then the narrative and the explanation might have to change. Let me illustrate this from my specialization in ancient history. As I have shown earlier in this book and elsewhere, when the history of India was written in the nineteenth century there was virtually no knowledge about Emperor Ashoka Maurya. Brahmanical sources are virtually silent about him. Kalhana in his *Rajatarangini* refers to him as an early ruler who included Kashmir in his kingdom. Buddhist texts referred to him but these at the time received little attention. For over ten centuries he was largely unknown to Indians, as his inscriptions appear to have been unread, so later rulers do not refer to him. With the decline of Buddhism even that source was silenced. His inscriptions were first deciphered in the early nineteenth century but none knew the identity of the author—Devanampiya Piyadassi. The identification with Ashoka was suggested when the Pali Buddhist chronicles of Sri Lanka were studied in the late nineteenth century. They refer to an Indian king Ashoka whose name was linked to this title. It was only in 1915 that an inscription was discovered which refers to Devanampiyassa Asokassa. The king's identity was revealed and Mauryan history changed. One never knows where a new clue may appear.

The search in historical study was not merely to use new sources to expand the narrative about the past, but also to provide new ways of correlating and analysing evidence. The other three of the four compulsory courses focused not on single societies but on the various concepts that are associated with different times and places. It is recognized that societies register social disparity and we took this as an entry point to the past. Societies were governed by chiefs of clans or by kings claiming to be of the upper castes. At the other end of the hierarchy were the slaves and the lower castes. The historian has to consider the entire range of the disparity and the hierarchy between the high and the low. But at the same time it was necessary to explain the context of such disparities and consider not just the disparities but other aspects of these societies as well.

We wanted students to read about Mesopotamian society and the later Greco-Roman. These were histories on which there had been, at that time, more accessible analytical study than on other ancient societies. How did these societies differ in their patterns of culture? What was the kind of culture that characterized these societies and how was it correlated to their histories? Who controlled resources and who laboured? The Greco-Roman is generally described as based on slave labour. Historians have investigated the different categories and how this imprinted the culture. The city state of Athens owned and employed individual slaves—the doulos—each unconnected with the other, whereas the city state of Sparta, had a separate society of slaves, the helots, who lived as families, separate from the free citizens, outside the city. This form has been compared with castes regarded as Avarna, excluded from caste society and living in ghettos outside the city. There are some similarities but of course many more dissimilarities. The question to be asked is what were the alternate organizations and did they function differently? Did this have an impact on other patterns of culture? Comparative studies can be helpful in sharpening definitions, and discovering new theories of explanation.

Some of these comparative studies of early societies had become vastly more challenging with the extensive use of archaeological data that gave some precision to the reconstruction of their pattern of life. This was data that was also becoming more available with reference to early India. Our intention was not to take up excavation since this required almost an additional department of archaeology, but to work on the data that was available as evidence of how early societies functioned. In this the insights of social anthropology were also useful. Differentiating between different categories of societies, and recognizing the forms and functions that went into the making of these different categories, assisted historians in recognizing some of these categories from the historical evidence. These were being brought to bear on the study of early societies in many parts of the world and such studies were helpful in formulating questions for the study of Indian material.

The redefinition of culture as a pattern of life in a society was undoubtedly a major input into studies of Indian society. Patterns of life are not restricted to elites and call for a discussion of the larger society. Hence culture was no longer confined to the texts, monuments, architecture, and art of royalty and the well-to-do, but required the study of not only objects but also social forms that characterized society as a whole. Therefore, studies of the economy, of caste, of gender relations, became essential to any definition of culture as an entity. Social history accommodated such changes. In terms of historical periodization it not only clarified but differentiated between the societies that were included in the early period and those of medieval times.

In many societies of the world, the period prior to the modern, is described as medieval. This is taken as a time when the social and economic structure is thought of as based on a feudal pattern although in some instances this pattern may be absent. We worked out a course on feudalism where the meaning of the concept and its variations were discussed, as also the degree to which it applied to a particular history. The variations are immense as is now being recognized. Almost every society has its own variation and that also became evident in studies of the extensive Indian subcontinent. Again comparative studies are helpful in understanding whether there was a particular kind of Indian feudalism, or more than one, and how the forms differed. Or indeed as is being discussed today for the European past, whether the use of the term as it is used, is valid.

The focus is more on land as a resource as compared to earlier times. Many questions arise such as who controls this resource, who labours on it to make it productive, and ultimately who profits from its productivity, and what is the associated cultural pattern? There is the juxtaposition of this activity with the forms taken by the cultural patterns that it supports.

The third of these courses, that on capitalism and colonialism, highlighted modern times. The attempt here was to show the interface between the two both in the colony and in the home country of the colonizer. British colonialism provided a clear example, although comparative studies of other patterns of colonialism were included. These were taken from European colonial control of other parts of the world. The degree to which this fostered capitalist development has to be ascertained. The interface between capitalism and colonialism has not always been sufficiently recognized even by those who have worked out detailed theories of explanation. Does the type of colonialism affect the way in which capitalism advances in the society of the colonizer? What is the difference between capitalism in the colonial societies and its arrival in the ex-colony? Can this be contrasted with societies that had not been colonies?

These four courses were what we called the 'core courses' and in a sense set out the concepts and concerns around which history was being debated in our times. This was made clear by showing how these societies were studied in the previous century and why they came to be studied differently. Readings had to be up-to-date and this forced students to have some idea of current debates in other histories. They provided a glimpse into other areas and pointed up the need to see different societies reacting to historical change that was partially similar and partially dissimilar. Coming to grips with the concepts basic to these courses prepared students to handle problems emerging from a range of historical situations. Since they were rather open-ended courses, it meant that the next person teaching the course could introduce other societies for comparison, provided the focus remained on the concepts, and could consider how even these are being refashioned in the light of advancing knowledge. The courses that we had worked out in the 1970s would, in present times, be asking additional questions based on more recent theories.

Since these courses were newly configured, we realized that some students would have initial difficulties with them. We were particular, therefore, in announcing at the start of the course that any student who wanted a further explanation of a topic, or who had problems with the explanations, or disagreed, was free to interrupt the lecture, and a discussion would follow. I recall one such occasion.

I was giving a lecture on fallacies in history, in the course on Historical Method. I had just started introducing the subject when a student stood up, took out a Bengali translation of the *Little Red Book of Mao Zedong*, and began to read from it. Both the class and I were perplexed. After ten minutes he closed the book and sat down. I asked him to explain what he had read since not all of us understood Bengali. So he explained as best he could what Mao's comments had been on Marx's theories of the modes of production being necessary to understanding a society. Some students said that that was not what I had been talking about, so where was the connection? Others attempted to make connections. This was followed by the liveliest of discussions with both agreement and disagreement. It went on for more than an hour with my trying to keep it on track in terms of the subject of discussion. Historical fallacies of all kinds were quoted, upheld or knocked down. Every student present had strong opinions on the subject, for and against. This was one of my most successful classes, not because it began from the *Little Red Book*, but because every student had argued vehemently. I was told that each one had later held forth with confidence in describing a historical fallacy!

The emphasis was very much on a readiness to discuss. This was so not only in the lecture room but also outside. Inevitably from history it extended to topics of contemporary interest when faculty and other speakers were invited to speak elsewhere on campus and strong opinions were expressed and debated. As everybody agrees, the university is a place that must allow freedom of speech and the freedom to debate any issue thought to be relevant. We wanted this to be effectively so in JNU and indeed it was so, until the last couple of years.

Theories of explanation in history are varied and many. Marx's periodization of history had perhaps a more orderly series of historical explanations than those, for example, of Max Weber. We discussed both and others, and made our choices. We were aware of the concept of modes of production not as the invariable explanations of Indian history but as a useful starting point to ask questions about social formations that might have given direction to historical events, and about causation and historical change in the context of the larger debates, and other issues significant to the study of history. Our concern was of course in discussing whether and how theories of explanation were applicable to Indian history, and perhaps more so with using them to trigger questions.

Much was said, and is being said, about JNU being Marxist in its orientation. These comments were also levelled at the CHS in those days. However, such comments fail to see that all theories of explanation have to be assessed for viability and therefore need to be prised apart. Discussing a theory does not necessarily mean that it is being endorsed. However, it does mean that it is being taken seriously and is being assessed, and that is what determines acceptance or not. Testing the application of a theory can become a form of asking new questions. That Marxism was much discussed in academic and intellectual circles the world over, half a century ago, meant that we also had to be familiar with what was being discussed elsewhere. In the process of examining one theory, obviously other theories were also looked at comparatively. It was not that everyone in JNU was or had to be a Marxist, but that JNU was unusual, because Marxism was treated neither as gospel nor as a taboo subject. There were the normal controversies over opinions about Marxist readings and these were argued over, generally analytically and sometimes acrimoniously.

I might add that one of the outcomes of teaching these courses was that they led to a widespread debate on the meaning of the concepts used, as well as the explanations they provided, and of course their applicability to Indian history. This debate by then was not restricted to JNU but was current in other institutions as well. For example, many Marxist historians argued in support of a feudal mode of production in Indian history. But it was Marxist historians again, some at JNU, who initially questioned the endorsing of this mode for the Indian past.

Marxists and non-Marxists of every hue had opinions on this debate and it went on for a few years. It was actually extremely useful to the study of medieval history. Regional history came into focus since much of the evidence comes from sources of regional history. Studies ranged from agrarian histories and varieties of tenancies to differing patterns of caste relations, to the inducting of local religions into the mainstream. The variations led to an interest among historians in aspects of environmental, socio-economic, administrative and cultural history. Medieval history, earlier regarded as the Dark Ages, with historians discussing only the politics of establishing sultanates and Mughal rule, was now illumined by other kinds of information and analyses. This debate has been a major departure in the study of premodern medieval Indian history.

Of the remaining twelve courses, three were the choice of the student. These could be courses in non-Indian history, or in other disciplines of the social sciences. Modern history students tended to study aspects of sociology and economics. Those working on premodern periods were encouraged to read social and cultural anthropology. Our sociologist colleague, Satish Saberwal, was a valuable asset for this, although there were others in the school whose courses were also taken. Incidentally, the term 'centre' was preferred over the conventional 'department', since each had multidisciplinary faculty linked to the general research interests of those that conformed to the main discipline.

The remaining nine courses focused on a broad period of Indian history. We debated in great detail whether we should follow the conventional periodization of ancient, medieval and modern. Historically it was defective since the breaks did not mark any major historical change, only a change in the religion of some dynasties in the twelfth century AD, and again with the arrival of British rule from the eighteenth. We were also well aware of the overlaps between one and the other. What stopped us from changing the periodization in the syllabus was the fact that most advertisements for teaching jobs in history specify one of these three periods, therefore if we had discontinued them our students would have had problems finding jobs. So we continued with the three but underlined continuities, overlaps and disjunctures, where needed, within and between each.

Specialization was required in one of these three periods. In each there was a set of core courses that taught students how to examine particular aspects of the history of that period—political, economic, social, religious and cultural and their interrelations. These courses required familiarity with the different kinds of primary sources relevant to each theme and training in how to consult them. The remaining four were optional courses on other aspects of the same period.

The intention of this course structure was that the student acquire a good idea of what is meant by historical context and background through a study of selected periods and themes; have some comprehension of the concepts that are used in historical analysis; and be familiar with the method of analysing the past and understanding what was meant when it was said that history explains the past. Methods of analyses such as these can be meaningful to research in almost any social science.

Let me mention some critical reactions to what we taught. Criticism came from a few Marxists for an insufficiency of theory—largely Marxist theory—in our courses. Our response was that theory was a means of understanding the past, but the focus could not be singular and it was equally necessary to be familiar with the nature and agenda of sources, and that such other aspects also required study. At the other extreme was some conservative and even liberal opinion, arguing that our history was far too theoretical. We were faced with reactions opposed to each other. These became even more intriguing when we discovered that some of our more vehement critics were including courses similar to ours in their own syllabi!

Historical explanations made greater sense where they drew from logical and secular explanations. This we saw as the contribution of the CHS. It was a time when the teaching of history explored little beyond political and religious factors and that too at a rather superficial level. Even those that claimed, and still claim, to be writing history from an indigenous perspective—whatever that meant or means—were actually basing themselves on colonial readings. We were critiquing the colonial versions of Indian history. Many of us subjected these versions to a secular and reasoned analysis. This became an alternative, if not a corrective, to the colonial reading of the past. This latter was a reading that nurtured a skewed history, and provided a justification, for example, for extreme religious nationalisms. These we demonstrated as being ahistorical and therefore untenable as history. We had our share of confrontations with fantasy playing at being history.

It is as well to remember that from the late 1960s Indian history was shifting from Indology and being inducted into the social sciences. In this mutation the role of the CHS was not insignificant. It was a pioneering effort that has had an impact in many areas of historical studies over the last half century. We were not looking for clones, but in a few universities new courses did begin to reflect a small change in this direction, in part because some of our students are teaching there, but much more so because it is becoming gradually an intrinsic change in the definition of history.

I have mentioned how the CHS started and its early life. People have come and gone and much has changed in JNU and inevitably in the CHS. I retired over twenty-five years ago. So I have been accused of being nostalgic about the early years. But I believe that much of what we started continues. Hopefully the foundations that we built will not be overturned in coming years, no matter how severe the current pounding becomes.

Establishing JNU was a challenge to see whether we could have a university which may not have the same material comforts as the better universities elsewhere but which would be respected for the intellectual quality of the students it produced and their research and that of its faculty. For the almost half century of its existence our students have met the challenge. Apart from the interest they evoke in other Indian universities, they are welcomed in the best universities outside India as generally being well-trained and thoughtful young people. Students have remarked on JNU having given them an understanding of the world in which they live, and even if there are some who have not experienced this, what they have experienced is different from the experience of any other university. Those who do not understand the function of universities in our society, or wish not to, resent this contribution, therefore an attempt is being made to convert a university from a place where one can think without restraint, to a shop where one can obtain degrees.

The content of education is a crucial factor in the cultural reflection of a society. It can be unquestioning and passive, subservient to belief about anything and everything, and pliant. This would suit those who wish to impose a particular way of thinking on people, resulting in an acceptance of a particular ideology. A different kind of content would make a society questioning and active, demanding a greater understanding of its world and making social ethics a primary concern. The culture that many endorse today is at a distance from a commitment to social ethics.

What the future holds cannot be predicted, barring a few hints of what may come our way. One is only too aware that the social sciences are at risk of being so diluted as to become ineffective as areas of knowledge, and especially in the better universities where they have been pushing the intellectual frontiers. Dismantling any one of the three, whether the humanities, the sciences, or the social sciences, will of course wreck the system of knowledge, since the three are interdependent. Those unfamiliar with the thought processes involved even in minimal research, are unaware that undermining the social sciences will be disastrous for the sciences as well, since the two are connected, not at the level of technology but at the level of both asking relevant questions and investigating the answers to questions that relate to advances in science. We would then be no more than purveyors of the thinking and activities of societies other than our own.

It does not require much wisdom to recognize that advances in the sciences come from exercising a critical enquiry into existing knowledge. This is often motivated by the questions posed in the social sciences. In every branch of knowledge it is critical enquiry that is at its root, whether we trace our thoughts to Socrates or the *Upanishads*. And knowledge in every field has to keep up with advances otherwise it becomes extinct.

To know the past of JNU is in part to remind ourselves that the university was created to advance knowledge, and to make it accessible to all those that want to access it. This involves questioning existing knowledge and being able to seek answers to questions in a free and unfettered manner. Knowledge is the heritage that we leave for those that will come after us. It has therefore to be cultivated and nurtured even against present political odds.

EPILOGUE

The epilogue, one is told, since it comes at the end should be what one wants to say finally but need not carry any conclusions. I shall abide by that.

Because cultures are thought to be rooted in the past, there is a considerable intermeshing of culture with history as I have tried to indicate in the initial chapter of the book. As with historical explanation that can change with the discovery of new sources or with new ways of analysing known sources, that which constitutes culture is also not a static concept. Since cultures are so deeply intertwined with history they too are bound to change. Both culture and history draw on narratives; each can refer to the other for supporting evidence; both are or can be, linked to power in divergent ways; both are concerned with identity and more narrowly with status.

What we frequently forget is that culture is not just a passive pattern of life nor does it remain so. Culture is also an agency of struggle especially where the pattern of living can involve forms of dominance and subordination. The question of freedom becomes central. The freedom to choose one's cultural idiom is of course in part conditioned by one's context, but there is also the aspiration to discard bondage of any kind and to be treated with dignity, at least the minimum dignity of being human. Resentment against being humiliated can be expressed in the idiom of culture when it is barred from being expressed in speech. Patterns of living when judged as cultures should consider the degree to which they respect this quality. Periods of history when resources have an inequitable distribution, and many people have to live precariously on the edge, are when essential freedoms and rights in law are threatened, or have been discarded. Even the right to aspirations are violated and trampled upon.

At such times, that which goes in the name of 'culture', has to be meticulously investigated. Coincidentally, this is also often the time when spurious histories are afloat, generated by those anxious to create a hegemonic culture to be used to control society in its entirety. Such controls fuel cultures as sources of struggle. The struggles are over the authenticity of the narrative relating to the past, but determined by requirements of the present; the source of power and the nature of identity, are aspects of the struggle. These are not unconnected with what goes into the making of what is then called national culture. As has been argued, the consent to a hegemonic culture has to come, less from the state but necessarily from civil society, so that such culture can claim that it has the moral consent of society. The questioning of this hegemonic culture often initiates the role of culture as a form of opposition. It also introduces another dimension in the study of history.

However history and culture can and do differ. History narrates and explains the past. Culture can invent the past more freely, without requiring the certification of historical evidence. Culture also draws on a collective memory, as does history in some cases. But with the latter this process has to be demonstrated through the use of reliable and tested sources, whereas with the former it can be more clandestine. Spurious history makes it that much easier. Such history assumes that major periods of history such as the Mughal period can be deleted from textbooks, even if the spectacular monuments of that time pepper the landscape, not to mention that they incidentally provide the largest income from tourism. Defeats in battle can be converted into victories. Poetic fiction, romanticizing heroines of the past can be treated as historical reality, and can become the idiom for justifying censorship and asserting the hegemonic culture.

Collective memory comes to the fore to support hegemonic cultures. Shards of what are believed to be memory are recollected and gathered from diverse sources and go into the making of cultural memory. More tangible fragments are located in museums. Museum displays are usually inadequate since their labels relate only to a fraction of the narrative. If every museum was complemented by a digital commentary available on the Internet, on each object, this could be the more effective way of both educating the public and encouraging individuals to explore a subject. This might also make curators in museums more thoughtful about what they are displaying and how, and what the narrative conveys.

What is perceived as culture by individuals or by communities, mutates. Nor are all cultures generated from a single source. But the diversity of these sources is not always averse to some form of integration. Most societies, barring isolated ones, experience the growth and extension of their cultures, both from within the society and from features originating elsewhere. These latter are, for various reasons, then imported and more often given a local gloss. Such societies cannot but have multiple cultures, and India is a significant example. The multiplicity can be due to continuity from the past and constitutes heritage, or it can be of more freshly minted forms of contemporary times. That which is defined as culture, can be claimed as having come from the past to the present, even if at times, it is found to be an invention of the present. Culture is not always a tangible pattern of living or an object from the past, therefore its forms arise from the interplay of many factors.

This questions the singularity of a culture, a singularity that is often upheld in nationalist claims. It is nevertheless, a debatable question as to whether such a claim to singularity characterizes a nationalist identity. Nationalism by definition is meant to be a collective, inclusive position, and would therefore have to incorporate the existing range of cultures. The singularity that emerges from such an integration, would be a different kind of innovation in identity, not conforming to any existing singularity. However, in its initial stages, it is frequently the articulation of the dominant group in society, as for example, an emerging middle class or a religious or linguistic majority. Consequently this is claimed as national culture although it is that pattern of life and thought that is associated with the dominant group. The question therefore of who is defining the culture of a society becomes a central question, since it decides on what is to be included and what excluded. The latter is often the elephant in the room. In this book I have tried to suggest some of the contexts that provide varied cultural forms and should be considered when defining culture, but which are frequently ignored.

It was not my intention to cover all the subjects that come under the rubric of culture and to provide an introduction to each. It was intended more as a critique of our frequently casual use of the word 'culture' without the attendant questions relevant to its comprehension. I was more concerned with drawing attention to a few of those aspects that form the contexts to cultures, but are often not consciously seen that way. These are generally neglected as being outside the purview of culture, and my attempt has been to suggest that they do form a contextual background. In popular explanations of the content of culture, a substantial presence of religion is included. I have written on this presence elsewhere and at some length in my earlier books, *The Past As Present* and *Indian Society and the Secular*, so I chose other themes for this book.

In defining culture I have highlighted some aspects that we have tended to either ignore or else to which we have given low priority. The earlier definition that focused on what has been called 'high' culture, changed in the late nineteenth and twentieth centuries to culture being seen as a pattern of living of any society. This was largely due to observing culture through the lens of the social sciences. This meant recognizing that links to power and to resources are also not only present in the making of cultural forms but determine in part the form it takes. To understand a culture it was necessary to know who were the patrons, how was it created and who internalized it. In order to know this, the articulation of culture could not be limited just to the patrons, generally the elite responsible for 'high' culture. The creators of the culture, no matter how diverse they may be, and those who lived in accordance with its patterns, had also to be inducted into its understanding. It was no longer seen as singular. Reference has therefore to be made to cultures (in the plural) to reflect the reality of societies such as those of the Indian past and the present.

The chapters on heritage and culture focus on aspects that are distanced from the usual objects and ideas that define culture—whether in literature and philosophy, or in the arts on display in museums, or in the architecture that dots the landscapes or in manuscripts. I have looked at some aspects that have much significance but have somehow not been too evident in studies of culture.

Concepts of time are basic to many activities that governed social functioning in the past, such as astrology and rituals that incorporate superstition about moments of time. Much of it still continues. Unfortunately the best of people have been recently assassinated for doubting the link. We take these beliefs and activities for granted but in order for them to be discontinued we have to know why they were, and still are, central to certain sections of society.

Many scholars of past times calculated concepts of time as a rationally ordered system that followed time-reckoning in a form that has been and continues to be, most helpful to our lives. In this as in other perspectives on the world, derived from rational knowledge, as for instance in mathematics and astronomy and to some degree in medicine, these were essential features of aspects of culture that we have tended to overlook. The measurement of time in myriad ways is an essential feature of every culture.

The variations continue these days. Festivals are calculated in lunar time whereas our daily lives are set by solar time, and there is always the awareness of professional uses of time that guide other activities.

Social structures define many cultural activities since these frame patterns of living. We recognize the role of the upper caste as providing the substance of 'high' culture, but there is less frequent mention of others, regarded as lesser beings according to the *Dharmashastras*, the social codes dictated by the upper echelons of society. The most obvious omissions are women, despite their having such a prominent position in the art and literature of what have been called classical periods of the past. Imagination has full play in calling up the pleasurable and romantic images of women in such sources, but there is little concession to their centrality in social reality. This was possibly because romanticizing the role of women can be an attractive exercise of the imagination, or even sometimes of social aspirations, but representing them in real life situations can point to a different story.

The other serious omission is that of the shadowy figures rarely given any clarity in discussions of culture—the excluded Avarna groups—the untouchable Asprishyas who lived on the edge, literally and metaphorically, and were despised. References to them in literature may be largely incidental but it is striking that they and their patterns of living and the artefacts they create, are seldom mentioned as part of any cultures either of the past or contemporary.

Whether culture is defined as that of the elite or includes the rest of society, one feature that is essential to its understanding is an assessment of the method a society chooses to educate itself. I did not discuss this with reference to past times, partly because access to education was varied among the different sections of society, as were the skills that were imparted through a range of educational or applied processes. To discuss this would require more than a single essay. I focused therefore on contemporary education. Its intention should be to make the educated aware of the many cultures that are juxtaposed in our society. This awareness comes not merely from being informed about the multiplicity of cultures, but through being taught to make relevant enquiries of them. It is equally necessary to understand the processes that go into investigating knowledge even of a primary kind, and to seeing them also as part of an on-going flow of knowledge that we have to be familiar with if we are to survive in the world of today.

Highlighting existing knowledge, and the questioning of knowledge that we focused on in our syllabuses in JNU, was intended both to impart existing knowledge as well as point to the new directions that the exploration of knowledge could reveal. Unfortunately in the present political ambience, the exploration of knowledge has been victimized. This obstructs the understanding of our many cultures and even more so the pursuit of the extension of knowledge. More than a century ago, Max Weber wrote extensively in defense of allowing every opinion to be aired in university discussions—be they of conservatives or of socialists and anarchists—and was strongly opposed to university authorities controlling appointments to university chairs. The current whittling down and devaluing of the social sciences in India whether by those in authority or in public opinion can only have a negative outcome.

The sources that we use for reconstructing cultures of the past are generally the sources that have survived and these almost inevitably reflect the views of the powerful and the wealthy. This condition is becoming a little less common now with new techniques of recovering the past from archaeological excavation, assisted very recently with laser images. DNA analyses are now being used in population studies but with some results still being somewhat controversial.

Written sources carry social differences such as those in the language of the royal courts and the learned, differing from the popular language. Record-keepers were common to kingdoms not only for maintaining a record of events and decisions, but also often as keepers of the traditions that legitimized the rulers. Who maintained the genealogies of the rulers, so necessary to their claims to status, even if sometimes fictional?

Education as I have argued is largely dependent on two factors: the content of what is taught and the language of communicating this content. What has always distinguished the educated person from the uneducated is the access to knowledge, through the ability to question theory and practice, and the ability to communicate it to others. Historically, in many societies education was viewed as a source of power and was therefore confined to the few. Modern societies have broken through these restrictions, but in some such as ours, the content of education lacks the thrust of questioning existing knowledge and the language of communication continues to be debated. Education therefore takes its own course. As is clear from the generally rather pathetic results from our system of education—with a few exceptions—this casual approach has not brought about the desired advance. One may well ask, what holds it back? Is it that what is taught done so in an irrelevant manner, or is the content of what is taught also irrelevant, barring in a few educational institutions? Is it the culture of merely repeating existing knowledge and not questioning it? Is this confounded by an inability to handle the language of socialization as different from the current language of knowledge? Or is it that since every child does not have access to education, the potential catchment area for those pursuing knowledge, remains reduced?

Was Sanskrit even in a simple form spoken widely, or were the variant Prakrits used more extensively in public discourse, as also for some religious and scholarly writing? Did any Prakrit incorporate the language of the Avarnas, such as the Chandala-bhasha? What was the relationship with other languages such as the Dravidian languages of the peninsula and the languages spoken by the Adivasis, some of whom lived in pockets contiguous with the areas of the major language? When and how did regional languages originate and why did they replace forms of Prakrit and Apabhramsha? What impact, other than the replacement of language, did this have on various cultures in terms of a wider reach of people accessing politics and social norms? Similar questions can be asked of the use of Persian as the language of the elite and the emergence of some of the regional languages such as Urdu. The same question may be asked of the use of English. Language as used in governance was also a form of maintaining the solidarities of power. This becomes obvious when centres of power changed from using Sanskrit to using Persian to using English in later times. Language can be an indicator of status although this may change from one period to another. What is vital to the process of learning as different from communicating, is knowing the language of contemporary knowledge.

The process of the inclusion or exclusion of social groups is an essential part of determining culture, as it also is in the structure of caste society. Caste was determined primarily from the intermeshing of access to power and economic resources with status, and the hierarchy that resulted was legitimized by claims to divine sanction or such like. This process continued through history although the constituents of castes changed as I have tried to show. This introduced some new categories of caste or allowed new occupations for existing castes. Given this there was some diversity in patterns of living.

There can be a clear-cut exclusion of those that have a distinctively different pattern of life, such as the Adivasis, those that live in forest settlements, who have always been kept away from mainstream society or have themselves remained isolated. The forest provides a powerful location for many aspects of Indian culture. In popular myths it is the haunt of demons, the rakshasas. However, there is a differentiated range of forest peoples, some who over time remain alien or others who became friendly. The forest people are sometimes linked to origin myths. Some Adivasi clans were given caste status.

In the epics, the forest is the place of exile. Those who for various reasons are to be exiled, are sent to the forest. These are largely members of the ruling families of adjacent kingdoms in the competition for succession—even if they are involved unwillingly. State administration has little to do with the forest dwellers except that the latter provide the administration with forest produce. The capturing of elephants, a major state enterprise, doubtless took the help of the forest people on occasion. The royal hunt in the forest was kept distinct and the focus was on animals without the intervention of local people. Even a ruler such as Ashoka, who gave priority to the welfare of his subjects, had a stern attitude towards the forest-dwellers.

Voluntary exclusion was taken up by wandering teachers who established their own settlements, given the easy availability of land. But such exclusion did not make any major impact on the ordering of society.

There is more than a hint of distancing from settlements, in the learning and scholarship among the Brahmanas being conducted ideally in relatively isolated retreats. The mathas were generally away from settlements and although they were not successful in being isolated, they were relatively so. Was this because in post-Gupta times they had begun to receive substantial grants from royal patrons that enabled establishing mathas, or was it a search for being far from the madding crowd? The Shramana monks established monasteries that by their very nature were at a reasonable distance from the settlement. Or was it generally understood that the pursuit of learning and knowledge required isolation? Needless to say the isolation became somewhat illusory when those living in mathas and monasteries came to be imbued with extraordinary powers and more than substantial wealth.

The large numbers that have an excluded position for entirely different reasons, are the Avarnas, those that are outside caste in contrast to the Savarnas, who are members of the four varnas and some of whom form the mainstream. In the utopian past there were no distinctions but with a decline in social mores, four differentiated varnas emerged. The hierarchy was said to be divinely ordained as mentioned in the *Bhagavata Purana* (9.14.48) and the *Mahabharata* (12. 59. 1 ff). From time to time the subordination of the Avarna was questioned, but the demand that they be treated with dignity and as equal members of society, remains a distant reality.

Migrants are often treated as excluded groups until such time that they are locally assimilated. The population history of the subcontinent has been a constant mix of varied people, both within it and coming from elsewhere. DNA analyses are beginning to confirm this. Migrations into an area or out of the area create their own cultures. Some come from and go to neighbouring lands and the cultural mixing differs from that which emerges when people travel far afield. What remains unpredictable is the point when migration is the signal for exclusion. Some who migrated into India many centuries ago such as the Arabs, Turks, Afghans, Mongols etc., and whose pattern of life is embedded in the region where they settled and generally intermarried, their descendants are now deliberately being treated as segregated groups for reasons of contemporary politics. It also happens that the adoption of a new religion such as Christianity and Islam by people already living in the subcontinent, is taken as indicating the arrival of a new population, which of course is not the case. This becomes clear from continuities in their patterns of living.

What is of interest and about whom we know so little are those who went as migrants from India to other parts of Eurasia and settled in more distant lands, from the Caspian to China and from the Red Sea to Indonesia. These were all places that have provided evidence of settlements of Indians resulting in fresh cultural forms emanating from their new patterns of life. Some of this is reflected in the occasional sculptured object or in a style of textile or is even marginally described in the texts that were written by the local people in these areas that hosted the migrants from India. The descriptions pertain more often to religious practices that came with them, and to the art and architectural forms, adopted by the elite in these places. But curiously we have virtually no Indian accounts of the places where Indians went or the life they led there. This is in striking contrast to the accounts of Greek, Chinese and Arab visitors to India, replete with descriptions of Indian cultural practices and forms. Were Indians that unconcerned with life around them, whether familiar or unfamiliar, that they were disinclined to describe what they saw or felt in the new environment?

Among the more adaptable articulations of culture are religious practices, since religious sects are quick to adapt themselves to local hierarchies and custom and to borrow rituals if need be. Rituals have a dual function. They are indicators of belief and they are signatures of status. The tendency therefore is for newer groups to suggest that they have adopted the rituals of people of high status and well-established. This does not always succeed, but it would be worth investigating rituals from this perspective.

Unless a ritual or a social form is anathema to a particular group, there is often a tendency to quietly incorporate it if it is emotionally attractive and socially helpful. The adoption or the amalgamation of selected rituals from major sects by those of lesser standing is not unknown, and continues to this day. What is adopted and why, makes for a fascinating study especially when it varies from region to region. The degree to which jati functions have been internalized by later societies is an indicator, although caste is of course not a ritual per se, even if it controls ritual functions, in accordance with the declared status.

One of the issues that is linked to religious belief and practice and that has resulted in contradictory actions and thought, is of course the question of social equality. Some religious sects of the Bhakti sants were firm in preaching social egalitarianism, and included among them were teachers of the Avarna category.

But the insistence on inequality has always been seen as stronger, doubtless because it had the backing of those that controlled the society and economy. It might be worthwhile to investigate in greater detail, which segments of society and persons supported equality. We may find a larger number than is generally thought, but obviously few from the elite or the dominant groups.

Aspects of culture can come in forms of accepted practices, often referred to as custom or customized law. Their strength lies in being located in precedents and conventions that are then accepted by the society in which they prevail. But practices are also codified and as we know there were many such codes in the form of *Dharmasutras* and *Dharmashastras*, and in other sects in the form of sharia codes, not to mention still others. Codified practices that were treated as laws often had a strong religious sanction in upper caste and conservative circles. The practices of some groups did not find mention in the texts but were treated as virtual law by those in the relevant occupation, as for example, the shreni-dharma, the code of the guilds. The *Arthashastra* [3.1.15;38] and some other texts do distinguish between custom and law. The interesting question remains as to why some practices remained customary whereas others were virtual laws. Again the context of each would be important. Those who knew the texts came to be seen as knowledgeable on the laws.

But with changed historical circumstances some laws did mutate. The commentaries on these texts—written in the second millennium AD—where the mutations are discussed, and either endorsed or negated, became sources encapsulating a process that was of central importance to upper-caste society and its cultural norms. Sometimes the laws were tweaked in order to consolidate new social groups. An interesting example of this is the discussion on who had the higher status—the Shrotriya or learned Brahmana or the priest of the temple. Temple priests naturally came into heightened importance when the large and wealthy temples boasted patrons of status and enormous wealth, generally from about the end of the first and the earlier part of the second millennium AD, the period when these questions were recorded. A new social category—that of the temple priest—had been created when temples became centres of worship and many acquired vast properties and wealth. Temple priests had to find their place in the status hierarchy.

My attempt has not been to discuss the many major aspects of history that go into the making of cultures, or for that matter all the activities that ultimately constitute cultures. My intention was to provide a few examples of what is often left out or treated casually as marginal or even irrelevant, to understanding culture. The cultural and historical forms can at the very least be juxtaposed, as they sometimes are these days, but it would be more illuminating if their interface were to be revealed. This is particularly important in current times when cultural forms are readily subjected to identity politics and many cultures are marginalized. Or, there is hesitation to study the cultures of other parts of the world thinking them to be of little consequence to our own. There is little interest, either general or intellectual, in researching and comprehending cultures outside the subcontinent, barring some reading on modern history as part of International Relations. This may be because there are hardly any facilities to encourage such an interest.

That cultures can be studied comparatively with each being analysed to observe its functioning, and that the analysis of the others can be used to further comprehend one's own, is still rare in our academic curriculum. The fundamental question of who is selecting that which is taken to be representative culture, remains crucial to all such studies; but the question is asked too infrequently. This is associated with the question of patronage. Patronage often sets the agenda of what represents the past and has to be protected, and what gives shape to contemporary culture. Since only fragments of the past are available in the present, it is the present that fits the fragments to create the past. This is a continuous activity indulged in by every generation. Each builds on the efforts of the earlier ones. This too embodies power, emphasizes its definition of the aesthetic, and creates cultural relationships sometimes embedded in physical forms. What emerges is the contemporary concept of the past. Some would accept it as it is. Others would subject it to historical scrutiny.

Cultural diversity does not annul the fact that both culture and diversity are linked to power. The question of diversity comes to the fore when what is perceived as national culture is confronted by regional or localized cultures or those constructed around the identity of religion or caste. How is a region to be defined, since making it coincide with the existing states that go into the making of the nation/country, is not feasible? Historically regions have been diverse because of their geography, ecology, social systems—as for instance their network of jatis—their religious sects, and the languages spoken. These constituents of a region vary in space and time. Their boundaries change and their forms are conditioned by natural and historical changes. Historically they have vacillated between being a part of a large kingdom or being small independent states. Their political and economic identities depend on what is basic to their functioning and what is excluded; vertical links may deepen certain forms such as exploitation of land resources, and horizontal links may create forms of exchange with other polities as in commerce. The cultural use of religion and language can be agencies that either unite or segregate societies, depending on usage.

The concept of a national culture tends to assume that all its constituent cultures are at base similar, and can therefore provide a foundation for a national culture. Where dissimilarities are observed there the problem arises of how these are to be fitted into the mould. Does the search for a national culture marginalize all that which does not conform to the dominant culture, relegating it to viable and necessary niches? Or does inclusion mean recognizing links? To what extent does the culture that we describe as the representative culture of an age, a period of time and history, actually represent the limited culture of dominant groups and elites? How are the cultures of the interstices to be represented?

Cultures can be real patterns of living, or alternately can be imagined patterns, representing the assumptions or the aspirations of a society. Here, mythology becomes one obvious form of creative expression that is based on fantasy and involves either only deities or deities and humans, in relationships that are sometimes predictable and sometimes quite unusual. The participation of animals and vegetation when personalized in mythology, adds to the fantasy. The imagination of cultural articulation can take the form of fantasy, but where culture is a pattern of living there reality intrudes. By its very nature mythology is distinct from history. At most it can hint at some social assumptions of the society.

Among the more unpredictable aspects of cultures are occasions when cultures meet or intersect. These are often treated casually and dismissed by referring to which 'influenced' which. What we call 'influence' is seldom direct and as easily recognizable as we like to believe. Therefore a claim to influence has to be prised apart and assessed in detail. Even if a feature is imported from another cultural stream its impact on what is subsequently created has to be explored far more fully than is generally done. Such intersections could well lead to the erosion of natural barriers and the blurring of characteristic peculiarities. This can happen by accident through the arrival of migrants, traders, missionaries and soldiers. Or else, it can be deliberate when particular items of culture or patterns of living are adapted or adopted from what are seen as distinctively different cultures but to be emulated. The controversies over the wearing of jeans in our days illustrates the point. It happened perhaps more casually in earlier times, such as the occasional common motifs in Achaemenid and Mauryan objects, or the borrowing of Mauryan forms in the Gupta period, or the wide-scale adoption of courtly fashion in dress among various elites during Mughal times.

Cultures can reflect the many new forms assimilated over the centuries. Some of this evolved as a matter of course and some of it came from those who originated in contiguous areas and settled in India in premodern times. They were therefore familiar and not unknown. Border regions of the subcontinent were invariably areas of mixed cultures. A quick headcount of substantial settlements throughout history provides a clear picture. The cultures of the Indus civilization were probably of local origin with an intervention in contiguous regions. The arrival of the Aryan speakers in the second millennium BC introduced new forms through the interface of existing cultures as for instance in the languages used and spoken. The proximity of Iranian forms goes back to the *Avesta* and to the Achaemenids in the first millennium BC. These were geographically contiguous. Hellenistic forms of the Indo-Bactrian Greeks succeeded these and extended to the Oxus plain. The arrival of the Shakas and Kushanas from Central Asia brought innovations. The Hunas left a small imprint. These migrants introduced changes in the cultures of the northwestern subcontinent but the rest was left much to its own devices. This was also the time when Indian traders, Buddhist missionaries and some Brahmanas, and doubtless some Indian craftsmen as well, travelled out and settled in Central Asia and Southeast Asia, creating a wide range of new cultural forms in these areas.

The Turks and Afghans who came in the second millennium AD made a noticeable impact in certain areas, and this is reflected even in their monuments scattered over the landscape, not to mention changes in languages and literatures, in technologies of various kinds and in trade patterns for a start. Arab traders settled as communities along the west coast and married locally giving rise to new socio-religious communities and sects, the admixture reflecting Muslim and Hindu practices and beliefs, that went into the making of customary law in these communities: a continuing pattern common to some other areas as well. The Mughals brought with them a host of other forms from Central

Asia and encouraged some that originated in Iran.

In every case those that came and those that went, through whichever channel, settled initially in the area of arrival and were the creators of new cultures. New forms of Christianity arose from the settlements of the Syrian Christians, in many ways different from the Protestant and Catholic missions that came later with the arrival of colonial traders and administrators. These earlier communities merged their own cultures of their locations and what had come to them from the arrivals, thus sprouting new cultural forms and communities. Whatever wealth they made was ploughed back into the locations and efforts were also made to encourage the interface between cultures. Such interfaces often took the form of incorporation, but did on occasion lead to a rejection of selected aspects of the other's culture. Both processes were evident and can be explained. Those that settled, whether in small or large numbers, did not go back to where they had come from. Their cultures grew from the soil where they had settled. Their communities grew with the induction of local peoples.

The cultures that evolved during the periods of these many early settlements and interactions, made their own comments on this varied experience, but these have received insufficient attention from historians and those writing on culture. They illustrate what might be called cultures transiting to finally emerging as established communities. They also raise the interesting question of who constituted the larger bodies of patrons and clients, in these cross-cultural communities? And who actually created the new cultural forms? The contribution of existing cultures and of those less touched by in-coming forms would have varied from place to place and needs to be assessed. More importantly, at what point did the transiting end and the cultures become internalized? Should we not focus on these questions? It does require greater attention to the context of an object, than the rather cursory treatment it often receives.

Let me quote an example or two that could be seen as unfolding this process. A coin is a small artifact and coinage has a role in economic transactions. It can also be a statement on other aspects of public life such as politics, social mores and religion. The kind of coin issued in a polity can relate to the history of the moment of issuance. It can also point to the context of other ideas.

Ghaznavid coins were issued in the northwest during the arrival of Ghaznavid power into the northern subcontinent, at centres such as the city of Lahore. Some coins refer to Mahmud's campaigns but others carry a different message. According to A. K. Bhattacharya, the legend on these was bilingual in Arabic and Sanskrit, the latter in the Sharada script that was the Kashmiri version of the late Brahmi script used for Sanskrit. The statement in colloquial Sanskrit reads: 'avyaktam ekam muhammad avatara nripati mahmud' (the unmanifest is one, Muhammad is his avatara, and Mahmud is the king). This was a considerable concession to local sentiment and status. It contradicts the Islamic rhetoric of some of the court chroniclers. But the point being made is perhaps to claim a continuity in authority as recognizable to the local people. This puts a different kind of emphasis on Ghaznavid rule and the introduction of new cultural forms.

Such concessions are recorded on other coins too. Early Ghurid coins carry Islamic titles as well as the Shaiva bull Nandi, and the legend, shri samanta deva. The use of this phrase says a great deal. It is suggestive of the local title, samanta, with claims to authority, the honorific shri is again local as is the use of the qualifier, deva. This was reflective of the status of a transitory position using familiar terms and icons. Gold coins of the Ghurids issued in Varanasi by Sultan Mu'iz-al-din Muhammad bin Sam, carried his name in Sanskrit, as was frequent in these coins when naming the ruler, and was obviously thought appropriate to kingship. The obverse has a stylized image of Lakshmi. Did the new money have to carry familiar features of the old in order to make it legal tender? Was this just an attempt to win over the local people? Was it to ensure the acceptance by traders as required by the economy? How did those using the coins react to this? Did they take it as normal for every new ruler to declare his power in this manner? Did his officers regard this as an expected move? What was the reaction of the mint-masters of the local mint in altering the coin legend but retaining the graphic? Was this also an attempt to weave the old into the new as seamlessly as possible, at least in some important practices?

Qutb-ud-din Aibak after his conquests started building in 1193, the Qutab Minar, a tall tower with an inner stairway to the top. The site was that of a Hindu temple converted into a mosque and the remains of the temple were part of the courtyard of the mosque. It is located in the vast fortress of the Qila Rai Pithora in Delhi and has been known as the Quwwat-ul-Islam mosque. The patron was the sultan and his successors, the clients were the elite who worshipped there and others who saw it as an idiom of the new power.

The inner walls of the Qutab Minar carry a number of inscriptions in Sanskrit, recording the fact that it had been struck more than once by lightning and each time had required repairs. The masons responsible for the repairs are likely to have come from the same community of craftsmen who had originally constructed it. One such inscription states that, 'In the reign of the Suratrana Pherojsahi [the Sultan Firuz Shah] in samvat 1426 [AD 1369], the *minar* was renovated. This work was completed by the grace of Shri Vishvakarma [the deity worshipped by craftsmen]. The sutradhara [the one in control] was Chahad, the son of Devapala, and the maternal grandson of............. The *shilpi sutra* [craftsman] was Nana Salha and the *darukarma* [carpenter] was Dharmuvanani.'

Another inscription gives the precise date of the damage during the reign of Pheroj Shahi and mentions that the masons who repaired it were Nana Salha, Lola and Lashamana.

Yet another inscription refers to the sutra Lashamana and Harimani Gaveri the son of Sahadhaira.

Post-Sultanate inscriptions of the sixteenth and seventeenth centuries may have stated something more than currently exists, but it has got erased. It is likely to have been a record of repairs since the style is similar to the earlier ones. The later ones also provide dates and names and it would seem that the minar was still being repaired when necessary. Some of the names mentioned in these inscriptions are Gopa and the stonecutter Sisha, the son of Hira, now referred to in Sanskrit as a sangatrasu, which has been explained as being a version of the Persian word sangtarash for a stonecutter. Another late inscription refers to Tulsi, Hira Devidas, Madholal, Badragu, and the sangatrasa, stone cutter, Rama of the Chandala-vamsha.

The names suggest members of the lower castes and this is confirmed in the inscription that refers to a stonecutter being a Chandala. As has been pointed out they are all Hindu craftsmen, barring the one Chandala. Yet interestingly the Chandala works on par with the other craftsmen. There are no Muslim names. What is also impressive is that these records are not of the patrons or the elite, but of the actual workmen, and express considerable confidence in being in control of the repairs and the maintenance of the structure. It is a statement of professional pride and of identity. The inscriptions are in Sanskrit but of a very colloquial kind and obviously making the point that despite being masons, artisans, craftsmen and stonecutters, they are embedding records in the royal structure and the inscriptions are claims to their professional status. Were they themselves literate in Sanskrit or were the inscriptions inscribed by a professional engraver? The text of the inscriptions and their locations suggests that the masons may well have been literate. That they use Sanskrit and not Persian points to the continuity of Sanskrit as the language of important records from the perspective of the workmen. Not only do the inscriptions indicate the cultural niche in which the work of these jatis was carried out, but it is also impressive that they unhesitatingly identified their culture and their deity on a monument linked to a different social patronage as well as social and religious practices.

Or the obvious question is, were they all that different? The dates are given in the samvat era used widely in India during the post-Gupta period, and not in the Hijri era as might have been expected in a monument of a sultan.

Further, there is no hesitation in attributing the success of the renovation to the deity Vishvakarma, this despite its being an Islamic monument decorated with verses from the Quran and closely associated with a mosque. The invocation known in temples was extended here to a mosque. Nor do they comment in any way on the fact that the associated mosque was built on the visible remains of an earlier temple. Had the deity of the temple not been part of the pantheon worshipped by the masons and stonecutters? Had the community of low castes been allowed to worship in the sanctum of this temple? Did they feel that having attributed the success of the repairs to their own deity, other deities were less significant? In trying to answer the question of what might have been their cultural context, a range of questions surface. In seeking the context of the Qutab Minar as a cultural monument, a different segment of cultural relations opens up. Presenting a wider context, this changes some of the contours of the cultural understanding of the monument.

Quranic verses were inscribed on the outer surface of the minar and this would have had to be done when the minar was first constructed. Were those engravers familiar with the verses and the Arabic script? Or were the verses traced on the stone by those who knew the Quran and Arabic, subsequent to which the surface of the stone was engraved by local engravers? It is unlikely that a guild of engravers and stonecutters would have been brought from West Asia to decorate these monuments. At most there would have been some that supervised the work. Did the engravers of the verses see themselves as culturally distinct from those who constructed the building? Or was this just another job requiring their engraving skills? Were they unconcerned with what they were engraving as long as they were doing it well?

Were the masons descendants of those who initially constructed the minar or engraved the verses?

These inscriptions read as normal records of repair-work carried out on a building struck by lightning a century or so after it was erected. It is likely that the same sutradhara who directed the repair on the Qutab Minar would have been contracted to build a temple, since he seems to have had skilled masons who were also capable of putting up inscriptions to record themselves and their work. Why did the craftsmen record their work? To acquire status, knowing that it would be read by those visiting the mosque and by posterity? Or to make a statement favourable to their profession? Perhaps we might give some thought to what might have been their conversations as they sat doing the repairs. Were they concerned about working on the site of a temple converted into a mosque—something that bothers some people in our times, but seems not to have bothered them. Or did it not matter since the work was bringing in an income and the minar had in any case been built more than a century earlier? These are questions worth asking. Through these questions the Qutab Minar becomes the work and concern of many, quite apart from those who were the patrons of its construction.

Such questions also lead to another, namely, who has the bigger stake in a cultural item? Is it the patron who made it possible financially and otherwise, but whose patronage may decline or even disappear after a few generations? Or is it the clients who use the cultural item either as an object of worship or see it as an idiom of power to which they pay obeisance? In the case of the Qutab, the records show that it was being looked after well into the Mughal period. Patronage was forthcoming although the patrons differed, and the reasons for the patronage may not have changed significantly. Why would the late-Mughals have ensured the maintenance of the minar? Was it that they thought preserving the monuments of the past would give them historical legitimacy? As recorded in the *Prabandha-cintamani,* this seems to have been one consideration when the minister Hemachandra advised Kumarapala, the Chaulukya king, to rebuild the temple at Somanatha. In earlier times, when heritage was being ascertained, clients would follow the gaze of the patrons or would give an ear to hearsay and act accordingly. In our times, tourism is increasingly commanding the stakes, on what constitutes heritage and is to be preserved.

Subsequent to these processes came the colonial cultural impact. This process is far more dramatically illustrated initially in the breaking away from earlier forms, and subsequently with the appropriation of colonial forms in objects and in ways of thought. At the level of externalities this continues to have an influence as, for instance, in some dress codes especially among Indian men in cities, in consumption patterns of food and drink, and more important in the use of many routine technologies that derive from non-Indian sources. A far larger percentage of Indians have been affected by the impact of this culture and at many more levels, than by other alien cultures in premodern times. The contradiction in a way is that the British, although they colonized India, were the only ones who did not settle in India, as did the earlier arrivals. What has engineered the continuity is the technology, the dependence on the market economy with the emergence of globalization, and the concept of modernity that registers a change in some lifestyles but remains essentially superficial so far. A change in mindset that will give priority to ensuring social equality, gender justice and human rights, is still awaited. Nevertheless what is spoken of as the difference in cultures needs enquiry.

The coming of the colonial powers, as the European colonizers of Asia, did not in essentials, conform to the pattern of creating new communities that merged into the existing populations and appropriated each other's cultures. The colonizers, with hardly any noticeable exception, did not settle in the colony. In the colonial empire, other than in Asia, colonial settlers stayed permanently and built new economies and on which they grafted their cultural norms. In Asia, they largely controlled and creamed off the wealth of an existing economic system, to be used to advance the economy of the home country. On acquiring the requisite wealth they made their way back to their own country in Europe, to invest the wealth in its development.

Was it because in Asia and in North Africa they met with existing cultures that resisted a cultural transformation? This experience had some similarity with the pattern of colonization by Spain and Portugal in Latin America. Some cultures were converted, others decimated. Comparative studies of these might illumine patterns of colonization. Where there was land available with a sparse local population, there the colonizers did settle and convert these areas into new economic systems. European colonialism did not colonize contiguous areas or areas with which they had had close contact over long periods. The colonies were distant places. The indigenous and the colonial cultures tended to remain distinct. The marginal exceptions were in the early years of contact when the British traders imitated the lifestyle of the local elite of rajas and nawabs, or when some among them became interested in studying in a systematic way, the cultures they were governing. Some of the more speculative of these studies have become the foundation of the cultural self-perception of the ex-colonized.

After the revolt of 1857 when the colony came directly under the crown, the distance between the colonized and the colonial authority became more formal, with a sharp demarcation between those governing and those being governed. This was evident in the setting up of the British cantonments, segregated areas in selected towns. Here a clearly worked out colonial lifestyle was established, in order to facilitate both governance and ways of living. Structures and systems that characterized cantonment culture were a short-lived experience, fading out with the end of colonialism. In effect, however, they have left remnants that have now merged into the ascendant contemporary cultures.

The cultures of modernism are sometimes explained as having been initially linked to nationalism. These are varied since nationalism led to the surfacing of diverse cultures in a range of communities. Nationalism requires subordinating all identities to the single national identity of the citizen loyal to the nation state. The individual subordinates her existing identity with a religious or caste or linguistic community, and makes her primary identity that of being a citizen of the nation. The nation state guarantees to the citizen her human rights, claim to civil laws, expectation of social justice and security, in the context of the equality of all citizens. Ideally a new relationship is established between the citizen and the state. Inevitably this brings with it a new pattern of living and of values and therefore new cultural forms. But this has to be thought about and choices made.

This does not happen in many modern states and is the cause of cultural struggles in most. Ex-colonial societies, by passing the essentials of a modern society—equal rights and social justice—often seek legitimacy for the dominant majority community in its access to power. Such a community claims to be the author of the fantasy utopian society of the past that is suggested as a role model. Interestingly this is generally based on the interpretation of the past made by colonial scholarship. It draws on the historical imagination of colonial thinking but insists that it is reflecting indigenous non-colonial views. The cultural forms determining this imagined past are a curious medley of contemporary desires and fears.

To those that understand its real meaning, nationalism does not mean going back to old identities or selecting the identity of the majority and calling it 'national'. Nationalism, if properly understood, should provide a new identity that is inclusive of all, both the dominant and the subordinate. This would give a sense of purpose to many, encouraging them in working towards a society with new cultural possibilities. The coming of globalization has however moved us away somewhat from this idea. It has introduced the sense of a nation being one of the many, but having to contest the many in maintaining an economic advance over others. There is a strong strand of insecurity in this contest. This has led to ideologies that propagate a wish to revert to the imagined utopia of the past that would allow national culture to be described as unique and incontestable. What it actually upholds is the reinvention of what is believed to have been the society and culture of the past golden age.

This reinvention is frequently guided by the vision of the upper class or the upper caste through the way in which it envisages such a past. The cultures of this vision emerge from these dominant groups but they have to carry the consent of civil society that in nationalist and post-nationalist times includes more than the dominant group. The consent has to be organized through the institutions of civil society rather than the state, since the state has a different relationship with citizens.

More often than not this results in selecting from past cultures those that support particular forms of contemporary cultures thought to be the most relevant. The garb of modernity—in dress, in food, in living styles—does not necessarily indicate a modern mindset. Much that conflicts with modernity in terms especially of social attitudes of premodern times, are described as 'traditional values' and treated as an inheritance, and therefore needing to be incorporated into the present, but on which are superimposed the rougher edges of a perceived and incomplete modernity. Since we are now a part of the global system as well, that leaves us with little choice to opt for other cultural patterns. What allows for optimism, is nevertheless, the fact that cultures can be changed and if there is enough determination to make a positive change, that change is not out of reach.

ACKNOWLEDGEMENTS

The contents of the chapters in this book have been drawn from some of my essays and lectures, published and unpublished. They are as follows:

Chapter 1: Cultures as Heritage
Lectures given at the Kalakshetra Foundation, Chennai, and at the Calcutta Museum in 2014. Unpublished.

Chapter 2: Heritage: The Contemporary Past
The Coomaraswamy Lecture, 'Heritage: The Contemporary Past' was given at the Chhatrapati Shivaji Maharaj Vastu Sangrahalaya, Mumbai, in 2016. To be published by the museum.

Chapter 3: Time Before Time
'Cyclic and Linear Time in Early India', lecture given at Darwin College, Cambridge, published in *Time,* edited by K. Ridderbos. Cambridge: Cambridge University Press, 2002.

Chapter 4: Science as Culture
'History of Science and Oikumenae' in *Situating the History of Science: Dialogues with Joseph Needham,* edited by S. Irfan Habib and D. Raina. New Delhi: Oxford University Press, 1999.

Chapter 5: Women Decoding Cultures
'Renouncers, Householders, Courtesans: Reflections on Women in Early India', Nandita Sahai Memorial Lecture, Centre for Historical Studies, JNU, 2016. Unpublished.

Chapter 6: The Culture of Discrimination
'Exclusion and Identity in the Context of Historical Change', Centre for the Study of Discrimination and Exclusion, JNU, Foundation Day Lecture, 2017. Unpublished.

Chapter 7: Knowledge as Heritage
'Education in Contemporary India', Amrik Singh Memorial Lecture, Bhai Vir Singh Sahitya Sada, Delhi, 2016. Unpublished.
'JNU's Contribution to the Nation—the Centre for Historical Studies', Lecture given at JNU, 2017. Unpublished.

REFERENCES AND FURTHER READING

INTRODUCTION

Anderson, B., *Imagined Communities: Reflections on the Origin and Spread of Nationalism*, London: Verso Books, 1983.

Berger, P. and Luckmann, T., *The Social Construction of Reality*, Harmondsworth: Penguin Books, 1966.

Beteille, A., *Caste, Class and Power: Changing Patterns of Stratification in a Tanjore Village*, Berkeley: University of California Press, 1965.

Bourdieu, P., *Outline of a Theory of Practice*, Nice, Richard, trans., Cambridge: Cambridge University Press, 1977.

Childe, V. G., *What Happened in History*, London: Verso Books, 1942.

Davids, T. W. and C. A. F. Rhys, ed. and trans., *Digha Nikaya, Sacred Books of the Buddhists, Vols. II, III, IV, Parts I to III*, London: Oxford University Press, 1971.

Frank, A. Gunder, *ReOrient: Global Economy in the Asian Age*, Berkeley: University of California Press, 1998.

———, and Gills, B. K., *The World System: Five Hundred Years or Five Thousand?*, London: Psychology Press, 1996.

Hall, S., *Cultural Studies*, Durham: Duke University Press, 2016.

Hobsbawm, E., *Nations and Nationalism since 1780: Programme, Myth, Reality*, Cambridge: Cambridge University Press, 1990.

Huntington, S., *The Clash of Civilizations*, New York: Simon and Schuster, 1997.

Kosambi, D. D., *An Introduction to the Study of Indian History*, Bombay: Popular Prakashan, 1956.

Rudolph, L. and S., *The Modernity of Tradition: Political Development in India*, Chicago: University of Chicago Press, 1967.

Saberwal, S., *Wages of Segmentation: Comparative Studies on Europe and India*, New Delhi: Orient Blackswan, 1995.

Thapar, R., *The Historian and her Craft,* Vol. I-IV, New Delhi: Oxford University Press, 2018.

Toynbee, A., *A Study of History*, abridged ed., by D. C. Somerville, London: Oxford University Press, 1961.

Wallerstein, I., *World-Systems Analysis : An Introduction,* Durham: Duke University Press, 2004.

White, L., *The Science of Culture: A Study of Man and Civilisation,* New York: Grove Press, 1949.

Williams, R., *Keywords: A Vocabulary of Culture and Society,* New York: Oxford University Press, 1976.

CHAPTERS 1 and 2

Fleet, J. F., ed., *Inscriptions of the Early Gupta Kings, Corpus Inscriptionum Indicarum* Vol III, Calcutta: Superintendent of Government Printing, 1888.

Flood, F. B., *Objects of Translation: Material Culture and Medieval "Hindu-Muslim" Encounter,* Princeton: Princeton University Press, 2009.

Gunther, R. T., *The Astrolabes of the World,* Vols. I and II, Oxford: Oxford University Press, 1932.

Higham, Charles, *The Civilization of Angkor*, Berkeley: University of California Press, 2001.

Hultzch, E., ed., *The Inscriptions of Asoka, Corpus Inscriptionum Indicarum* Vol I, London: Clarendon Press, 1888-1925.

Kangle, R. P., *The Kautiliya Arthasastra*, Bombay: Motilal Banarsidass, 1965.

Kothari, A., 'Revisiting the Legend of Niyamgiri', *The Hindu,* 2 January 2015.

Lorenzen, D., *Bhakti Religions in North India : Community Identity and Political Action,* New York: SUNY Press, 1995.

Morrison, J., *The Astrolabe,* Great Shelford: Janus, 2007.

Merutunga, *Prabandhachintamani*, Jinvijaya, Muni, ed., Tawney, C. H., trans., Shantiniketan: Vishvabharati, 1933.

Ram, R., 'Ravidass Dera Sachkhand Ballan and the Question of Dalit Identity in the Punjab', *Journal of Panjab Studies,* 16 (1). 2, 2009. Santa Barbara: University of California, 2009.

Raychaudhuri, H. C., *Political History of Ancient India*, Calcutta: University of Calcutta, 1923.

Thapar, R., *Asoka and the Decline of the Mauryas,* New Delhi: Oxford University Press, 1997.

———, 'Death and the Hero' in Humphreys, S. and King, H., eds., *Mortality and Immortality: The Anthropology and Archaeology of Death,* London: Academic Press, 1981, pp. 293-316.

———, *The Past Before Us: Historical Traditions of Early North India,* New Delhi: Permanent Black, 2013.

———, *Somanatha : The Many Voices of a History*, New Delhi: Penguin Books, 2004.

Trautmann, T. R., *Kautilya and the Arthasastra: A Statistical Investigation of the Authorship and Evolution of the Text,* Leiden: Brill, 1971.

CHAPTER 3

Bechert, H., ed., *The Dating of the Historical Buddha*, Vols. I and II, Goetingan: Vandenhoeck & Ruprech, 1991.

Benjamin, W., *Illuminations,* London: Random House, 1968.

Eliade, M., *The Myth of the Eternal Return: Cosmos and History,* Princeton: Princeton University Press, 1971.

Epigraphia Indica, Vol. VI., p. 11 Aihole Inscription.

Landes, B., *Revolution in Time: Clocks and the Making of the Modern World,* Boston: Belknap Press, 2000.

Olivelle, P., ed. and trans., *Manu Dharmashastra,* New Delhi: Oxford University Press, 2005.

Ruesen, J., *Time and History: The Variety of Cultures*, New York: Berghahn Books, 2008.

Thapar, R., *Time as a Metaphor of History: Early India*, New Delhi: Oxford University Press, 1996.

———, *Somanatha: The Many Voices of a History*, New Delhi: Penguin Books, 2004.

Whitrow G. J., *Time in History: Views of Time from Prehistory to the Present Day*, Oxford: Oxford University Press, 1980.

Wilson, H. H., trans., *The Vishnu Purana: A System of Hindu Mythology and Tradition,* Calcutta: Punthi Pustak, 1840, 1961 (reprint edition).

CHAPTER 4

Bernal, J. D., *Science in History: The Scientific and Industrial Revolution,* Vols. I to IV, London: Watts, 1954.

Childe, V. G., *Man Makes Himself*, London: Mentor Books, 1951.

Gould, S. J., *Ever Since Darwin: Reflections in Natural History*, New York: W. W. Norton and Company, 1977.

Hobsbawm, E., *Nations and Nationalism since 1780: Programme, Myth, Reality*, Cambridge: Cambridge University Press, 1990.

Ifrah, G., *A Universal History of Numbers: From Prehistory to Computers*, New York: John Wiley & Sons, 2000.

Joseph, G. G., *The Crest of the Peacock: The Non-European Roots of Mathematics*, Princeton: Princeton University Press, 2000.

Kuhn, T., *The Structure of Scientific Revolutions*, Chicago: University of Chicago Press, 1962.

Needham, J., *Science and Civilization in China*, Cambridge: Cambridge University Press, 1954 sq.

Pingree, D., 'The Logic of Non-Western Science: Mathematical Discoveries in Medieval India', *Daedalus*, 132, 4, 2003, pp. 45-54.

Sarma, K.V. ed., *Lilavati of Bhaskaracara with the Commentary Kriyakramkari*, Hoshiapur: Vishveshvaranand Institute, 1975.

Uberoi, J. P. S., *Science and Culture*, New Delhi: Oxford University Press, 1978.

Varamihira, *Brihat Samhita*, Bhat, M. R., Sastri, P. V. S., trans., Bangalore: V. B. Soobbiah & Sons, 1946.

CHAPTER 5

Basham, A. L., trans., *Mricchakatika, The Little Clay Cart*, New York: SUNY Press, 1994.

Basu, A., *Two Faces of Protest: Contrasting Modes of Women's Activities in India*, New Delhi: Oxford University Press, 1993.

Chakravati, U., *Gendering Caste Through a Feminist Lens*, Kolkata: Sree, 2002.

Dumont, L., *Homo Hierarchicus: The Caste System and its Importance*, Chicago: University of Chicago Press, 1970.

Hallisey, C., trans., *Therigatha: Poems of the First Buddhist Women*, Cambridge: Harvard University Press, 2015.

Hawley J. S., ed., *Sati, The Blessing and the Curse: The Burning of Wives in India*, New York: Oxford University Press, 1994.

Keith, A. B., trans., *Aitareya Brahmana, Rigveda Brahmanas*, Patna: Motilal Banarsidass, 1971.

Marglin, F. A., *Wives of the God-King: The Rituals of the Devadasis of Puri,* New Delhi: Oxford University Press, 1985.

Menon, N., *Seeing Like a Feminist,* New Delhi: Penguin Books, 2012.

Olivelle, P., ed. and trans., *Manu Dharmashastra,* New Delhi: Oxford University Press, 2005.

Power, E., *Medieval People,* New York: Doubleday, 1924.

Radhakrishnan, S., trans., *Brihadaranyaka Upanisad: The Principal Upanisads,* London: George Allen and Unwin Ltd., 1953.

Roy, K., *The Power of Gender and the Gender of Power: Explorations in Early Indian History,* New Delhi: Oxford University Press, 2010.

Sangari, K. and Vaid, S., eds., *Recasting Women: Essays in Colonial History,* New Delhi: Kali for Women, 1989.

Sarkar, T., and Butalia, U., eds., *Women and the Hindu Right: A Collection of Essays*, New Delhi: Kali for Women, 1995.

Schopen, G., *Buddhist Nuns, Monks and Other Worldly Matters: Recent Papers on Monastic Buddhism in India,* Honolulu: University of Hawaii Press, 2014.

Shah, K. K., ed., *The Problem of Identity: Women in Early Indian Inscriptions,* New Delhi: Oxford University Press, 2001.

———, *History and Gender: Some Explorations,* Jaipur: Rawat Publications, 2005.

CHAPTER 6

Ahmed, I., *Caste and Social Stratification among Muslims in India,* New Delhi: Manohar, 1978.

Ambedkar, B. R., *Annihilation of Caste,* Jullundar: Bheem Patrika Publications, 1968.

Banabhatta, *Harshacharita,* Cowell, E. and Thomas, F. W., eds. and trans., *The Harsacarita of Bana,* London: Royal Asiatic Society, 1897.

Cowell, E. B., ed. and trans., *Jataka, The Jatakas,* Cambridge: Cambridge University Press, 1905.

Desai, A. R., *Peasant Struggles in India,* Bombay: Oxford University Press, 1979.

Faxian, *A Record of Buddhist Kingdoms,* Legge, J. ed. and trans., Oxford: Clarendon Press, 1886, 104 ff.

Davids, T. W. Rhys, trans., *Milinda-panha, Questions of King Milinda,*

Sacred Books of the East, Vols. XXXV and XXXVI, Oxford: Oxford University Press, 1890-94.

Dumont, L., *Homo Hierarchicus: The Caste System and its Importance,* Oxford: Oxford University Press, 1970.

Gupta, D., ed., *Social Stratification,* New Delhi: Oxford University Press, 1992.

Gopal Guru, 1993, 'Dalit Movement in Mainstream Sociology', *Economic and Political Weekly*, 28 (14) 3 April, 370-73.

Gopal Guru, ed., *Humiliation: Claims and Context*, New Delhi: Oxford University Press, 2011.

Jaffrelot, C., *India's Silent Revolution: The Rise of the Lower Castes in North India,* London: C. Hurst and Co., 2003.

Jha, V., Candala: *Untouchability and Caste in Early India*, New Delhi: Primus, 2017.

Karve, I., *Hindu Society: An Interpretation,* Poona: Deccan College, 1968.

Klass, M., *Caste: the Emergence of the South Asian Social System*, Philadelphia: Institute for the Study of Human Issues, 1980.

Megasthenes, *Indica*, McCrindle, J. W., trans., *Ancient India as Described by Megasthenes and Arrian,* London: Trubner and Co., 1877.

Omvedt, G., *Dalit Visions: The Anti-Caste Movement and the Construction of an Indian Identity,* New Delhi: Orient Blackswan, 1995.

Parasher-Sen, A., *Subordinate and Marginal Groups in Early India,* New Delhi: Oxford University Press, 2004.

Shah, A. M., *The Household Dimension of the Family in India: A Field Study in a Gujarat Village and a Review of Other Studies*, New Delhi: Orient Longman, 1973.

Sharma, R. S., *Shudras in Ancient India*, Patna: Motilal Banarsidass, 1980.

Singh, Hira, *Recasting Caste: From the Sacred to the Profane,* New Delhi: Sage Publications, 2014.

Singh, K. S., *Tribal Ethnography, Customary Law and Change,* New Delhi: Concept Publishing Company, 1993.

———, *Tribal Society in India: An Anthropo-Historical Perspective,* New Delhi: South Asia Books, 1985.

Srinivas M. N., *Caste in Modern India and Other Essays*, Bombay: Asia Publishing House, 1999.

Thapar, R., *The Aryan: Recasting Constructs*, New Delhi: Three Essays Collective, 2008.

Weber, Max, trans., *The Religion of India: The Sociology of Hinduism and Buddhism*, Glencoe: The Free Press, 1959.

Zelliot, E., *From Untouchable to Dalit: Essays on the Ambedkar Movement,* New Delhi: Manohar, 1992.

CHAPTER 7

Desai, S., and Kulkarni, V., 'Changing Educational Inequalities in India in the Context of Affirmative Action', *Demography*, Vol. 45, 2, 2008, 245-270.

Jayatillake, K. N., *Early Buddhist Theory of Knowledge,* London: George Allen and Unwin Ltd., 1963.

Kumar, K., *Prejudice and Pride: School Histories of the Freedom Struggle in India and Pakistan*, New Delhi: Penguin Books, 2001.

Mohanty, J. N., *Reason and Tradition in Indian Thought,* Oxford: Clarendon Press, 1992.

Sgharfe, H, *Education in Ancient India*, Boston: Brill, 2002.

EPILOGUE

Bhattacharya, A. K., 'Bilingual Coins of Mahmud of Ghazni', *Journal of the Numismatic Society of India,* XXVI, 1964, pp. 53-56.

Chattopadhyaya, B. D., *Representing the Other?*, New Delhi: Manohar, 1998.

Dreijmanis, J., *Max Weber's Complete Writings on Academic and Political Vocations,* New York: Algora Publishing, 2008.

Flood, F. B., *Objects of Translation: Material Culture and Medieval 'Hindu-Muslim' Encounter,* Princeton: Princeton University Press, 2009.

Gramsci, A., *Selections from The Prison Notebooks*, New York: International Publishers, 1971.

Gupta, P. L., *Coins*, New Delhi: National Book Trust, 1969.

Hall S., *Cultural Studies 1983: A Theoretical History,* Durham: Duke University Press, 2016.

Hobsbawm, E., *Nations and Nationalism since 1780: Programme, Myth, Reality,* Cambridge: Cambridge University Press, 1990.

Lubin T., 'Custom in the Vedic Ritual Codes as an Emergent Legal Principle,' *Journal of the American Oriental Society*, 136, 4, 669-87, 2016.

Prasad, P., *Sanskrit Inscriptions of Delhi Sultanate, 1191-1526,* New Delhi: Oxford University Press, 1990.

Skinner, Q., ed., *The Return of Grand Theory in the Human Sciences,*

Cambridge: Cambridge University Press, 1990.

Thapar, R., *Somanatha: The Many Voices of a History*, New Delhi: Penguin Books, 2004.

———, *Cultural Pasts: Essays in Early Indian History,* New Delhi: Oxford University Press, 2008.

———, *Indian Society and the Secular: Essays,* New Delhi: Three Essays Collective, 2016.

———, *The Past as Present: Forging Contemporary Identities through History,* New Delhi: Aleph Book Company, 2013.

———, *Talking History,* New Delhi: Oxford University Press, 2017

INDEX

Abhijnana Shakuntalam, xix
Ad Dharm, 36
Adivasis, 33, 105, 118, 123, 186–187
Ajivika sect, 42
Akbar, 14
Akka Mahadevi, 98
Al-Biruni, 80
alchemy, 48, 70–71, 73, 75–76
Ambapali, 91
ancestry, 7–8, 32, 57, 90, 105, 107
Andal, 98
Annales group, 61
anthropological studies, xiv
Apabrahmsha, 150
Arabian Peninsula, 31
Arabs, xxx, 29
Arnold Toynbee, 61
Arthashastra, xxxii, 6, 34, 94–95, 122, 191
Aryabhatta, 64
Arya-Mlechha duality, 108
Aryan, 66, 105, 107, 194
asceticism, 84–85
Ashoka, 14, 17, 22–24, 26–27, 34, 37, 50, 89, 103–104, 108, 149, 166–167, 187
Ashokan inscription, 24, 26
Ashokan pillars, 14, 25–27
Asprishya, 100, 105, 112, 118, 120–121, 124–125, 127, 184
astrologers, 29, 77
astronomy, xiii, xxxix, 29–30, 41–43, 50, 59, 63, 70, 77, 119, 127, 150, 152, 183
Atavika, 34, 104, 118
Avarna, xvi, xxvi, xxxi, xxxix, 100–102, 104, 112, 120–121, 125, 127, 129, 132, 168, 184, 188, 190
Ayurvedic, 64, 74
Ayyanar, 30–32
Azes I, 50

Babri Masjid, xxxii, 18, 165
Banabhatta's *Harshacharita*, 34, 118
Beghampura, 36-37
Benjamin, Walter, 21
Bhadda Kundalakesa, 90
Bhagavad Gita, 58, 108
Bhakti sants, xxviii, 35, 119, 126, 190
Bhakti, 13, 35–36, 98–100, 127, 130
Bharhut, 89
Bhaskara's *Lilavati*, 70
bhikkhuni, 88–89, 92
bhishaja, 73
Bingen, Hildegard von, 97
Borobudur, 10
Brahman dharma
Brahmana Kalkin, 46
Brahmanical sects, 94, 96
Brahmanical tradition, xxiii, 23,

94–95, 100
Braj Bhasha, 16, 151
Brihadaranyaka Upanishad, 87
Brindavan, xxviii
Buddha Maitreya, 46
Buddha, xxviii, 46, 50–52, 89–90, 107, 121, 145
Buddhism, xxiv, xxx–xxxi, 10–12, 17, 23–24, 46, 99, 108, 116, 130, 146
capitalism, xxx, xxxiii, 65, 67–69, 164, 169–170
Centre for Historical Studies (CHS), 135, 156, 159
Chalukya, 14, 21, 51
Chamar, 36
Chandala, xxvi, 104, 112, 121–122, 130, 150, 186, 198
Chandravamsha, 48, 117
Charaka, 73
Charita literature, 53
Charvakas, 23, 130, 146
Chikitsaka, 73
Childe, V. Gordon, 65
China, 9, 11–12, 60, 65, 67, 71–72, 77, 80, 129, 189
Chinese culture, xx
Chinese science, 60
Chokhamela, 130
citizenship, 135, 145
city state, 167
civilization, vii, ix, xii–xiii, xviii, xxxiii, xxxvii, 1–2, 8–12, 15–16, 19, 38–40, 60–62, 69–71, 76, 79–80, 105, 126
classical age, 9, 12, 15
classical Indian music, xxix
Colebrooke, Henry Thomas, 47
colonial reconstructions of the past, xxv
colonialism, xii, 65–68, 151, 158, 164, 169, 202–203
communication, xi, xiii, xv, xvii, xx, xxiii, 10–11, 65–66, 139, 151, 153, 161, 186
Confucianism, 12
cosmology, 40, 43, 55, 76–77
courtesan, 88, 90–95
craft, xiii–xv, 29
cultural crisis, xxxv
cultural heritage, xxxiv, 2
cultural identity, xix
cultural innovation, 16
cultural socialization, xxxix
cyclic time in India, 39

Dalit community, 35
Dalit Sikhs, 36
Dasas, 105–106, 108
Dasi, 87–88, 92–93, 107, 113–114
Dasiputra Brahmanas, 88, 113
delineation of civilizations, xiii
Devadasis, 90
Devanampiya Piyadassi, 26, 167
Devanampiyassa Asokassa, 26, 167
Dhamma, 23
Dharmashastras, xxv, xxiv, xxix, 46–47, 82, 84–85, 94, 96, 101, 108, 110–111, 114, 122–123, 125, 184, 190
Dipavamsa, 89
Dongria Kondhs, 30, 33–34
Dumont, Louis, 84
dynastic chronicles, 54
dynasties, 13, 47, 49–50, 55, 57–58, 115–117, 150, 173

early historical societies, xxiv
educational institutions, 134–135, 137, 186

Eileen Power, 97
elite cultures, xi, xx, xxxvii, 3, 19
Epigraphia Indica, 55
equality, idea of, x
eschatology, 40, 46
ethnic/ethnicity, xxiv, xxxiv–xxxv, 68–69
European culture, xx
European Enlightenment, 2
European science, 69, 72, 79
evolution, xii, xv–xvi, xxv, 13, 59, 65–67, 70–72, 77, 80, 85, 120, 144

Faxian, 104, 124
four-fold system of caste society, 3
Frank, Andre Gunder, xviii

gana-sanghas, 86
Ganikadhyaksha, 94
Ganikas, 90–91, 95
Gargi, 89
genealogies, 40, 47–50, 53–56, 58, 111, 185
generational time, 47–49
gift-giving, xxxvi, 77
globalization, xxxvi, 66, 79, 201, 204
Gotami, 89
Gotra, 113
Greco-Roman civilization, 12
Gregorian calendar, 52
Grihapatni, 86–88, 92–93, 99
Gulbarga, 24
Gupta period, 12, 20, 24–25, 28, 105, 114–117, 120–121, 125, 129, 194, 199
Guru Nanak, 36

Harappan, xv, 123
Harun al-Rashid, 42, 72
Hellenistic astronomy, 41
Hellenistic forms, 4–5, 194
Hetaera, 91
Hierarchy, viii, x, xii, xiv, xxiii–xxiv, 3, 12, 36, 74, 91, 99, 103, 108–109, 111, 113, 124–125, 159, 161, 167
high culture, vii, xi–xiii, xviii, xxxiv, 2, 70, 74, 182–183
Hindu science, 71, 79
Hinduism, xxviii, xxx, 11–13, 98–99, 114, 119–120, 129, 147
Hindutva nationalism, 79
hunter-gatherers, xv, 3
Huntington, Samuel P., 61

identity of community, xxiv
Ikshvaku, 94
inclusive identity, xxv
Indian mathematics, 42, 71
Indo-Aryan language, 149
Industrial Revolution, 65–67
Industrialization, 67–68, 71
inequalities, x, xxiii
inscriptions, 11, 21, 24, 26, 32, 40, 49–50, 52, 54–56, 89–90, 94, 104, 106, 108, 115, 117, 126, 149–150, 166, 197–200
inter-religious marriages, 81
Islamic science, 79
Itihasa-Purana, 49

Jabala, Satyakama, 87
Jahangir, 26
Jainas, xxiv, xxx, 11, 23, 99, 146
jatis, x, 109–111, 118, 122–125, 192, 199
Jawaharlal Nehru University (JNU), xl, 135, 139, 155–159, 162, 164, 171–172, 175–177, 185
Jones, William, 47

Kakshivant Aushija, 113
Kalhana, 23, 28, 39, 54, 166
Kali Yuga, 34, 44, 46–47, 49, 55
kalpa, 42–43
Kanaganahalli stupa, 24
Kanvas, 116
Kauravas, 63
Kavasha Ailusha, 113
Kayastha, xxiv, 151, 155
Khan, Ras, xxix, 147
khanqahs, xxxvi, 53, 186
Khatri traders, 4
Khatri, 111
Khusrau, Amir, 29
kirti-stambha, 31
Krita era, 50
Krittibas's *Ramayana*, xxviii
Kshatriya, 4, 45–49, 56, 108, 111–112, 114–117, 126
Kuhn, Thomas S., 59
Kumarapala, 14, 21
Kurukshetra, 49

Lal Ded (Lallesvari), 99
Latha Bhairon, 25
Lysenko, Trofim, 144

Madhavacharya , 147-148
Maha Parinirvana, 50–51
Mahabharata, xix, xxiii, xxix, 10, 46, 49, 105, 108, 122, 188
Mahavihara Monastery, 89
mahayuga, 43, 46, 54, 57
Maitreyi, 89
Maitri Upanishad, 74
Malava era, 50
Manimekhalai, 90
Manu, 43, 46, 48, 82, 85, 92, 95–96, 100, 106–107, 122
manvantara, 43
Mao Zedong, 170
Marxist theory, 174
mathas, xxxvi, 99, 119, 146, 188
Mauryas, 41, 116
McNeill, William H., xviii
medical knowledge, 73–75
Megalithic cultures, 13
Megasthenes, 104, 124
Mehrgarh, 65
memory, xxxv, 17, 22, 37, 180–181
Menander, 116
Merutunga, 13–14, 21
migrant communities, 6
Mirabai, 99
Mircea Eliade, 40
Mleccha, xxvi, 10, 106, 116, 118, 125
Mohenjo-daro, 20
Mridhra-vac, 105
Mughals, xvii, xxx, xxxiii, 14, 26, 151, 195, 201
mythology, xi, xxxix, 22, 38, 193

Nagasena, 116
Nastaliq, 26
nation state, xxiv, xxvii, 68–69, 203
national culture, xxvii, xxxi, xxxiii–xxxvI, 180, 182, 192–193, 204
national heritage, 18–19
national identity, 78, 143, 203
nationalism, xxvi–xxvii, xxxi–xxxii, xxxiv, 68–69, 78–79, 82, 145, 165, 181, 203
natural heritage, 2, 20
Needham, Joseph, 59, 73, 80
Neolithic Revolution, 65
Niyamgiri Hill, 30, 33
Non-European sciences, 70
non-violence, 17, 27–28

oral history, 131, 143
Orientalists, 39, 47

Panini, 6, 122, 149
Parthasarathi, G., 158
pathashala, 159
patriarchy, xxiii, 81, 87, 89, 91, 101
patronage, xi, xxviii, xxxvi–xxxvii, 13, 16–17, 21–23, 68, 100, 116, 119, 144, 192, 199–201
Pattanam, 142
Pauranika, 76–77
plastic surgery, 63
pollution and impurity, 125
popular culture, 151
Prakrit, 5, 11, 24, 149–151, 186
primitive societies, xviii
Prinsep, James, 26
print capitalism, 69
Protestant, 67, 195
Puranas, 23, 26, 34, 42, 46–48, 50, 52, 54, 56–57, 64, 76–77, 96
Purohita, 113
Pushpaka Vimana, 63

Qawwali, xxx, 29

race, xii, xxv–xxvi, 61, 69, 130
Rajatarangini, 23, 28, 39, 54, 166
rakshasa, 10, 105
Rama Katha, 18
Ramayana, xxviii–xxix, 10, 19, 48
rationality, 61, 67, 77–78, 148
Ravidas, 35–37, 120, 130
rayo asoko, 24
religious categories, xvi
religious nationalisms, xxiv–xxv, 175
Renaissance in Europe, 30
renouncers, xx, 83–85, 97, 100
renunciation in Christianity, 97
Rigveda, xxix, 105, 107–108
royal biographies, 56–57

Saberwal, Satish, 173
samnyasa, 84–85
sangha, 51, 84, 86, 88–90, 92–93, 95, 100
Sanghamitta, 89
Sannathi, 24
Sanskrit, xxix, 5–6, 10–11, 14, 16, 21, 24, 29, 38, 41, 71–74, 96, 106, 118–119, 142, 149–152, 164, 186, 196–199
Sarasvati River, 88, 113
Sariputta, 90
Sarvadarshana-sangraha, xxviii
Sayana, xxix, 106
scientific knowledge, 62–63, 70, 72, 77
Scopes Monkey Trial, 144
Secularism, 68
Seleucids, 41
semester system, 160
sex worker, 91–93, 95
Shah, Bulleh, 5
Shah, Firuz, 14, 25, 29
Shah, Waris, 5
Shakta traditions, 100
Shramana dharma, 11, 23, 146
Shramanas, xxiv, xxx–xxxi, 23, 83–84, 93, 96, 100, 130, 146
Shudras, 45, 74, 108, 110, 112, 122, 149
Shungas, 116
Simeon Stylites, 97
social differentiation, 96
social ethics, xxiv, 23, 27, 129, 131, 176
social groups, xvi, 22, 187, 191
social justice, xxiv, 69, 133, 135, 203

social sciences , xv, 145, 151–152, 156–158, 164, 173, 175–177, 182, 185
socialization, x, xxxix, 152, 155, 186
Somanatha temple, xxxii, 14, 21-22
Somayaji, Nilakantha, 29
South Asian culture, 16
specialized knowledge, 151
Stridhana, 87
subcultures, xi
Sufis, xxix, 5, 119, 151
Sung period, 72
Suri, Mahendra, 29
Suryavamsha, 48, 117
Sushruta, 73

tangible heritage, 20–21
Tantric practices, 76
Tarikh-i-Firuz Shahi, 25
technological innovations, 4
textbooks, 22, 137, 140, 14, 180
Theophrastus, 75
transmission of knowledge, 77
Tughlaq, Muhammad bin, 106
Tughlaq, Sultan Firuz Shah, 14, 25
Turushka, xxvi

Ujjain, 51
Upanishads, 113, 145, 177
Upasikas, 90, 93
Ussher, James, 39
utopias, xxxviii, 34–35

vaidya, 73
Vaishnavism, 46
Vaishyas, 108, 112
Vallabhacharya, xxviii
Vamshanucharita, 47
Varahamihira, 70, 116
varna, xvi, xxiii, 4, 103–113, 115–118, 123, 125
varna-ashrama-dharma, 103, 108, 110, 116
Vedic Brahmanism, 11, 23, 98, 114, 120
Vedic mathematics, 71
Vedic rituals, 114, 120
Velar community, 31
Vellalars, 111
victimization, xxix, xxxi, 147
viharas, xxxvi, 145
Vikrama era, 50–51
Vikramaditya, 51
vira-kal, 31
Virtual Reality (VK), xxi
Vishnu Purana, 17, 47, 49–50, 55, 58, 115, 117
Vishvamitra, 122, 130
Vitthala, 32

Wallerstein, Immanuel, xviii
Weber, Max, 40, 61, 67, 69, 95, 171, 185
Wells, H. G., 26
Wilson, H. H., 47

Yangshao, 65
Yavana, xxvi, 116, 125
yuga, 34, 42–47, 49, 55

Zoroastrianism, 46